This book explores the political sig[n]
context of cultural studies. It applies

MW00567222

Lacan to film studies, and asks how political responsibility can be reconciled with the concept of the university as a democratic institution. Art and the university, Patrick McGee claims, share a common feature: they are usually regarded as autonomous realms that resist the determination of economic and political interests, while they still play a crucial role in ethical and political discourse. Through detailed reference to Neil Jordan's *The Crying Game*, McGee shows how film can be both a product of the culture industry and a critique of it. He goes on to analyze the function of the university in producing interpretations of political art-forms and in determining the limits of critical discussion. McGee links Adorno with popular culture and film studies to provide new ways of thinking through the claims of political criticism. He reconfigures Derrida's theory of undecidability, which has been criticized by Habermas and others as politically irresponsible, to address some of the most crucial debates on freedom and the ethics of intellectual work in social institutions like the university.

Cinema, theory, and political responsibility in contemporary culture

Literature, Culture, Theory

❖❖❖

General editor

RICHARD MACKSEY, *The Johns Hopkins University*

Selected series titles

Cinema, theory, and political responsibility in contemporary culture

❖❖❖❖❖❖❖❖❖❖❖❖❖❖❖❖❖❖❖❖❖❖❖❖❖❖❖❖❖❖❖❖❖❖❖❖❖❖❖

Patrick McGee

Louisiana State University

CAMBRIDGE
UNIVERSITY PRESS

PUBLISHED BY THE PRESS SYNDICATE OF THE UNIVERSITY OF CAMBRIDGE
The Pitt Building, Trumpington Street, Cambridge CB2 1RP, United Kingdom

CAMBRIDGE UNIVERSITY PRESS
The Edinburgh Building, Cambridge CB2 2RU, United Kingdom
40 West 20th Street, New York, NY 10011-4211, USA
10 Stamford Road, Oakleigh, Melbourne 3166, Australia

First published 1997
Printed in the United Kingdom at the University Press, Cambridge

Typeset in Palatino 10/12.5, in Poltype™ [VN]

A catalogue record for this book is available from the British Library

Library of Congress cataloguing in publication data applied for

ISBN 0 521 58130 3 hardback
ISBN 0 521 58908 8 paperback

For Joan and Sean

Contents

Contents

Preface

On a rainy afternoon in late December 1992, I walked from one side of Manhattan to the other in order to see *The Crying Game*. I had been attending a meeting of the Modern Language Association and wanted to escape the chaos of the academic marketplace for a few hours by sitting in a dark theater with other moviegoers. I have loved movies all of my life and believe that the pleasure one takes from the cinematic process derives in part from being with others and participating in their most intimate fantasies without violating them or being violated by them. In the darkness of the movie theater, our fantasies somehow manage to coexist, perhaps because the community of moviegoers is so absent-minded. In any case, something happened as I watched the movie that afternoon. It was nothing mystical or mysterious but more like an experience of concentrated distraction. Yet when I left the theater, I could not get the experience out of my mind. Though it started as a distraction, it soon became an obsession; and out of my need to say something about it, I began to write this book. Though I can never convey to the reader what the experience was (and have not ruled out the possibility that it is a myth), I know that in some form it has entered into the intellectual process that lies behind this work.

With the increasing normalization of cultural studies within the university (and, despite their disclaimers, I would include new historicism, recent versions of poststructuralism, and the new theories of gender and race in this category), it is important that we return to the question of reading and the place of interpretation within contextual research. Reevaluating the theories and the objects of literary and cultural study in this way enables us to avoid the inevitable tendency toward routinization that plagues any intellectual field. Precisely because of the new and utterly necessary emphasis on history in English and the other humanities, we need to pay attention to what actually constitutes the text–context relationship in order to avoid the reductionism that limited earlier versions of historicism, including Marxism. As I argue in the following chapters, Theodor Adorno's concept of the aesthetic monad and Jacques Derrida's speculations on intellectual responsibility offer crucial models for understanding the political and ethical functions of critical work, including close reading as a form of contextual analysis.

I discuss Adorno's relation to the general field of cultural studies in chapter 1 and analyze aspects of his *Aesthetic Theory* in chapter 2. However, the goal of my reading of Adorno lies in chapter 3 on *The Crying Game*. The experience of this film somehow suggested to me the importance of Adorno's work and called into question the usual understanding of his cultural theories. In effect, I argue that *The Crying Game* is *both* a work of art *and* a product of what Adorno called the culture industry. Though this may be true of any contemporary work, *The Crying Game* illustrates this duality in unusually powerful ways. It unabashedly seduces its spectators through an overt deception and organizes itself structurally around a series of narrative ruptures and displacements. This film, as Adorno said of the work of art in general, is a system of contradictions. Though it may seek to transcend the social context that determines its commodity form, it also projects onto the spectators an experience of disappointment that requires what Adorno called a *second reflection*. This involves a reading that must adapt itself to what is singular in the work as the articulation of a specific historical context.

Not every art work is plugged into its context in the same way. *The Crying Game* indirectly responds to Irish history, colonial and postcolonial Caribbean history, British history, the histories of sexuality and race, and, most important, the history of the concept of the nation. My analysis does not want to subordinate the work to a stable context but to situate it in relation to the social processes of which it is a part. The work as symptom or windowless monad is not a reflection that can be adequate or inadequate to its context. *It is the context*. It is a cultural commodity that nevertheless discloses its commodity form as the fetish that defetishizes itelf. It articulates the fundamental experience of art as one of disappointment, that is, of our disappointment in the failure of art to transcend history. Through that failure, art discloses its unconscious historiography as a symptomatic formation.

Preface

After passing through Adorno and *The Crying Game*, I return, at the beginning of chapter 4, to the work of Derrida and to the question of responsibility that haunts all of contemporary criticism and the culture wars that have been waged, in the view of some, over the grave of deconstruction. Specifically, I try to elaborate a deconstructive concept of freedom and autonomy through a reading of, and response to, some of the critics of Derrida's work who have been influenced by Jürgen Habermas. At various points, this discussion brings me back to Adorno and requires me to clarify the relationship between his concept of critique and deconstruction as a form of political intervention. While Adorno is not a deconstructionist, his theory of the autonomous work of art presupposes a concept of undecidability that finds its fullest elaboration in Derrida's work.

Chapter 4 concludes with some speculations on the university as the site of literary and cultural studies, as an institution which plays a role in creating the social conditions of freedom. The university grounds freedom not by formulating its law once and for all but by giving space to the undecidable as the condition of social and political responsibility. This responsibility means leaving an ear open to the voice of the other who would criticize any specific formulation of freedom as law. True freedom is not identical with the law that grants it, though it works through the law as an ongoing process of dialogue, social exchange, negotiation, and compromise. Because the aim of freedom is something that can never be defined once and for all, it lies beyond commitment. Yet, for that reason, the call of freedom requires that we make a decision and commit ourselves to one side or the other at each historical juncture. It has never been more important to think about the requirements of freedom and political responsibility than it is today. As the world grows smaller and our cultural contradictions more visible, it is important to remember William Blake's insight that applying one law to the lion and the ox, one measure to the incommensurable differences that make up human society, is oppressive. Freedom remains possible because the law, as a response to the history of human desire, is *not one*. It is an ongoing process of rewriting and recontextualization.

Acknowledgments

This study, in its theoretical concerns, owes something to Gregory Jay's criticisms of the original manuscript of my second book. I thank those individuals who have read and responded to this work at various stages or have supported me through their friendship: Granger Babcock, Anthony Barthelemy, Murray Beja, the late Bernard Benstock, Ricky Blackwood, Robert Con Davis, Michael Dietz, John Fischer, Eric Halpern, Ellen Carol Jones, Bernhard Kendler, Karen Lawrence, Veronica Makowsky, Michelle Massé, Elsie Michie, Dana Nelson, Leslie Roman, and David Wills. I thank all of my anonymous readers for their helpful criticisms and Louisiana State University for the Summer Research Fellowship and Sabbatical Leave during which I wrote a first draft of the manuscript. I offer my special thanks to Ray Ryan, my Cambridge editor, and to Michael Sprinker, the co-editor of the "Literature, Culture, Theory" series.

My greatest debts are still to my son Sean and my wife Joan who keep me laughing, who tell me when I make a mistake, and who never permit me to lose confidence in myself. They are my toughest critics and closest friends. This book is dedicated to them.

Abbreviations

AT   T. W. Adorno, *Aesthetic Theory*, ed. G. Adorno and R.
     Tiedemann, trans. C. Lenhardt (London: Routledge and
     Kegan Paul, 1984).

E   J. Lacan, *The Ethics of Psychoanalysis 1959–1960*, book 7 of
     The Seminar, ed. J.-A. Miller, trans. D. Porter (New York:
     Norton, 1992).

ND   T. W. Adorno, *Negative Dialectics*, trans. E. B. Ashton
     (New York: Continuum, 1973).

NJR Neil Jordan, *A Neil Jordan Reader* (New York: Vintage,
     1993).

1

Redeeming contradictions: from critical theory to cultural studies

Adorno, culture, and film

The reification of a great work of art is not just loss, any more than the reification of the cinema is all loss ... Both bear the stigmata of capitalism, both contain elements of change ... Both are torn halves of an integral freedom, to which however they do not add up.

Theodor Adorno wrote these words from London to Walter Benjamin in a letter dated March 18, 1936.[1] They articulate the promise of a unified culture that expresses "integral freedom" although they dismiss the possibility of realizing this promise as the simple addition of the two halves of culture, high and popular or mass culture, in a capitalist society. Some years later, in the essay "Cultural Criticism and Society," written in the United States before his return to Germany at the end of the forties,[2] Adorno expressed his reservations about the concept of culture itself, by which he means, in this context, high culture. He suggests that cultural criticism makes culture into a fetish by isolating it from larger social processes. Neither art nor philosophy, when they are true, are ever complete in and of themselves. They always stand "in relation to the actual life-process of society from which they distinguish themselves." They present themselves as independent and autonomous through their "rejection of the guilt of life which blindly and callously reproduces itself." Yet this

---

[1] E. Bloch et al., *Aesthetics and Politics* (London: NLB, 1977), p. 123.
[2] P. U. Hohendahl, *Prismatic Thought: Theodor W. Adorno* (Lincoln: University of Nebraska Press, 1995), p. 22.

1

rejection of the realm of purposes and interests carries within it "the promise of a condition in which freedom were realized. This remains an equivocal promise of culture as long as its existence depends on a bewitched reality and, ultimately, on control over the work of others."[3]

In these comments, Adorno virtually identifies autonomous art and philosophy with a "bewitched reality," the very reality that Horkheimer and Adorno described as a form of mass deception in the essay on the culture industry written in the forties. The paradoxical and ambivalent nature of Adorno's dialectical thought displays itself in these formulations. For the work of art is authentic and the philosophy true only insofar as they are able to make visible their fundamental inauthenticity and untruth, insofar as they implicate themselves in the "guilt of life" by their very insistence that they are separate from the society that produces that guilt. They "blindly and callously" insist on their own integral autonomy, or being-in-itself, as the promise of freedom; but this promise contains the essence of their being-for-something else, for that bewitched reality that makes such authenticity and truth possible through the production of its other. Adorno has frequently been criticized for his horror at the inauthentic spectacle of mass culture and for his belated defense of the autonomous work of art associated primarily with modernism and the avant-garde. But the most unrelenting critic of Adorno was always Adorno himself. In the same essay, he describes modern bourgeois cultural criticism in terms general enough to include his own. He refers to the comfort such criticism takes in the division between high and low culture, which results from both "an uncompromising opposition to being-for-something else" and "an ideology which in its hybris enthrones itself as being-in-itself." Adorno did not have to wait for the student movements of the sixties and the New Left to learn that his work was a form of modern bourgeois cultural criticism. The self-subversive moments in his work make this judgment implicitly and consistently, from the period of his debate with Benjamin to the end of his life. "Cultural criticism," he concludes, "shares the blindness of its object."[4]

From the perspective of Adorno's version of critical theory, in other words, culture is a lived contradiction. There is no question

[3] T. W. Adorno, *Prisms*, trans. S. and S. Weber (Cambridge, Massachusetts: MIT, 1981), p. 23.   [4] *Ibid.*, p. 27.

but that Adorno himself, as so many of his critics have pointed out, was élitist in his aesthetic predispositions. As he wrote in *Minima Moralia*, near the time he and Horkheimer were writing *Dialectic of Enlightenment*, "Every visit to the cinema leaves me, against all my vigilance, stupider and worse."[5] Many critics of the Frankfurt school have tried to explain this élitism as a response to the different historical contexts and events that shaped the life and work of Adorno and the other members of the school. The events which initially inspired this cultural formation were the collapse of working-class movements and organizations in Western Europe after World War I, the transformation of German leftwing parties with a mass base into reformist movements dominated by Moscow, and the rise of Stalinism, fascism, and Nazism after the promise of the Russian Revolution had failed. Adorno witnessed first-hand what the Nazis were able to accomplish through the manipulation of mass culture; and when he went to the United States, he was shocked by the extent to which mass culture had already become what Fredric Jameson would now call the *dominant cultural logic*.[6] He surely feared that such a powerful mass culture would achieve exactly what Jameson believes postmodernism has achieved: an erasure of the difference between high and popular culture in a way that would force the two to add up to something monstrous in its implicit enforcement of standardization and normality. Such a homogenization of culture would be a parody of the integral freedom that was the true promise of cultural division itself. As Diane Waldman argues, the division between autonomous art and popular art articulates and participates in the class divisions of capitalist society. "Thus Adorno's critique of the culture industry," she concludes, "is based on its attempt to reconcile the contradiction by absorbing light into serious art and hence mystify class antagonisms."[7]

It serves no purpose to excuse or rationalize Adorno's élitist predispositions, especially as they took shape in his categorical

[5] T. W. Adorno, *Minima Moralia: Reflections from Damaged Life*, trans. E. F. N. Jephcott (London: Verso, 1978), p. 25.

[6] F. Jameson, *Postmodernism, or, The Cultural Logic of Late Capitalism* (Durham: Duke University Press, 1991), p. 6.

[7] D. Waldman, "Critical Theory and Film: Adorno and 'The Culture Industry' Revisited," *New German Critique* 12 (Fall 1977), 52. For a related defense of Adorno's critique of the culture industry, see A. Huyssen, "Introduction to Adorno," *New German Critique* 6 (Fall 1975), 7.

rejection of jazz as an inferior, regressive form of musical art[8] and of film as an art-form completely determined by its economic and technological conditions of production. When he says that he felt "stupider and worse" everytime he went to the cinema, he responds to what Benjamin described as "reception in a state of distraction," which "finds in the film its true means of exercise." But Benjamin's response to this aspect of cinematic experience was not completely negative. Because film causes the aura or cult value of the traditional work of art to recede, it has the effect of "putting the public in the position of the critic"; but, at the same time, it eliminates, or at least makes very difficult, the act of critical concentration as a form of reception. In the cinema, according to Benjamin, "The public is an examiner, but an absent-minded one."[9]

To employ a popular figure of speech that Adorno uses himself, we should not throw out the baby with the bath-water in analyzing Adorno's response to Benjamin and to film as a form of mass culture. If any form of culture, high or low, is to have a positive political effect, it requires an engaged and critically active form of consumption that does not necessarily accept the cultural product or commodity strictly on its own terms. As the quotation from Adorno with which I began suggests, every form of culture in late capitalist society undergoes reification; but no cultural object is ever totally identical with its own status as a commodity. In the section of *Minima Moralia* which bears the heading "Baby with the bath-water," Adorno challenges the notion that any form of culture can ever be reduced completely to its function as ideology. He concludes that "To identify culture solely with lies is more fateful than ever, now that the former is really becoming totally absorbed by the latter, and eagerly invites such identification in order to compromise every opposing thought."[10] In other words, it would be a misreading of Adorno's own extremely negative critique of the culture industry to assume that a cultural object,

---

[8] For a contextual explanation of Adorno's negative view of jazz, see M. Jay, *The Dialectical Imagination: A History of the Frankfurt School and the Institute of Social Research 1923–1950* (Boston: Little Brown, 1973), pp. 186–87, and S. Buck-Morss, *The Origin of Negative Dialectics: Theodor W. Adorno, Walter Benjamin, and the Frankfurt Institute* (New York: Free Press, 1977), pp. 109–10.

[9] W. Benjamin, *Illuminations*, trans. H. Zohn (New York: Schocken, 1969), pp. 240–41.

[10] Adorno, *Minima Moralia*, p. 44.

4

even an object of mass culture, can be completely contained by the culture industry. In the forties, Adorno thought that culture as a way of life was becoming totally absorbed by the culture industry as a business. For this reason, mass-cultural objects no longer pretended to be art, and the fact that they were just business had become the ideological justification of their status as cultural things that need not be analyzed critically.[11] This ideology of the complete identity of mass culture with the culture industry is promoted not by Adorno but by the culture industry itself. If one accepts that ideology, then one has thrown out the baby with the bath-water by refusing to analyze the mass-cultural object from a perspective that foregrounds its contradictory relationship to its own status as a commodity of the culture industry.

As Adorno continues the passage from *Minima Moralia*,

> If material reality is called the world of exchange value, and culture whatever refuses to accept the domination of that world, then it is true that such refusal is illusory as long as the existent exists. Since, however, free and honest exchange is itself a lie, to deny it is at the same time to speak for truth: in face of the lie of the commodity world, even the lie that denounces it becomes correct.[12]

Adorno suggests that exchange value is the material reality that underlies capitalist culture. It is not the economic system *per se* but the system of commensurable values that has almost totally absorbed culture as a way of life. In effect, the world of exchange value claims to be the totality of culture. Yet Adorno suggests that there is something in culture that refuses the domination of exchange value, that posits a world beyond exchange value. This world is a false one insofar as it belies the reality of the world of exchange value and, as Marcuse suggested, affirms a freedom from exchange value within capitalist culture. The truth is that even our ability to imagine such a utopia is contaminated by the world of exchange value, whether that utopia is expressed through a work of art that proclaims itself autonomous or through a product of the culture industry that advertises itself as a commodity. But the world of exchange value is also a fiction that derives from the overall effect of commodity fetishism; and the concept of free enterprise as a "free and honest exchange" is the

---

[11] M. Horkheimer and T. W. Adorno, *Dialectic of Enlightenment*, trans. J. Cumming (London: Allen Lane, 1973), p. 121.

[12] Adorno, *Minima Moralia*, p. 44.

centerpiece of this ideological construction. Therefore, the cultural lie or illusion that calls into question the lie of the commodity world speaks the truth through its negation of the other that is its own condition of existence. This truth is precisely what refuses the domination of exchange value. If the latter is the commensurable in capitalist culture, then it can only be opposed by the incommensurable.

For Adorno, the incommensurable in any cultural object, including those that we call works of art, is the moment of its self-contradiction. This moment does not emerge from the attempt to eliminate the division between high and low culture or from the enforcement of a false equality between all cultural objects. The contradiction lies *within* cultural division which every cultural object absorbs and expresses as the ideology of its form. In the canonized work of art, it is the contradiction between its claim to aesthetic autonomy and its revelation of the social content of aesthetic form. In the product of the culture industry, it is the contradiction between the object's self-advertisement as a commodity and its revelation of the illusory nature of the commodity world. For Adorno, the tendency toward aesthetic judgment, a tendency which Adorno himself exemplifies in his constant effort to distinguish between true and false works of art, derives from the incommensurable in art itself: "Even someone believing himself convinced of the non-comparability of works of art will find himself repeatedly involved in debates where works of art, and precisely those of highest and therefore incommensurable rank, are compared and evaluated one against the other." This self-contradictory remark, which almost begs the question it poses, is autobiographical, since Adorno believes both that art is incommensurable and that this quality is the distinguishing mark of works of the highest rank. Adorno must evaluate that which cannot be evaluated because "This compulsion to evaluate is located ... in the works of art themselves."[13]

Despite Adorno's best efforts to classify film as a pure product of the culture industry without any redeeming value as art, his own insistence on the incommensurability of true art makes it impossible to enforce such a distinction absolutely. As long as it is possible to produce an analysis, or immanent reading, of the

---

[13] Adorno, *Minima Moralia*, p. 75.

cultural object, a reading that must necessarily contradict the ideology of the culture industry that tries to undermine such a critical reception, then it is possible to locate a redeeming contradiction in the mass-cultural object. This redeeming contradiction is the baby that should not be thrown out with the bath-water which signifies the culture industry itself. Throughout his career, Adorno showed little sympathy with reception studies; and though we should not align ourselves with this viewpoint, we should understand why he insisted on the value of immanent criticism. In recent years, sociological methods of literary scholarship have made it possible to demonstrate that the public reception of mass-cultural objects can be more critical and oppositional than Adorno was willing to concede. Still, reception remains a field of contention, a field in which there are political stakes as to what constitutes the meaning of the cultural object. Though the intervention of the critic or theorist in that field should not claim an authority that supersedes all forms of popular reception, it does play a role in foregrounding or making visible the incommensurable in the cultural object as the moment of its self-contradiction. Adorno's insistence on the necessity of immanent criticism should not be read as an argument *against* reception studies but as an argument *for* a particular kind of reception. Such a reception "takes seriously the principle that it is not ideology in itself which is untrue but rather its pretension to correspond to reality. Immanent criticism of intellectual and artistic phenomena seeks to grasp, through the analysis of their form and meaning, the contradiction between their objective idea and that pretension."[14] I will try to demonstrate how this process works through the consideration of a film that Adorno would surely have considered an exemplary product of the culture industry.

Analyzing *It's a Wonderful Life*

Frank Capra's 1946 movie classic contains at its center one of the most bizarre scenes of a marriage proposal in film history. George Bailey, the hero of *It's a Wonderful Life*, is undergoing a crisis, not his first or his last, as he learns that his brother Harry has a wife and no real intention of coming back to Bedford Falls to take over

[14] Adorno, *Prisms*, p. 32.

the Bailey Bros. Building and Loan Association. George has already given up a trip to Europe and a college education for the family business, and once again he can see no way out of his dilemma. He is torn between the family commitment to a concept of social responsibility within the capitalist system and his own desire for adventure and self-gratification. George wants to leave Bedford Falls, see the world, get his degree in engineering, and build things. At the same time, he feels obligated to keep the Building and Loan alive and out of the hands of Mr. Potter, the richest man in town, who would destroy any form of economic activity that does not contribute to his own accumulation of wealth. On the surface, this conflict looks like the classical opposition between the good capitalist, George, and the bad one, Potter. Though the film does posit such a distinction (the good capitalist is a minor character, George's high school friend, Sam Wainwright), it also suggests a conflict within George Bailey that complicates his relation to capitalist culture altogether.

As Potter says in the segment of the film in which George has to take over the Association, "Peter Bailey [George's father] was not a businessman; that's what killed him." George accepts the view that neither he nor his father fully subscribes to the rules of capitalist culture, though he does not realize that such an implicit refusal to participate in the system carries a certain risk. As far as George is concerned, the people who "do most of the working and paying and living and dying in this community" deserve the credit that will give them "a couple of decent rooms and a bath," that is, some degree of personal comfort so that they can enjoy life. Potter, on the other hand, wants to liquidate the Building and Loan and criticizes its social function as producing "a discontented lazy rabble instead of a thrifty working class." Ultimately, George and Potter embody two different forms of economic desire under capitalism: the desire for expenditure and the desire for accumulation, or, from a psychoanalytic perspective, desire under the rule of the pleasure principle and desire under the rule of the death drive. For Potter, the aim and justification of life is accumulation that produces interest through its submission to the death principle; for George, the aim of life is expenditure that redeems the deathly interest of accumulation by transforming its exchange value into use-value – its abstract value into concrete joys and pleasures.

8

But in order to guarantee the community's desire for the good life, George must sacrifice the object of his own desire. On the night of his brother's return from college, George wanders away from the homecoming party. Though his mother urges him to visit Mary Hatch, his future wife, he walks off in the opposite direction toward the main street of Bedford Falls. He encounters Violet, a young woman who functions as a sexual magnet in the community. (Notice the difference in the names of the women. "Mary Hatch" suggests a maternal figure whose primary function is to nurture things to life. Violet's name contains the root *viol*, which suggests that she attracts violence, violation, or rape.) When George half-ironically invites her to join him for an adventure on Mount Bedford and suggests they take their shoes off and go swimming in the dark, Violet looks horrified and rejects his proposal. George may not be serious, but he toys with the idea of sexual gratification without social responsibility. Some years before, on the night he and Mary fell into the swimming pool at the high school dance, George walked Mary home when all she had to wear was a bathrobe. As he started to kiss her, Mary ran and inadvertently slipped out of her robe. Ironic as ever, George circled the hydrangea bush she hid in and mused over this "very interesting situation." The scene typifies the culture industry's "pornographic and prudish" representation of sexuality[15] but still articulates the dialectic of desire in capitalist culture. As George approaches the naked woman in the hydrangea bush, he is prohibited from enjoying her by the call of social responsibility. He abruptly learns from a passing car that his father has had a stroke.

After leaving Violet on the night of the marriage proposal, George ends up at Mary's house in an angry mood. To the question "What do you want?" repeated by Mary and her mother, George replies irritably that he does not want anything; but when Sam Wainwright calls to court Mary himself and to offer George a future in plastics, George clarifies the aim, though not the object, of his desire. He says to Mary, "I don't want any plastics and I don't want any ground floors and I don't want to get married ever to anyone. I want to do what I want to do." In the next shot, he is walking down the aisle with his new bride. The story of George's life is that he always wants *what he wants* but always does *what*

---

[15] Horkheimer and Adorno, *Dialectic*, p. 140.

9

others want. He never really proposes to Mary on the screen; he merely protests against the contradictions of his own desire. George wants to leave the small town and see the world; but instead, after his wedding, he ends up saving the Building and Loan from bankruptcy and moves into the old Granville house that he said he would not live in even as a ghost (though, in the end, George becomes a sort of ghost who wants nothing more than to return to his house). Mary, on the other hand, has dreamed of living there all her life. He saves the Building and Loan by convincing the depositors not to think of the institution as a place where their money is kept but as a means by which they are able to invest in, and realize, one another's dreams. "We have to have faith in each other," he concludes.

Ironically, the only person who really understands George is his nemesis, Potter, who finally tries to buy him off. The money he offers is not as important as his attempt to manipulate George's desire. As Potter astutely asserts, George "hates his job, hates the Building and Loan almost as much as I do." In a sense, Potter knows George better than George knows himself; for if, as Potter recognizes, George "never makes a dime" out of the Building and Loan, Potter himself rarely *spends* a dime out of the capital he has accumulated. They are mirror images of one another. Potter has been made immobile by his confinement to a wheelchair, and George is paralyzed and permanently entrapped by the community of Bedford Falls. If Potter, as his name suggests, is the one who gives shape to the emptiness at the center of capitalist culture, George is the one who fills the emptiness – that is, who makes the system work by redeeming the death drive as the destructive tendency of capitalism to subordinate all forms of individual desire to the accumulation of capital itself. George's final crisis comes in response to the revelation of the truth about the capitalist accumulation of wealth. When Potter fails to return the eight thousand dollars he inadvertently takes from Uncle Billy, he clarifies his true identity by showing that capitalist accumulation is really a form of theft. George does not know and never learns the truth about what happened to the money, but he knows the truth about his own desire – that it will never be realized, that it is the hole in his being. With the decision to commit suicide, George is ready to surrender that desire to death – to reduce himself to capital as the net worth of his life insurance.

Still, before George can kill himself, he is granted a vision by his guardian angel, Clarence Oddbody. He sees what the world would look like if he had not been there to prevent everything from being absorbed by Potter's black hole of accumulated wealth. Bedford Falls is now Pottersville; and this segment of the film, shot in *noir* style, presents it as a world without pleasure. People go to the neighborhood pub not to enjoy the company of others but to get drunk as quickly as possible. On the main street of town, both the theater and the Building and Loan have been transformed into nightclubs and striptease palaces, suggesting that the few who take pleasure from this world do so at the expense of others. Mary is a childless old maid, and George's mother is cynical and bitter. But the most haunting object in this nightmare is the graveyard that would have been Bailey Park, the housing project George and his father created for the working poor. Just before George goes there, Clarence warns him that "one man's life touches so many other lives and when he isn't around he leaves an awful hole." These words are spoken over an extreme close-up of James Stewart's anxious face. In the next scene, George looks into the hole created by his own absence from the world.

In my view, the meaning of this sequence, and of the film's predictable ending, is not the condemnation of capitalism but rather the recognition that hope within capitalist culture lies precisely in its contradictions. George Bailey is bailed out – that is, literally spared from having to go to prison – by the people to whom he has bailed the property that has been the basis of their good life. I use the word "bail" in the specialized sense of delivering something in trust to another for a special purpose and for a limited period. This concept bears comparison with the term "usufruct" which means the right to use or enjoy something without owning it. "Usufruct" is one of the possible meanings of the French term, *jouissance*, which can be thought of as a pleasure irreducible to exchange value.[16] George Bailey embodies the promise of the post-Depression, post-World War II capitalist society in which hope and the good life are founded on credit and the promise of infinite prosperity. He is the symbolic father of the new suburbia for ordinary working-class people, a vision that will dominate the American landscape in the fifties and sixties. In this

[16] J. Gallop, *The Daughter's Seduction: Feminism and Psychoanalysis* (Ithaca, New York: Cornell University Press, 1982), pp. 49–50.

world, no one really owns anything except in the abstract form of credit; and the new basis of class distinction is access to credit (which has never been distributed equally) as the collective fantasy of individual ownership.

Though there is something real behind George, he promotes what amounts to a fantasy because the reality he makes possible for some belies the black hole of capitalist accumulation that ultimately makes the full realization of human potential impossible for all. At the same time, this lesson is the meaning of George's life. According to Terry Eagleton, the foundation of Marx's ethical philosophy lies in the belief that living well involves the concrete actualization of one's potential in interaction with the self-realization of others. George's life suggests that within capitalist culture there is a contradiction between utopian desire for self-actualization and responsibility to others. As Eagleton points out, even in Marxist theory, there is a restriction on human self-realization. According to the ethical norm he refers to, individuals should develop only those powers that are consistent with the collective good, or the social guarantee of everyone's right to self-actualization within the limits determined by the norm.[17] On the one hand, George embodies the alibi of humanism, or the myth of benevolent expenditure, that serves to veil the dominating death drive of capital accumulation. On the other, he exhibits the contradiction between individual desire and the ethical good of the other that may be the only hope within capitalist culture. As long as the principle of capital accumulation contradicts the ethical norms of capitalist culture, there is hope for a better world than the artificial one promised by the angels of the culture industry.

It could be argued, of course, that this content-centered reading contradicts the intention of Adorno's concept of immanent analysis which focuses more on form. In response to such a reservation, I would point out two things. First, though Adorno argued for the necessity of immanent analysis as a ground of cultural criticism, he produced very little of it himself apart from his significant body of music criticism. In his studies of music, Adorno insisted on a more direct identity between form and content than is possible in literary and cinematic texts. Perhaps

---

[17] T. Eagleton, *The Ideology of the Aesthetic* (Oxford: Basil Blackwell, 1990), pp. 224–26.

the best example of the analysis of such texts in Adorno's own work is the essay on Beckett which could be taken as a detailed close-reading that pays as much attention to thematic content as it does to the significance of form.[18] My second point is that our perception and appreciation of both cinematic and literary techniques is neither transcendent nor ahistorical. To use literary examples, the significance of form to the first readers of *Tristram Shandy* or *Moby Dick* was not immediately apparent; and these works, to different extents, had to await the modernist revolution in literary form before they could be fully appreciated as the brilliant technical experiments that they are.

No one today who views a Hollywood film from the forties can see it with the eyes of its original audience. As Miriam Hansen has pointed out, Adorno's negative response to Hollywood films largely had to do with their "techniques of illusionism": "The deceptive identity of image and referent validates the detail in itself and instantly links it to the cultural system as a whole, thus dispensing with its mediation through the structure of the individual work which, in Adorno's view, still provides an element of negation in autonomous art."[19] To restate this more plainly, when Horkheimer and Adorno said that "real life is becoming indistinguishable from the movies,"[20] they meant that the cinematic image has naturalized itself by effacing its difference from the world it represents. Yet, by today's standards, Hollywood techniques of editing from the thirties and forties no longer have the effect of simulating reality and have been employed by contemporary directors like Steven Spielberg and George Lucas to produce exactly the opposite effect. In a retrospective viewing of *It's a Wonderful Life*, one becomes aware that the film never permits us to forget that it is a film. As Hansen paraphrases Adorno, "For a film to become art ... it would have to inhibit the photographic iconicity of the image flow by means of cinematic techniques that make it 'resemble the phenomenon of writing,' that would fracture the illusionist self-identity of the moving image and make it an object of immanent construction, figuration and decipher-

[18] T. W. Adorno, *Notes to Literature*, ed. R. Tiedemann, trans. S. W. Nicholsen, 2 vols. (New York: Columbia University Press, 1991), vol. I, pp. 241–75.

[19] M. B. Hansen, "Introduction to Adorno, 'Transparencies on Film' (1966)," *New German Critique* 24–25 (Fall–Winter 1981–82), 189.

[20] Horkheimer and Adorno, *Dialectic*, p. 126.

ing."[21] Ironically, the Hollywood style of *It's a Wonderful Life*, even as it derealizes the darker implications of the film's social content, forces us, from our position as spectators in the late twentieth century, to recognize the film as coded or symptomatic writing that must be decoded or interpreted in relation to its historical context.

When James Stewart first appears on the screen as the adult George Bailey, the frame freezes on his image. Meanwhile, the spectators hear the voices of angels, who have been represented as artificial-looking heavenly bodies in the "celestial suture" of the film's opening shots.[22] The winged angels discuss George's character with his wingless guardian, Clarence Oddbody. As the celestial spectator of George's cinematic life, Oddbody models the desire of the audience to identify with the reality of the film, even to the point of intervening in its world by entering the cinematic frame itself. In the nightmare sequence, George aligns himself with the perspective of Oddbody and sees the world from the viewpoint of the absent other – in Lacanian terms, the barred subject. This barred subject is also the position of the spectator who, in some sense, sees the cinematic image as the articulation of a world without the spectator as subject. George and the spectators become odd bodies, not because the nightmare is the truth from which they are excluded, but because the truth lies in the contradiction between the ideology of capitalist humanism and the reality of capitalist accumulation, between George's wonderful life and the real that makes this fantasy necessary.

One could go much further into the context of *It's a Wonderful Life*. Capra's politics were a contradictory blend of economically conservative republicanism and democratic populism. Despite his conservative leanings, the writers he worked with tended to be liberals and radicals. According to Joseph McBride, Capra did not arrive at his formula for filmmaking until he began collaborating with Robert Riskin in the early thirties. It was Riskin who wrote the screenplay for Capra's first independent production in 1941, *Meet*

---

[21] M. B. Hansen, "Mass Culture as Hieroglyphic Writing: Adorno, Derrida, Kracauer," *New German Critique* 56 (Spring–Summer 1992), 45. See also T. W. Adorno, "Transparencies on Film," *New German Critique* 24–25 (Fall–Winter 1981–82), 201.

[22] K. Silverman, *Male Subjectivity at the Margins* (New York: Routledge, 1992), p. 93.

John Doe, his most risk-taking and politically radical film. The
original screenplay version of Philip Van Doren Stern's *The
Greatest Gift* was written by Dalton Trumbo and revised by
Clifford Odets and Marc Connelly. Capra bought this material in
1945 from RKO for a second attempt at an independent production. It became *It's a Wonderful Life* through the work of two
liberals, Frances Goodrich and Albert Hackett, with contributions
from Michael Wilson, Jo Swerling, and Dorothy Parker. In later
years, according to McBride, Capra selectively remembered this
screenwriting process in order to purge the film of any dangerous
political connections. In truth, out of eight screenwriters, six,
including Capra himself, became victims of the Hollywood inqui-
sition that began in 1947. (Trumbo and Wilson were blacklisted.) A
complete analysis of *It's a Wonderful Life* would have to take into
account the film's articulation of these contextual factors, particularly by analyzing the differences between the final version of the
film and the darker screenplay by Trumbo. But from what I have
said here, it should be clear why, retrospectively, a film that has
always been seen as a Christmas classic can also be seen, in the
words of Emanuel Levy, as "one of the gloomiest movies ever
made."[23]

Aesthetic Theory and political responsibility

It's a Wonderful Life virtually negates its own promise as a
commodity of the culture industry. Life, it says, is not so wonderful after all. Furthermore, analysis has the effect of subverting its
commodity form, which is reflected in the Christmas-card quality
of the framing images. Though over the last half-century the film's
commodity form has probably dominated the mode of its reception as a Christmas movie that reaffirms the humanist values of
capitalist culture, analysis reveals that another mode of reception
is possible and perhaps has already taken place. It reveals in the
work a tendency toward autonomy which offers resistance to the
pressures of the culture industry that would reduce the film to an
object completely subsumed by the profit-making calculations of
business. Such autonomy is not pure in the sense that it can

[23] J. McBride, *Frank Capra: The Catastrophe of Success* (New York: Simon and
Schuster, 1992), pp. 292, 510–12; and E. Levy, *Small-Town America in Film: The
Decline and Fall of Community* (New York: Continuum, 1991), p. 92.

completely negate the commodity fetishism of the culture indus-try. But insofar as the film can be made by immanent analysis to disclose the contradiction between its meaning and its commodity form, it becomes an absolute commodity that is impelled by its own internal contradictions to the moment of an explosion or self-negation. From this perspective, even *It's a Wonderful Life* anticipates and illustrates the argument Adorno makes in his final major work, *Aesthetic Theory.*

When this work was originally published in 1970, conservative and moderate critics praised it while leftist critics kept their distance. As Peter Uwe Hohendahl suggests, the interpretation and critique of Adorno's work in the early seventies was guided by the conflict between the student movements and the West German establishment. In a context where the New Left was trying to create political alliances and a political practice, Adorno took a position that seemed antithetical to such goals by arguing against the unity of theory and praxis and for the necessity of defending theory against an uncritical positivism.[24] In retrospect, the New Left quest for a political praxis may seem more impracti-cal than Adorno's insistence on the autonomy of theory. I would argue, however, that the two positions are not inconsistent as long as one believes that social change is not something that happens all at once, or that revolution, even if it were just around the corner (which it appears not to be), is never enough in and of itself to bring about a liberating social transformation. Adorno's "philo-sophical strategies of hibernation," as Jochen Schulte-Sasse calls them,[25] may be seen not as a rejection of the efficacy of political practice but as an argument for the necessity of critique. The latter is essential to any long-term social change or what Raymond Williams has called the long revolution. Critique is a form of political responsibility that must precede and follow any form of praxis if such praxis is not to become rigidified into purely ideological categories.

Adorno's work seems to be completely at odds with the work of

---

24 P. U. Hohendahl, *Reappraisals: Shifting Alignments in Postwar Critical Theory* (Ithaca: Cornell University Press, 1991), pp. 79–80. See T. W. Adorno, *Kritik: Kleine Schriften zur Gesellschaft* (Frankfurt am Main: Suhrkamp, 1971), pp. 145–50.

25 J. Schulte-Sasse, Foreword, *The Theory of the Avant-Garde*, by P. Bürger (Min-neapolis: University of Minnesota Press, 1984), p. xviii.

someone like Edward Said who has written: "cultural forms are hybrid, mixed, impure, and the time has come in cultural analysis to reconnect their analysis with their actuality." Said recognizes that this concept of the hybrid cultural artifact goes against the grain of traditional cultural criticism which is usually organized under such categories as the creative writer, the autonomous work of art, national literatures, genres, and other abstractions "that have acquired almost fetishistic presence."[26] In my view, he correctly criticizes the Frankfurt school in general for remaining silent on the question of imperialism, although he sees this as true of most European and American cultural theory, with the exception of feminism and the work of cultural studies critics influenced by Raymond Williams and Stuart Hall. Nevertheless, Said's own emphasis on the fetishistic character of the traditional aesthetic categories points toward the historical pertinence of Adorno's work.

In *Aesthetic Theory*, the autonomous work of art does not transcend history but is a specific historical form. Adorno's theory depends on the division between the social and the aesthetic within bourgeois culture that dates back to the eighteenth century. "By historicizing the major categories of aesthetic theory," writes Hohendahl, "Adorno brings these realms closer together again. Ultimately, art and society belong to the same stream of history."[27] Still, the critic who rejects out of hand any division between art and society necessarily fails to grasp the historical form of either in the context of capitalist culture. If one ignores the autonomy of the work of art, then one assumes that the relation between the work and its context is unmediated and transparent. One assumes that the message of the work is contained in its meaning; and once that meaning has been deciphered and situated in the field of cultural antagonisms, the work has been defined in terms of its political effects. Such an approach, however, either ignores or oversimplifies the symptomatic relation of the art work to its post-Enlightenment historical context.

When Adorno describes the work of art as a windowless monad, he does not mean to detach it from the social field but to articulate its social form. According to Said, to the extent that this

---

[26] E. Said, *Culture and Imperialism* (New York: Alfred A. Knopf, 1993), pp. 14, 315.
[27] Hohendahl, *Reappraisals*, p. 82.

social form is unique to the West, it is a mistake to argue that "the 'other' non-European literatures, those with more obviously worldly affiliations to power and politics, can be studied 'respectably,' as if they were in actuality as high, autonomous, aesthetically independent, and satisfying as Western literatures have been made to be."[28] But this kind of thinking entails its own risks. It leads to the depreciation of the aesthetic pleasures that can be derived from reading so-called *postcolonial* or *Third-World* literature, while it suggests an aesthetic simplicity in such work that belies, in my view, its actual complexity and sophistication. For example, Ngũgĩ wa Thiong'o has been rather notorious in his recent fiction for his overt engagement with political and ideological issues. At the same time, Ngũgĩ has been a self-conscious craftsman in drawing on Western models and African oral narratives to produce works like *Devil on the Cross* and *Matigari* that could bear comparison with the work of Brecht in their insistence on both aesthetic experimentation and didactic purpose. Particularly in *Matigari*, Ngũgĩ uses techniques that detach the work from its immediate context in Kenya in order to emphasize not the universality of its themes but rather their translatability into different historical contexts both in Africa and throughout the world. To some extent, the hybrid nature of cultural forms makes no sense unless one presupposes their autonomy. It is precisely the autonomy of art as an institution that gives Ngũgĩ the authorization to take his aesthetic material from wherever he wants and to construct a work that does not have to conform to a preconceived political or aesthetic ideology. I do not mean, of course, that autonomy should become an alibi for political irresponsibility or quietism. In Ngũgĩ's case, it becomes the ground of responsibility in the face of a state that tries to enforce its own interpretation of the world on the artist and eventually exiles him for choosing to write in his native language. Yet Ngũgĩ also takes into account the commodity form of the art work and quite intentionally exploits that form in order to reach the widest audience for his work, both in Gĩkũyũ and in English.

But if the concept of aesthetic autonomy cannot be limited exclusively to the West, the *worldly affiliations* of the autonomous work of art cannot be ignored in the so-called *metropolitan*

[28] Said, *Culture and Imperialism*, pp. 316–17.

literatures. When Adorno reminds us that the "Greek military junta knew only too well why it banned Beckett's plays in which not a word is said about politics," he makes the point that the politics of art cannot be reduced to voluntarism or simple commitment (*AT* 333). He suggests that one of the ways in which art criticizes the world is by dispelling its own mystique as art, by making itself useless for appropriation by an authoritarian state. Adorno would not disagree with Said that the autonomous work of art has acquired a fetishistic value; but, he would add, "The fetish character of art works is a condition of their truth, including their social truth" (*AT* 323).

Art today is both affirmative and critical. It participates, as Marcuse stresses, in the affirmative culture

of the bourgeois epoch which led in the course of its own development to the segregation from civilization of the mental and spiritual world as an independent realm of value that is also considered superior to civilization. Its decisive characteristic is the assertion of a universally obligatory, eternally better and more valuable world that must be unconditionally affirmed: a world essentially different from the factual world of the daily struggle for existence, yet realizable by every individual for himself "from within," without any transformation of the state of fact.[29]

Every work of art could be considered affirmative to the extent that it legitimates the division between mental and physical labor on which artistic production depends in almost any context. For example, Ngũgĩ's Gĩkũyũ writings may have led to his exile from Kenya, but in translation they have received a positive reception in Britain and the United States. Yet, as a writer, Ngũgĩ insists that the neocolonial system which exists in so many African states directly expresses the interests of Euro-American capital and culture. The stylistic techniques and literary forms that have enabled Ngũgĩ to challenge this system also indirectly affirm the very cultural imperialism he struggles to defeat.

For Adorno, there is an element of risk in any artistic production, however critical it may be of its social context, since it can always be appropriated and institutionally manipulated in such a way as to affirm the authority of the state and the status quo. The university in particular seems to be the site of such an intermeshing of affirmation and critique. Since the nineteenth century,

[29] H. Marcuse, *Negations: Essays in Critical Theory*, trans. J. J. Shapiro (Boston: Beacon, 1968), p. 95.

literature as an institution has made its home in the university and has come to include, by this late date, not only classical and vernacular literatures but forms of popular or mass culture as well. Such an institutional formation in and of itself has the effect of affirming cultural norms that may or may not be open to the possibility of critique. Critique itself becomes affirmative insofar as it finds its institutional authorization within the university. Nevertheless, if criticism wants to articulate the political effect of art, that is, to bring art back to the recognition of its worldliness, it must squarely face the dilemma that Adorno describes so well: if art "lets go of autonomy it sells out to the established order, whereas if it tries to stay strictly within its autonomous confines it becomes equally co-optable, living a harmless life in its appointed niche" (*AT* 337).

The method of cultural studies

By contrast with those who reject Adorno's *Aesthetic Theory* as a belated expression of modernist ideology, I believe it should be a resource for contemporary cultural studies. It is not enough to harangue against the political irresponsibility of art or the artist, or, for that matter, of criticism itself. We have to understand, or at least to pose the question of, what art is. Adorno's theory of art yokes together two seemingly irreconcilable tendencies that have divided the field of the humanities in recent years: tradition and culture. Defenders of tradition argue that the autonomy of art is not historical but universal; it expresses transcendent values that cannot be reduced to any specific context (though background, including historical background, is required as the condition of access to the universal). By contrast, defenders of culture suggest that there is no distinction to be made between art and any other cultural product; aesthetic autonomy is simply a metaphysical illusion without any historical validity.

Adorno's position is not a compromise between tradition and culture. On the contrary, *Aesthetic Theory* should be aligned with the project of cultural studies precisely through its refusal of the idealization of art as an object imbued with transhistorical value. Adorno nevertheless differs from many cultural theorists by insisting that art's negative autonomy is the means by which it criticizes the world. He even goes so far as to argue that the autonomous work of art can have a greater political impact on the social field than a more overtly engaged work that identifies itself with specific positions in that field. While art should never be read as if it were divorced from the social context, it also should not be reduced to that context as if context were something that determines the work from the outside. Art is the symptom of history, and it can be made to reveal its historical truth only through a critical intervention that lays bare the context in the text, the immanent form of its historical determination. Adorno yokes together tradition and culture by articulating the fundamental contradiction in the art work between the one and the other.

In his essay, "Cultural Studies and its Theoretical Legacies," Stuart Hall addresses the tension between theory and practice in cultural studies, a subject also important in Adorno's late writings. According to Hall, this new field, now that it has been popularized in America, represents the academic triumph of a "privileged object of study: culture, ideology, language, the symbolic." While Hall recognizes many positive advances in the field brought about by what he calls the *linguistic turn*, with its emphasis on discursivity and textuality, he also identifies a threat to the characteristic that would distinguish cultural studies from other intellectual disciplines: its political mission. He insists that cultural studies, while it may have been radically transformed by the influence of theory, has no identity or purpose if it loses the critical tension between political commitment and theoretical speculation. Still, it is not always clear what the political commitment of cultural studies is a commitment to, except insofar as the field has always affiliated itself with the question of class and, more recently, with the political issues of gender and race. As Hall points out, while cultural studies was from the beginning influenced by Marxism, there was never a "perfect theoretical fit."[30] Is it appropriate to say that cultural studies proper is a rigorous intellectual discipline that seeks to promote the development of democratic socialism through cultural analysis?

Hall suggests another way of understanding the relation between theory and politics. Speaking of textuality as the object of cultural analysis, he insists that cultural studies asks us "to say

[30] S. Hall, "Cultural Studies and its Theoretical Legacies," in *Cultural Studies*, ed. L. Grossberg, C. Nelson, and P. A. Treichler (New York: Routledge, 1992), pp. 279, 283.

'yes' and 'no' at one and the same time." Culture will always operate through the medium of its textualities (which, in this context, does not refer exclusively to written texts but to any cultural artifact or encoded object); but such textuality as a thing in itself is not the aim of cultural production. The identity of this aim has become the stumbling block of cultural studies, which has never been able to produce a complete theory of culture detailing its internal relations and effects. Yet, without such an account, how is it possible to determine the precise political effect of cultural theory and practice? Hall describes culture's *displacement* of the social, or its relative autonomy, as a quality that makes it difficult to determine the impact of cultural work on other social and political issues that cannot be reduced to questions of critical textuality. Thus, for Hall, cultural studies has become important among the contemporary intellectual fields not because of its brilliant theorizations (which less political poststructuralisms can probably surpass) but because of its articulation of theory and politics in "an ever irresolvable but permanent tension." Indeed, it articulates the contradiction between theory and practice without surrendering the necessity of both to social transformation. Without this recognition of tension or even contradiction, there is always the danger that cultural analysis will posit some concept of power as "an easy floating signifier which just leaves the crude exercise and connections of power and culture altogether emptied of any signification."[31] The problem, of course, is that this tension in and of itself does not constitute a political program that would lead in any obvious way to human liberation, nor does it clearly define what it is that humans need to be liberated from. If the Birmingham Centre of Contemporary Cultural Studies aimed at creating organic intellectuals who would align themselves with the emergence of a historical movement, it failed in that goal because the historical movement never materialized. The intellectual worker in the broader field of cultural studies has no guarantee that his or her practice of theory will necessarily produce positive political effects.

Nevertheless, in my view, the field of cultural studies is the necessary starting point for any contemporary cultural politics that would try to account for what passes as the autonomous work

---

[31] Hall, "Cultural Studies," pp. 284–86.

of art. Within cultural studies, it is possible not only to defend the usefulness of that category but, perhaps more problematically, to engage in what will appear to be *close readings*. Such a move could be said to reverse the direction in which cultural studies has developed since the sixties. As Dennis Dworkin narrates, "by the late 1960s, cultural researchers and theorists at the Centre had grown dissatisfied with the theoretical foundations of their project. They recognized that their method of close readings must be anchored in a wider understanding of society, an understanding that could only come from social theory."[32] While I agree in principle with this movement away from the simple application of literary critical methods to the field of culture in general, I still believe that reading and some form of immanent analysis are the necessary prerequisites to understanding the political effect of writing and other forms of cultural production. Against the reductive models of close reading, Hall has similarly noted that there is a significant difference between the rejection of any final, absolute meaning and the rejection of any meaning whatsoever.

Hall describes the requirements of reading in the modern context. He begins by calling into question the possibility of closure in the analysis of meaning. Since no reading is ever final, critics should engage in "the semantic raids that Benjamin proposed – to find the fragments, to decipher their assembly and see how you can make a surgical cut into them, assembling and reassembling the means and instruments of cultural production." Such an improvisational analysis is a defining characteristic of the modern and postmodern worlds. Yet while this methodology shatters the concept of univocal meaning and opens critical discourse up to "the infinite plurality of codes," it does not suggest that reading ever transcends the process of encoding, which "always entails the imposition of an arbitrary 'closure.'" On the contrary, the meaning of a text or any other cultural object is actually enriched by such a self-conscious interpretive closure because "we understand meaning not as a natural but as an arbitrary act – the intervention of ideology into language." Still, reading is not *totally* arbitrary in the sense that any signifier can go with any signified. The arbitrariness lies in the absence of any

[32] D. L. Dworkin, "Cultural Studies and the Crisis in British Radical Thought," in *Views Beyond the Border Country: Raymond Williams and Cultural Politics*, ed. D. L. Dworkin and L. G. Roman (New York: Routledge, 1993), p. 47.

natural connection between the signifier and the signified or between the text and its meaning. Reading as an ideological intervention recognizes a given text or document as the ground of contention between different ideological tendencies within a specific historical situation, tendencies that can lead to different articulations of meaning. Hall's theory of articulation thus clarifies our understanding of the politics of reading. According to Hall, the unity of any discourse is "the articulation of different, distinct elements which can be rearticulated in different ways because they have no necessary 'belongingness.'" Yet this unity is not completely random and involves a linkage between the "articulated discourse and the social forces with which it can, under certain historical conditions, but need not necessarily, be connected." The concept of articulation describes both the internal relationship between ideological elements that can be said "to cohere together within a discourse" and the external relationship between such an articulated discourse and certain political subjects and contexts.[33] It suggests a technique of reading that avoids the New Critical concept of the work as organic whole with a unique and self-contained meaning.

In other words, within the field of cultural studies, an immanent reading involves the reconfiguration of the elements of a text at two different, though mutually interdependent, levels. First, the reader links together those elements of a text which constitute not so much a unity as a configuration of meaning. Such a configuration is not necessary or absolute for all time, but it has to suggest some form of coherence or closure that can make sense to a reader in a specific historical context. Virtually any interpretation, whatever its ideological underpinnings, produces a configuration of elements to constitute a meaning, although a naive interpretation would mistake this configuration for the organic structure of the whole. The second step of this process is more complicated and could actually be said to precede and yet somehow to follow from the first step. There can be no internal articulation of the elements of a text without the introduction of an element from the outside. Such an element could be a political perspective, a cultural norm, a theoretical model, or another text. When I say that the element

---

[33] S. Hall, "On Postmodernism and Articulation: An Interview with Stuart Hall," ed. L. Grossberg, *Journal of Communication Inquiry* 10.2 (1986), 49–50, 53.

must come from the outside, I mean that it must be possible to identify the element as a part of the social context from which the text differentiates itself; but this does not exclude the element from an immanent position within the text. Reading as a form of articulation is thus necessarily a political intervention because while there is no *natural* linkage between the different elements of a text or between the text and its context, it is not possible to articulate any two elements at random. An articulation is always the symptom of the historical context in that it embodies the material limits of that context; it suggests through its success or failure both what can be understood and cannot be understood at a given moment in historical time.

This practice of articulation also bears a striking resemblance to the concept of constellation that governs the critical practices of both Benjamin and Adorno. That concept, according to Eagleton, posits

a form of criticism so tenaciously immanent that it would remain entirely immersed in its object. The truth of that object would be disclosed not by referring it in rationalist style to a governing general concept, but by dismantling its component elements through the power of minutely particular concepts, then reconfigurating them in a pattern which redeemed the thing's meaning and value without ceasing to adhere to it.[34]

Such a dismantling and reconfiguration, however, necessarily involves a dialectical interplay between the text and the context. As the aesthetic object is dismantled, the individual elements regain their status as contextual fragments that can have no meaning until they are linked to other elements derived from the same context. The constellation is precisely the form of meaning that refuses metalanguage or any metaphysically stable referent. "Ideas," wrote Benjamin in *The Origin of German Tragic Drama*, "are to objects as constellations are to stars."[35] They are not abstractions but the configuration of the particulars that make up the object. These particulars have no necessary belongingness but suggest historical meanings through the way in which they are linked to one another and to the context from which they derive. This concept of meaning as the effect of a particular arrangement or configuration of elements (which could be phenomena or

[34] Eagleton, *Ideology*, p. 328.
[35] W. Benjamin, *The Origin of German Tragic Drama*, trans. J. Osborne (London: NLB, 1977), p. 34.

signifiers) brings us to the Lacanian concept of meaning as a *point de capiton*, the arbitrary linkage of signifier with signifier.

Lacan, sublimation, and *The Age of Innocence*

Lacanian theory plays a significant role in the reading of Adorno's concept of mimesis in chapter 2 of this study. Should readers imagine that this linkage has no textual ground, they should keep in mind this remark from Jacques Lacan's seminar, *The Ethics of Psychoanalysis*:

> works of art imitate the objects they represent, but their end is certainly not to represent them. In offering the imitation of an object, they make something different out of that object. Thus they only pretend to imitate. The object is established in a certain relationship to the Thing and is intended to encircle and to render [it] both present and absent.
>
> (*E* 141)

These formulations anticipate Adorno's understanding of mimesis as adapting or correlating behavior. The work of art never simply copies or reflects its object but rather adapts to it in the sense of making something different out of the object through *a process of incorporation* or, to use the language of cultural studies, *articulation*. Mimesis is a form of linkage or articulation that expresses "the non-conceptual affinity of a subjective creation with its objective and unposited other" (*AT* 80). How art makes the objective other render what Lacan calls *das Ding* requires a more complicated explanation.

A work of art can articulate a relationship to what is not art, or its objective other, through two means: symptom-formation and sublimation. In the first case, the true object of aesthetic representation is evaded through the substitution of another object or signifier that takes its place in such a way as to repress the other. As Lacan notes, "A symptom is the return by means of signifying substitution of that which is at the end of the drive in the form of an aim." Sublimation, by contrast, refers to the "paradoxical fact that the drive is able to find its aim elsewhere than in that which is its aim – without its being a question of the signifying substitution ... of the symptom as compromise formation" (*E* 110). One could hypothesize that the symptom articulates the conservative dimension of art: its refusal to surrender the aim of the drive that propels artistic production by giving ground to the chain of signifying substitutions that constitutes the play of desire. *Finnegans Wake* would be a model of such a process because in its linguistic play, its constant repetition of the "seim anew," it never surrenders its desire, even though it can never finally say what that desire is a desire for. This silence, in fact, is the condition of desire. The aim of the drive that this desire articulates relentlessly through its metaphorical substitutions is impossible, and it is the very impossibility of that aim that desire refuses to concede or give ground to. Consequently, desire displaces the drive and appears to draw it away from its aim; but in this way it actually keeps that aim alive through the signifier.

Although Slavoj Žižek insists that the symptom should be distinguished from what Lacan calls in his late work, with the specific example of Joyce in mind, the *sinthome*, he does not explain how the latter term should be related to the former. The symptom, he says, is "the coded message to be deciphered by interpretation," while the *sinthome* is "the meaningless letter that immediately procures *jouis-sense*, 'enjoyment-in-meaning,' 'enjoy-meant.'"[36] It seems to me that these two terms are related to one another in this sense: the *sinthome* results from the subject's identification with the symptom. As Žižek explains, "To 'identify with a symptom' means to recognize in the 'excesses', in the disruptions of the 'normal' way of things, the key offering us access to its true functioning."[37] In *Finnegans Wake*, Joyce has identified with his symptom to the extent that it is no longer the illusion of meaning that the work seeks to produce, the illusion that is the essence of the symptom, but rather the pleasure that derives from the play of meaning-production. The critical edge of the *Wake* lies in its material realization that the excesses of its language are historically more important than the possible meanings they may harbor. These excesses disclose the truth about meaning-functions in the normal or ideological use of language, the truth that meaning gives pleasure. The *sinthome* is the truth about the symptom, the truth that its metaphorical substitutions are nothing less than a strategy for continually taking pleasure from the impossible aim of the drive.

[36] S. Žižek, *Looking Awry: An Introduction to Jacques Lacan through Popular Culture* (Cambridge, Massachusetts: MIT, 1991), pp. 128–29.
[37] S. Žižek, *The Sublime Object of Ideology* (London: Verso, 1989), p. 128.

Sublimation is something different from the symptom and, as I will try to show in a moment, something not that different from the *sinthome*. By providing the drive with "a satisfaction different from its aim," sublimation "reveals the true nature of the *Trieb* insofar as it is not simply instinct, but has a relationship to *das Ding* as such, to the Thing insofar as it is distinct from the object" (E 111). The drive is ultimately something more than the instinct; it is what Freud called the death drive but not in the sense that death is the true aim of the drive but in the sense that death is nothing in itself, something that cannot be known objectively, or the Thing. According to Lacan, "the Thing is that which in the real, the primordial real ... suffers from the signifier" (E 118). Though it cannot be known as an object, it is that in the object that makes an object, the subject's absolute Other that is supposed to be found again but cannot be found, though it is known through "its pleasurable associations" (E 52). The Thing is something that is always already missing and that "will always be represented by emptiness, precisely because it cannot be represented by anything else – or, more exactly, because it can only be represented by something else" (E 129–30). The Thing is not strictly the aim of the drive in the sense that *the aim of all life is death*, to use Freud's formulation. Death, in this sentence, is just another signifier; and insofar as death is the aim of the drive, as in the case of someone who feels compelled to risk his or her life repeatedly, it becomes the ground of symptom-formation. Sublimation does not substitute one object for another with the same aim but changes the aim of the drive and provides a kind of satisfaction completely different from that of the symptom. "Sublimation," writes Lacan, "raises an object ... to the dignity of the Thing" (E 112).

I will try to illustrate the process of sublimation through a consideration of Edith Wharton's *The Age of Innocence* and the film version of Martin Scorsese. Although Scorsese does an interesting job of translating the book into film, he makes a few problematic changes. For the most part, in Scorsese's version, the woman is presented exclusively as the symptom of the man. Newland Archer, who is engaged to marry May Welland, falls in love with her cousin, the Countess Olenska, who has left her husband in Europe. There are rumors that she has had an affair after leaving him, and this scandal marginalizes her position in New York high society. In two critical scenes, one before Archer's marriage to May and one after, he confesses his love to Countess Olenska. In both cases, she reciprocates verbally but insists that there can be no consummation of this love because of May and the others whom it would hurt. Finally, the privileged society that both characters respect conspires to separate them with the full participation of Newland's wife. Ellen Olenska returns to Europe to live the rest of her life apart from both her husband and her relatives in New York. For Archer, she becomes the symptom par excellence: "When he thought of Ellen Olenska it was abstractly, serenely, as one might think of some imaginary beloved in a book or a picture: she had become the composite vision of all that he had missed."[38] In Archer's eye, Ellen Olenska is a signifier of the lack in the Other, of what is missing from his world.

Still, in the novel, Ellen's own view of the situation differs dramatically from Archer's. In the key scene before Archer's marriage, Ellen explains to him that it is too late for their love, and he does not understand. "You don't understand because you haven't guessed how you've changed things for me," she says, and then describes what had been her innocence about New York society before Archer's interventions saved her. The book then suggests that what has been changed is not so much her position in society as her relation to something else. Originally, Ellen had wanted the divorce that would liberate her from a bad marriage; but while her family could not dissuade her from this desire, Archer inadvertently showed her another way. As she says,

The very good people didn't convince me; I felt they'd never been tempted. But you knew; you understood; you had felt the world outside tugging at one with all its golden hands – and yet you hated the things it asks of one; you hated happiness bought by disloyalty and cruelty and indifference. *That was what I'd never known before – and it's better than anything I've known.* [my emphases]

The words emphasized are in the film, but they have been decontextualized almost beyond recognition. Their meaning is distorted by the fact that we hear Ellen softly speak them while Archer kisses her slipper, an image which virtually overpowers and mystifies the meaning of the words. Ellen broaches this subject again when the two meet in Boston after Archer's marriage: "it was you who made me understand that under the

---

[38] Edith Wharton, *The Age of Innocence* (New York: Macmillan, 1992), p. 347.

dullness there are things so fine and sensitive and delicate that even those I most cared for in my other life look cheap in comparison." Though she cannot explain herself, she realizes now "with how much that is hard and shabby and base the most exquisite pleasures may be paid." Archer responds bitterly, "Exquisite pleasures – it's something to have had them!"[39]

In truth, Ellen has given up one form of exquisite pleasure for another, *better than anything she has ever known*, though admittedly this new pleasure is more properly a *jouissance* that transgresses the boundary between pleasure and pain. Archer, by contrast, clings to the aim of his drive, or the signifier of everything he lacks in the way of physical and spiritual pleasure – that is, a substitute-formation. For Ellen, Archer is not the signifier of a lack but rather the sublime object that has been raised *to the dignity of the Thing*. Ellen has implicitly come to realize what Archer will learn, if he ever learns, only at the novel's end: that the sexual relation does not exist. Archer's *méconnaissance*, his commitment to a romantic dream that is as ordinary as the completely conventional life he leads, causes him to turn his back on the Real when he finally has the chance to be with Ellen Olenska, that is to say, with the real person who could never possibly live up to Archer's fantasy of her. It is the signifier he wants and not the Thing itself.

One could argue that Madame Olenska, after she buries herself alive in Paris, resembles the figure of Antigone who has been reinterpreted by Lacan as the realization of the death drive in its purest form. Furthermore, Sophocles' play as a whole, through its focus on the image of Antigone, maps out the visual economy that defines desire: "She has a quality that both attracts us and startles us, in the sense of intimidates us" (*E* 247). Antigone's beauty, which virtually brings desire to a stop, is the signifier of her death drive; and the ambivalence of our reaction to her corresponds to the ambivalence of our response to the death drive that she channels. As the final scene of *The Age of Innocence* demonstrates (in both the novel and the film), Archer's attraction to Madame Olenska is ultimately ambivalent. In effect, she seems to split his desire just as Lacan says that beauty splits "desire strangely as it continues on its way, for one cannot say that it is completely extinguished by the apprehension of beauty" (*E* 248–49). Lacan is

---

[39] Wharton, *The Age of Innocence*, pp. 171, 241.

suggesting that readers of *Antigone* are confronted by a fascinating object that lures desire with the promise of an end to it and yet supports desire with the failure of its promise. *The Age of Innocence* reveals the same structure of desire. Insofar as Ellen Olenska is the object of Archer's obsession, she is the symptom or lure of his desire, the promise of its extinction, which she evades by refusing to be the symptom and forcing him to confront his own relation to the Real that lies beyond society as he knows it. Beyond society lies that for which all of society is a detour, call it death or the Thing that is nothing. It is that which cannot be represented and therefore cannot exist because it brings the subject who confronts it back to the truth of the impossible demand for love or for the total satisfaction of needs that would transcend every form of division, including the division between life and death. Desire continues on its way because it cannot face the terrifying beauty that is the true object of desire insofar as desire is the desire of the Other, of nothing that can be named. Ellen, like Antigone, dies a symbolic death before her real death, so that she can take pleasure from the *sinthome*, from a life that has become like a work of art. Archer, on the other hand, refuses to identify with the symptom, to recognize in its excesses the key to the pleasure he takes from it.

The film version of *The Age of Innocence* transforms the novel in another way. Under Scorsese's direction, from the very beginning, Archer is presented as a sublimated figure, while in the book he must undergo a change before he appears in that form. Initially portrayed in the novel as just another vapid dilettante in the New York high society of the late nineteenth century, he is gradually transformed into a sublime object of desire. In the frame of the novel as a whole, moreover, Archer becomes a synecdoche for the whole of New York society, which is transformed into the sublime object of Wharton's novel. This does not mean that Wharton has idealized that society in the way that Archer idealizes Madame Olenska as the symptom of his lack. On the contrary, as Žižek observes, "there is nothing intrinsically sublime in a sublime object – according to Lacan, a sublime object is an ordinary, everyday object which, quite by chance, finds itself occupying the place of what he calls *das Ding*, the impossible–real object of desire.'[40] In effect, New York society as the sublime object of desire

[40] Žižek, *Sublime Object*, p. 194.

articulates the desire for the Thing as the desire for the Real itself. It is not society that is desired anymore than it is Archer who is desired by Madame Olenska (though her love for him, which is neither puritanical nor platonic, channels her desire); it is the Thing, the metaphysical emptiness that is channeled through the representation of a sublime object. This emptiness is not the lack in the Other that produces Archer's symptom, his desire for something that will fill the emptiness and take away the gaze of the Real. The emptiness is the thing itself, the Real that exists beyond all the possible representations of culture, the Thing that makes cultural change possible. The gaze of the Thing calls into question the necessity of any status quo, of any system of values, of any structural law. It points to the contingency of these cultural forms. According to Lacan, "All art is characterized by a certain mode of organization around this emptiness [*das Ding*]" (*E* 130).

Lacan would agree with Adorno that art is an illusion insofar as it is incomplete, insofar as it punctures its own claim to represent a totality; but in that very incompleteness it leads us back to the Real in the sense of all the possibilities of cultural and social organization that have been excluded by the status quo as a system of symbolic values and relationships. Lacan observed that, as a work of art, even "a box of matches is not simply an object, but ... in the form of an *Erscheinung* ... it may be a Thing" (*E* 114). For Adorno, *Erscheinung*, or apparition, is that force within the illusion (*Schein*) of art that destroys the illusion by bringing into visibility the historical contradictions and antagonisms that determine it at the level of form. *Erscheinung* destroys the illusion of art as an end in itself, the object of desire as the substitute-formation that tries to resolve all the contradictions and fill all the gaps within society as it actually exists. Even a work of art that operates like a symptom can be transformed into a sublime object through the artist's or even the reader's identification with this structure. In other words, the *sinthome* is itself the change of object, the change of the drive's aim, that punctures the illusion of the symptom, the illusion that it possesses some final meaning.

Lacan's theory of sublimation makes it perfectly clear why the individual work of art is, in Adorno's sense, a windowless monad. It is not that art transcends the social or can ever be anything more than a commodity of a particular sort. On the contrary, sublimation means that human subjects have the power to transform their desires into commodities that can be traded on the economic or cultural marketplace. Furthermore, the correct value of sublimation in art can only be determined by recognizing that "all artistic production ... is historically situated" (*E* 107). Art changes the world even when it represents it most faithfully because it changes the aim of our desire for the object. Art – at least, the work of art that is true – destroys its own illusion and directs the thought of the subject toward that which lies beyond illusion – not reality in the sense of an absolute interpretation of the world but the Real as the ground of all possible interpretations.

Derrida and the responsibility of interpretation

The last chapter of this study contains a lengthy discussion of Jacques Derrida's concept of critical responsibility. In this section, however, I need to explain why I continue to see a relationship between Lacan and Derrida in the field of cultural studies. Žižek, for example, constantly insists on an absolute and irreconcilable difference between these two thinkers, a difference that defines Derrida as a poststructuralist and Lacan as not: "Poststructuralists see the Lacanian theory of the *point de capiton*, of the phallic signifier as the signifier of lack, as an effort to master and restrain the 'dissemination' of the textual process." Derrida, he concludes, faults Lacan for transforming the lack into an affirmation of the phallus, into an idealization of the missing whole that always returns to the same location. This idealized trajectory of the phallus presupposes "a point of exception" which somehow guarantees the closure of the system of signifiers, the totalization of the symbolic. It posits symbolic castration as the condition of identity, with the phallus as its signifier.[41]

In dismissing Derrida's critique of Lacan, Žižek calls it a defense of linguistic dissemination, as if to suggest that, for Derrida, *dissemination* is some sort of liberation from language, rather than the disturbing fact of the historically contingent nature of meaning. Of course, Derrida does read the Lacanian theory of the phallus as an idealization; and in my view there is no question but that in some contexts it is. But, as I have argued elsewhere,[42]

[41] Žižek, *Sublime Object*, p. 154.
[42] P. McGee, *Telling the Other: The Question of Value in Modern and Postcolonial Writing* (Ithaca: Cornell University Press, 1992), pp. 64–78.

Lacan's theory as a whole and the style in which he conveys it also suggest the contingency of the phallic signifier. I believe that it is the privileging of the phallus within the context of a specific reading of Poe that Derrida calls into question (whether one agrees with him or not) and not all of Lacanian theory. In any case, Lacan's critique of metalanguage, his insistence on the impossibility of stabilizing the signification process in its own terms, implies the Derridean theory of dissemination. For Lacan, as for Derrida, meaning can never be transparent to itself in the medium of language because language can never circumscribe itself or lay down the limits of its own system.

As Žižek puts it, metalanguage is "*Real* in the strict Lacanian sense – that is, it is impossible to *occupy* its position." Stated somewhat differently, metalanguage refers to the fact that language, quite apart from its signifying functions, is made up of something irreducible, something that cannot be symbolized, something that is missed in every attempt to capture the totality of the linguistic system. Metalanguage is language that points to the Real through its failure to remain self-adequate and whole. Metalanguage is language about language and therefore, in some sense, is the condition of meaning. In my view, it is impossible to live in a world without meaning, but meaning can never be adequate to the Real which is the absolute limit of representation. Meaning is imaginary or ideological, but it is also an essential component of any subject's lived relation to the world. It is through the register of the Imaginary that we suture the Symbolic to the Real in order to construct a reality from which we derive pleasure and purpose. The Real could be called the meaning of meaning in the sense that it is the goal at which all meaning aims. Still, as Žižek suggests, the Real can never be captured by language, nor can a relation to the Real be avoided through language. The only way to articulate the Real in language is "to produce an utterance of pure metalanguage which, by its patent absurdity, materializes its own impossibility: that is, a paradoxical element which, in its very identity, embodies absolute otherness, the irreparable gap that makes it impossible to occupy a metalanguage position."[43] The irreparable gap between language and the Real divides language from itself, insofar as the signifiers that

---

[43] Žižek, *Sublime Object*, p. 156.

make up the linguistic system are themselves pieces of the Real that have been charged with symbolic value. For Derrida, however, it is not the concept of *the lack* as the formal incompleteness of the linguistic or any other symbolic system that is the problem. It is the postulation of a master signifier that can govern the lack and virtually eliminate any excess or remainder that derives from its own signifying process. If the phallus always returns to the location of the lack, then the lack has been transformed into an idealization of itself, a universal truth transcending history. But the whole point of Lacan's concept of *das Ding* is that no symbolization ever completely escapes its historical situation; the phallus, as the Freudian thing, is nothing in itself – and therefore cannot be the penis *per se* – because it is historically contingent. The master signifer is Imaginary as the articulation of universal truth, but the signifying Thing is Real. As Lacan's own theory of sublimation reminds us, anything can be *das Ding*. The master signifier is any signifier.

Derrida does not deny the existence of meaning, even the meaning of the phallus as a contingent signifier that attempts to totalize the systems of language and culture in a specific historical situation. In my view, the Derridean concept of the undecidable makes no sense (and it does make sense, as I argue in the last chapter of this book) unless one presupposes the necessity of totalization, of taking a systematic position, and, in effect, of positing a Lacanian *point de capiton*. Such a meaning is fixed or constructed through an articulation of elements or signifiers. Though one cannot imagine a thought that does not posit a center of meaning as such, one can always subject this center to a deconstructive reversal and displacement. Every system of meaning, however normalized it may be as ideology, remains incomplete; and this term *incomplete* strikes me as politically more useful than the term *lack*, though ultimately they are two sides of the same coin. I prefer the term *incomplete* because it emphasizes the dialectical relation between human desire and historical actuality. I cannot explain desire; and, like the Thing that is its ultimate goal, it is probably nothing in itself. Yet it is the relation of desire to history that creates the human sense of incompletion. Historical understanding may be the purest expression of desire, since it presupposes a human subject whose present is split between the past and the future as the ground of its meaning. That split is the contradiction between need and demand, between *what has been necessary for survival* and *the goal of an end to the necessity of surviving*. The subject redeems that contradiction without transcending it through its split formation. The subject is not the origin of desire but the expression of a redeeming contradiction that arises from the difference between need and demand. Desire is that difference or division. It is not a lack, though it conveys the sense that history is not yet finished. It is not the absence of something but the hope that comes from nothing.

If we take the phallus as the master signifier instead of the historically contingent signifier of patriarchal culture, we actually destroy the true significance of the Lacanian *point de capiton*, which resides in its arbitrary nature. In other words, there is no way of localizing the lack without symbolic violence, without the enforcement of meaning (*à la* Humpty Dumpty). At the same time, there is no escaping this violence insofar as we are the subjects of history. We can, however, take responsibility for the violence. Such responsibility is the ethical condition of interpretation and the ground of all possible hope.

Cultural studies is the methodology of hope. If it has not been able to forge a perfect theoretical fit with Marxism or with the other theories it has absorbed (including psychoanalysis, deconstruction, and feminism), it has made visible its own internal contradictions as the basis for its intervention in cultural politics. There are many critics today who would like to make cultural studies consistent with itself by denying the influences and forms of intellectual kinship I have foregrounded in this essay. In my view, they would eliminate the redeeming contradiction that makes cultural studies possible as a form of interdisciplinary desire. Cultural studies will never overcome the tension or, as I would prefer to say, the contradiction between theory and practice or thought and commitment. For this reason, it can never be a systematic theory or a pure discipline. Cultural studies is rather an inflection of intellectual work with the responsibilities of desire. It has a transformative effect on every theory and discipline that comes into contact with it because it insists on taking into account *real* human desires and the *other* voices that are both constituted and repressed by disciplinary and theoretical discourses. Like deconstruction and psychoanalysis, it unlocks every closed meaning; but it also constructs meaning as a form of political responsibility. Though it is not often described in this way, cultural studies articulates the experience of the undecidable as the instability of disciplinary and intellectual boundaries. However, it distinguishes itself from nihilism or universal relativism by insisting on the historical necessity of making a decision in the face of the undecidable. It promotes not the decision itself, which in one form or another is unavoidable, but the responsibility for the decision as the basis of commitment in intellectual work. Without this responsibility, human freedom as a form of ethical relationship between human subjects is impossible.

2

Art as the absolute commodity: the intersubjectivity of mimesis in Adorno's *Aesthetic Theory*

> True art challenges its own essence.
>
> Adorno, *Aesthetic Theory*

The aesthetic thing

The true work of art is never politically correct.

Such a statement is not meant to comfort or support the neoconservative critic in higher education today who makes it his or her business to reduce the unmanageable and sometimes irresponsible power of art to some sort of apolitical pap for nourishing the illusions of the status quo. Such an institutionalized art reinforces the belief in a transparent social reality by insisting on the absolute difference between art and life. Reality, it says, is concrete and particular, while art is abstract and universal. No one worships at the altar of the universal with greater show of devotion than the traditionalist; but at the same time the traditionalist secretly laughs at the intellectual Don Quixote who imagines that those things which are universal have anything to do with the way people are required to live in a world that was not constructed to be a work of art. Art, says the traditionalist, is contemplative and useless – a sort of second thought about the course of history after it is no longer possible to do anything about it.

On the other hand, art is not simply an instrument for those on the left who seek a formula for social change and human liberation. It is necessary to resist programmatic politics. The true Marxist today may not be the one who wears the label "Marxist" but rather who poses the questions, "Are we Marxists? Do Marxists exist?" These words belong to Gramsci who further says, "Marx did not write a nice little doctrine, he is not a Messiah who left a string of parables laden with categorical imperatives, with absolute, unquestionable norms beyond the categories of time and space."[1] Marxists, however, are not the only ones on the left who can be seduced by normative thinking. The left today is a complicated category in which it is not uncommon to find feminists, deconstructionists, new historicists, and materialists of every stripe who think they have all the answers locked inside the crystal ball of their methodology. Too often such thinking is contaminated by the very logic it attempts to resist. The world gets divided up into the different versions of the Manichean myth: capitalism against socialism, colonizer against colonized, white against black, straight against gay, men against women, and so forth. Of course, these divisions are not arbitrary or paranoid but derive from the experience of history, from acts of historical violence. Nevertheless, when these historical conflicts and contradictions are translated into sociological and sometimes even metaphysical categories, that is to say, when they come to be regarded as a sort of second nature, then they become abstractions that can be manipulated in such a way as to blind the victims of social violence and inequality to the concrete particularity of their historical situations. The vocabularies of critical discourse, which are the sedimentations of historical experience, suggest ways to name and explain the world, but they should not be confused with the aesthetic means by which the social context makes an imprint on the work of art.

The art work is never politically correct because the politics of art is immanent and not referential. Let me try to clarify what I am saying. It is certainly possible for an art work to contain material and convey messages that would be considered politically correct by one camp or another in a social debate. It may be appropriate, depending on the context, to evaluate a work of art for its contribution to the dissemination of a political message. The artist could even publicly declare that he or she intends to send a politically correct message to a specific audience, although there is

[1] Antonio Gramsci, *An Antonio Gramsci Reader: Selected Writings, 1916–1935*, ed. D. Forgacs (New York: Schocken, 1988), p. 36.

no guarantee that such a message will in fact be considered politically correct by that audience. It may just as easily turn out that an audience regards as a politically correct message something in an art work that was never intended by the artist to be political in any sense whatsoever. And yet I would argue that art, insofar as it is art, is necessarily political. Art may not be universal in the sense of transcending the historical, but it results from an articulation of the historical that cannot be reduced to a straightforward reflection. The work of art congeals the historical process into a form that is the effect or symptom of that process but not a representation of it. As Theodor Adorno writes in *Aesthetic Theory*, such a work is "the windowless monad of society" (*AT* 64).

According to Adorno, the art work is an object. As an object which has effaced the socio-economic relations and technical forces that make its production possible, it is also a commodity. Yet art is different from other commodities; it is the "absolute commodity" that "rids itself of the ideology inherent in the commodity form" (*AT* 336). At least, that is its structural intention. In a move that looks contradictory at first, Adorno asserts that even the absolute commodity does not completely escape being ideological. The contradiction may not be in Adorno's argument but in the immanent structure of art itself. The work of art, he says, "puts before us a picture of an antagonistic totality, of a whole which is made up of contradictions." The work nevertheless tries to transcend this system of contradictions, its historical content, through the medium of expressive form. Such a form mediates or transcodes the effects of social antagonism, or contradiction itself, rather than trying to resolve the conflict by privileging one side of the equation. The artistic subject does not posit contradiction or generate it out of the mind: rather, contradiction is an objective social relation that has left a trace in the subject. The objectivity of art derives from this process: "The subject can vanish meaningfully in the aesthetic object because it in turn is mediated by the object, as well as being immediately objective *qua* moment of suffering in expression." Social antagonisms enter the art work through technical means, through the *métier* of the artist. It is possible to interpret these antagonisms "in terms of tensions that exist outside of art" that can be said to shape it, though these tensions are not explicitly "reproduced or copied in the work of art." For Adorno, aesthetic form hinges on the dialectical relationship between technique and the social contradictions that deter-mine it (*AT* 446).

The primary antagonism that the art work embodies – not reflectively but immanently – is the contradiction between its objective form as a commodity in the market of cultural goods and its resistance to that objectivity through a disclosure that simulta-neously brings to light and disrupts the boundaries of the commodity form as a social process. The aesthetic object or thing has a relation to the outside world insofar as it is a thing, but that relation is not one of representation but of mediation. It is the first impulse of art to transform the outside world of which it is a part from within. It attempts to transcend the condition of its produc-tion by overcoming the division between art as a process and art as an institutionalized form. Only because art has become an institu-tion in real historical time – that is to say, because it has achieved a degree of autonomy as a thing-in-itself in post-Enlightenment society – can it make explicit through visible form and technique the process that institutionalization in some sense tries to efface.

Historically, art as a social process can be subjected to purely rational analysis only after the art work has achieved autonomy. The history of the commodification of art and the history of art's resistance to commodification are parallel tendencies within the same historical process. Modernity is the revolution in social production that enabled the art work to posit its own internal contradictions in order to transcend them through the means of technical innovation. Hypothetically, this process of innovation should be infinite in scope; but in practice it seems evident that it reached a saturation point during the period of modernism and that postmodern art grounds itself on a more negative relation to technique. The postmodern artist frequently innovates by refusing to innovate or by reproducing, in new combinations, familiar or outmoded techniques. Such technique is the means that art uses to transcend its own internal contradictions which are rooted in its antagonistic relation to society. These internal contradictions derive from objective traces in the artist, including the artistic skills and dispositions that she or he has learned and the social understanding of art that determines the artist's relation to her or his work. The art work materially expresses the imprint of society that constitutes the artist as a subject within the institutional field of aesthetic production. For this reason, it becomes possible and necessary to interpret the art work in terms of the social tensions that exist outside of it. This interpretation means unraveling or disclosing the process of determinate negation by which art constitutes itself in opposition to society. Determinate negation describes the aesthetic process and not the status of art as an institution. The true work of art tries to negate its own status as a work of art or its institutional form. As Adorno stressed, "The work of art is both a result and a process that has been arrested" (*AT* 257). Determinate negation in art is the process that has been arrested. Interpretation that is not just a ritual act of cultural reproduction must explode the boundaries of the art work to reveal its negative force, its negative autonomy. It must reveal the moment of anti-art, or determinate negation, in the work of art.

The artistic subject is objectively a "moment of suffering in expression." Throughout *Aesthetic Theory*, Adorno implies that suffering takes the form of determinate negation in the artistic process. Stated another way, determinate negation expresses suffering. Although expression is usually thought of as originating in the autonomous subject, as the immediate articulation of its will, desire, or feeling, for Adorno it articulates the social content of the subject: "Expression in works of art is the non-subjective in the subject; it is not so much the subject's expression as it is its impression, in the sense of imprint" (*AT* 165). The work of art does not represent suffering with the hope that such a representation will put an end to suffering by making it visible. Nor does it attempt to capture and convey the sensation of pain that we attribute to suffering. It is determined negatively, in its mimetic impulse, by suffering. Suffering in this context is not something that we feel or experience in ourselves as a response to something outside of us; it is the experience of that thing outside of us as being inside. Antagonistic social relations (and it is only through art and thought that we are able to imagine any other kind of social relations) do not merely cause physical or mental pain in a pure and autonomous subject that struggles to escape suffering by liberating itself from those relations. The subject is constituted by those relations and only through the determinate negation of its own constitution can it give expression to suffering as its objective form.

The autonomous subject of late capitalist society – *the free democratic subject* – faces a world over which it must claim responsibility insofar as it is free and to which it must be responsible insofar as it recognizes the freedom of others. Yet when the freedom that positively determines the identity of such a subject fails in its promise, it forces the subject to recognize its truth as an ideological construction or reification, which participates in the commodity culture that dominates the world around it. Obviously, the fulfillment or the failure of freedom varies according to one's relation to the social antagonisms and contradictions that make up the world. Although the promise of freedom does not automatically fail for every member of a particular class and may even survive in the ideology of class identity, the experience of the failed promise necessarily becomes one of the determinations of class tendency. At the same time, suffering is not the result of a choice. One could put it this way: freedom as a concept, whatever its origin and history, never lets go of the subject for whom its promise has objectively failed. In *Negative Dialectics*, Adorno argues that freedom as a concept arises from the subject's "need to lend a voice to suffering" as the condition of its truth. Suffering is objective because it results from the determination of the subject at its core, in the very experience of subjectivity, by social contradictions (*ND* 17–18). For Adorno, the artist objectively mediates the contradictions of society, or suffering, through the production of art.

Instrumental and communicative reason

As a way of proceeding to the heart of Adorno's theory, I want to consider what is perhaps the most compelling criticism of Adorno in the last twenty years: that of Habermas. According to Habermas, Adorno's thought never manages to avoid the contradictions of the philosophy of consciousness whose paradigm is "a subject that represents objects and toils with them." Against the philosophy of consciousness, Habermas would favor the models of linguistic philosophy which privilege intersubjective understanding or communication.[2] Habermas aims his criticism primarily at Horkheimer and Adorno's *Dialectic of Enlightenment* which extends Lukács's reification theory to the general critique of instrumental reason. Whereas Lukács derived "structures of reified

---

[2] J. Habermas, *The Theory of Communicative Action*, vol. 1: *Reason and the Rationalization of Society*, trans. T. McCarthy (Boston: Beacon, 1984), p. 390.

consciousness" from the "form of objectivity specific to capitalist society," namely, the commodity form, Horkheimer and Adorno give these structures such an "abstract interpretation" that they virtually cover "not only the theoretical form of identifying thought but even the confrontation of goal-oriented acting subjects with external nature." In their argument, the concept of instrumental reason as a form of self-preservation subsumes capitalist reification and appears to be identified as a transhistorical tendency. Reification loses all of its historical specificity and becomes a subcategory of human nature, the reflection of a mechanism that must already be present "in the anthropological foundations of the history of the species, in the form of the existence of a species that has to reproduce itself through labor."[3] As John Brenkman summarizes, Horkheimer and Adorno reconceived instrumental or analytical reason as the general human capacity for representation, conceptualization, and objectivity.[4] Habermas argues that Horkheimer and Adorno rewrite the history of reason so as to posit a radical divorce between a reason that pursues truth and one that aims at the self-preservation of the subject. In fact, the latter subverts the former in its origins so that even the concept of truth-seeking universal reason becomes utopian. Yet this original reason would seem to have left a trace in modern culture: this is the capacity of *mimesis*, which Horkheimer and Adorno discuss as if it were an irreducible natural process which defies full rational explanation.

For Habermas, the critique of instrumental reason "denounces as a defect something that it cannot explain in its defectiveness because it lacks a conceptual framework sufficiently flexible to capture the integrity of what is destroyed through instrumental reason." Horkheimer and Adorno use the word *mimesis* to name what is destroyed by instrumental reason; but they cannot explain mimesis theoretically within a framework that posits the global and monolithic power of instrumental reason. Mimesis would be the polar opposite of reason, its antithesis, some sort of irrational impulse. According to Habermas, Adorno's aesthetic theory wants to show that mimesis gives art a power to open or unlock the social structures from which it derives; but this opening up can

[3] Habermas, *Communicative Action*, vol. i, pp. 378–79.
[4] J. Brenkman, *Culture and Domination* (Ithaca: Cornell University Press, 1987), p. 15.

have no practical result because it has no rational force of its own. Consequently, Habermas insists that the history of cognitive-instrumental reason does not tell the whole story of human rationality. In the context of modernity, what remains in need of explanation is no longer "the knowledge and mastery of an objective nature, but the intersubjectivity of possible understanding and agreement – at both the interpersonal and intrapsychic levels." This means that the focus of critical investigation must shift from instrumental reason as the ground of objective knowledge to "communicative rationality." The latter no longer centers its epistemology on the relation between the autonomous subject and the world of objects, subject to representation and manipulation, but on the paradigm of intersubjectivity. The latter foregrounds the process by which speaking subjects arrive at an agreement about the facts of the world as the ground of ethical human action.[5]

In *The Theory of Communicative Action*, Habermas is not primarily concerned with Adorno's aesthetic theory but with the implications of the critique of instrumental reason for social theory in general. While his critique is compelling when applied to some of the apparently ahistorical assumptions underlying the *Dialectic of Enlightenment*, it does not take a full measure of the argument in *Aesthetic Theory*. In particular, Habermas's understanding of intersubjectivity within the frame of communicative rationality does not do justice to the intersubjectivity of art as Adorno presents it. I realize that "intersubjective" is not a major term in Adorno's argument (except in its restricted meaning of consensus), but I would suggest that underlying Adorno's concept of mimesis is an implicit theory of intersubjectivity.

Before I elaborate that theory, however, I need to specify where art as a process fits into Habermas's mapping of the human world. In *The Philosophical Discourse of Modernity*, Habermas takes for granted a historical view of enlightenment, derived from Weber, as a process leading to "the desocialization of nature and the denaturalization of the human world." Through the destruction of myth, humankind ceases to regard human nature as a fact of nature and starts to take responsibility for society as the outcome of practical human activity. Habermas postulates that, through the

---

[5] Habermas, *Communicative Action*, vol. I, pp. 382, 390–92.

process of enlightenment, the external world is divided into the objective and the social, a world of things and a world of norms (which regulate interpersonal relationships); and these worlds posit as their other the internal world of subjective experience. As a result, the validity relations that pertain to each of these worlds are released from the demands of the empirical and become differentiated internally with respect to the propositional determination of truth, normality, and authenticity.[6] According to Habermas, this process of separation and autonomization represents a critical advance for human culture because such a rationalization of the lifeworld (the intersubjective context and interpretive horizon of communicative action) makes possible the emergence of the subsystems, money and power. The ground of Habermas's critique of Marx lies in this conviction. Marx did not recognize "the *intrinsic* evolutionary *value*" of the media-steered subsystems. He did not see that the state and the economy as autonomous apparatuses, even though they no longer directly express and may even contradict human needs, nevertheless represent "a higher level of system differentiation, which simultaneously opens up new steering possibilities *and* forces a reorganization of the old, feudal, class relationships."[7]

As this last remark indicates, Habermas's enormous critical project hinges on the assumption that differentiation means progress for human culture, even though this progress entails some dangers. He retains the critique of instrumental rationality insofar as it means that privileging norm-free system integration over social integration rooted in consensus damages the lifeworld. In other words, there is the danger that steering systems like the economy, which originate in normatively grounded social institutions, will forget their origins and try to set the limits on what can be thought, said, and done within those institutions. Habermas implicitly claims that his theory is better able than Adorno's to analyze and correct a defect in the social world because it can situate that defect within an overall context of normality. Norm-free systems derive from normatively based social institutions that

[6] J. Habermas, *The Philosophical Discourse of Modernity: Twelve Lectures*, trans. F. Lawrence (Cambridge, Massachusetts: MIT, 1987), p. 115.

[7] J. Habermas, *The Theory of Communicative Action*, vol. II: *Lifeworld and System: A Critique of Functionalist Reason*, trans. T. McCarthy (Boston: Beacon, 1987), p. 339.

represent progress in social organization. Eventually, progressive social differentiation leads to what Habermas calls the uncoupling of system and lifeworld. Pathologies emerge when this process is reversed, when system and lifeworld are de-differentiated, and the system begins to colonize the lifeworld. Still, it can also be shown that Habermas regards any gesture that reverses the process of social differentiation as regressive.

The three linguistic worlds that derive from the rationalization of the lifeworld are each specialized according to one validity claim. The propositions of science aim at truth; the propositions of morality aim at normative rightness; and the propositions of art aim at subjective truthfulness. Habermas makes it clear that he regards such specialization as the outcome of progressive social differentiation. As a purely expressive medium, art gives institutional embodiment to the autonomy of the subject. Although Habermas surely recognizes that the autonomous subject represents a historical development, he seems not to allow for any ambivalence in its construction or in its relation to expression. In fact, Habermas's concept of communicative rationality grounded in intersubjective validity claims takes for granted the autonomous subject as an originary category. As he presents it, this form of reason presupposes "the central experience of the unconstrained, unifying, consensus-bringing force of argumentative speech, in which different participants overcome their merely subjective views and, owing to the mutuality of rationally motivated conviction, assure themselves of both the unity of the objective world and the intersubjectivity of their lifeworld."[8] The possibility of such a rational experience presupposes a subject that is able to transcend itself: it can question the underlying assumptions of its own position in an argument *vis-à-vis* another subject and can recognize validity claims made by another subject that have to be answered with a yes or a no. It can come to an agreement with another subject about the rules or norms governing an argument, about the empirical tests that will determine the truth of propositions about the objective world, and about the criteria of authenticity in a work of art. It even recognizes that it does not know itself entirely, that it interprets the world according to values and traditions that are not immedi-

---

[8] Habermas, *Communicative Action*, vol. I, p. 10.

ately available to it as objective knowledge but are the intersubjective contexts of knowledge. For Habermas, the ethics of communication relies on the assumption of a "formal ideal of mutual understanding in language," or the *ideal speech situation* as it is usually called. This principle of "universal discourse" resides in "the very structure of language, it is no mere demand of practical reason but is built into the reproduction of social life."[9] Nevertheless, this ideal of an unlimited and undistorted communication community presupposes the absolute autonomy of each individual subject as the sender and receiver of messages that make normative validity claims which cannot be reduced to the interests of power-formations but reflect a rationally achieved consensus. The concept of undistorted communication makes no sense without the presumption of the sovereign autonomy of the subject.

Habermas's claim that the ideal of undistorted communication lies in the very structure of language commits him to the implicit belief that the autonomy of the subject is guaranteed by the metaphysical essence of language. Though he recognizes that the emergence of the bourgeois subject is a historical event, he implicitly attributes to it the same *intrinsic evolutionary value* that he attributes to the media-steered subsystems in capitalist society. If the historical emergence of the autonomous subject reflects an intrinsic value of language, then that principle was always present in language even if it was not realized by cultures in the past. If the history of human culture has tendencies that express intrinsic values (rather than constructed values), then it is necessary to posit a metaphysical essence of the human, both biologically and culturally. Thus language must have its own metaphysical essence that is realized through the unfolding of human history which will finally culminate in the undistorted or ideal speech situation posited by the very structure of language itself. Habermas has not really escaped the paradigm of the philosophy of consciousness that he sees as the structural flaw in Adorno's social and aesthetic theory. He has transposed the Hegelian dialectic onto the ground of social evolution and has substituted for the unity of subject and object in absolute knowledge the *ideal speech situation* which presupposes the self-identity

[9] Habermas, *Communicative Action*, vol. II, p. 96.

of the subject in an act of undistorted communication. If Habermas's hidden commitment to the philosophy of consciousness is recognized, his view of cultural tradition takes on a different significance.

John Brenkman has argued that, for Habermas, cultural traditions register two almost contradictory historical effects: first, they represent the sedimentation of *forms of life* that derive from human intersubjectivity through linguistic understanding and exchange; second, their communicative capacity can be exploited in order to legitimate domination.[10] Brenkman wants to explain why Habermas, in his debate with Gadamer, accepts the latter's concept of cultural tradition as a continuous universe of meanings. As Brenkman sums up, "Gadamerian hermeneutics misunderstands its constructed tradition as *the* cultural tradition." Identifying tradition with a set of classical texts and timeless art works, Gadamer's interpretive procedures systematically occlude the art work's historical implication in social relations and practices that determine its meaning and form; they replace the individual work's immanent and problematic claim to universality (which would amount to its practical translatability into other historical contexts) with the interpreter's assumption that every work of art *categorically* possesses universal validity. According to Brenkman, Habermas understands the preservation–transmission of cultural traditions by hermeneutical understanding in the same way as Gadamer.[11] Human subjects who seek to understand and communicate with one another supposedly require stable cultural traditions. Consequently, the communicative infrastructure of the lifeworld is threatened not only by what Habermas calls *"systemically induced reification"* (or the colonization of the lifeworld by norm-free steering systems) but by *"cultural impoverishment"*:

The lifeworld is assimilated to juridified, formally organized domains of action and simultaneously cut off from the influx of an intact cultural tradition. In the deformations of everyday practice, symptoms of rigidification combine with symptoms of desolation... The latter, the dying out of vital traditions, goes back to a differentiation of science, morality, and

[10] Brenkman, *Culture and Domination*, p. 46. See J. Habermas, "Walter Benjamin: Consciousness-Raising or Rescuing Critique," in *Philosophical-Political Profiles*, trans. F. G. Lawrence (Cambridge, Massachusetts: MIT, 1983), p. 158.

[11] Brenkman, *Culture and Domination*, pp. 37–38.

art, which means not only an increasing autonomy of sectors dealt with by experts, but also a splitting-off from traditions; having lost their credibility, these traditions continue along on the basis of everyday hermeneutics as a kind of second nature that has lost its force.[12]

This passage clarifies the fundamental contradictions underlying Habermas's position. On the one hand, the norm-free steering systems have an intrinsic evolutionary value derived from the process of rationalization that differentiates science, morality, and art from the lifeworld. On the other hand, this increasing autonomization of institutions, which entails the growth of expert cultures, damages the lifeworld's communicative infrastructure and lays the ground, so to speak, for reification. In effect, what is damaged by institutional autonomy is the cultural unity that would guarantee the authority of the autonomous subject. Habermas wants to construct a social theory that rigorously accounts for this originary autonomy in order to explain the subject's ability to enter into communicative exchanges with other autonomous subjects who share common values and traditions. At the same time, he wants to justify the function of instrumental reason as a specialized form of communicative reason. From an evolutionary viewpoint, since communicative reason is elaborated through the rationalization of the lifeworld, it eventually gives ground to instrumental reason. The rationalization process, however, damages the lifeworld in two ways: either through the continuing differentiation of institutions grounded in communicative reason or through the de-differentiation of instrumental reason turned back against the rational institutions that unleashed it.

Although Habermas successfully challenges Horkheimer and Adorno's critique of instrumental reason as reason *per se* by showing its historically subordinate relation to communicative rationality, he ends up with a scenario that posits the same dead end for human culture as that posited by the *Dialectic of Enlightenment*. Communicative rationality, through its own by-product, instrumental reason, results in the destruction of cultural authority, that is to say, of universal and continuous cultural traditions. As long as communicative rationality must be justified through an appeal to the ideal speech situation inherent in the structure of language, then culture itself must be identified with a universal

---

[12] Habermas, *Communicative Action*, vol. II, p. 327.

tradition. As Brenkman concludes, Habermas's normative diag-
nosis of the impoverished cultural traditions that have resulted
from capitalist modernization fails to recognize the constructed
nature of tradition, which leads to different versions of cultural
history with their "ideologically relevant conflicts of interpretation."[13] In effect, Habermas endorses a view of human nature and
history that fails to take into account the plurality of subject-
positions produced by conflicting interpretations within different
areas of social and political contention. He presupposes the ideal
of a universal subject that in practice would find its nearest
realization in the European subject. Rationalization would become
indistinguishable from the process of cultural imperialism that
insists that all cultures bow to the interests of the most advanced
culture in terms of evolutionary progress.

Mimesis

When Adorno speaks of the objectivity of suffering in the expressions of art, he gestures towards a concept of intersubjectivity that
is radically different from that of Habermas. In a section of
Aesthetic Theory entitled "Mimesis and Rationality," Adorno
comments that in art, "the subject, depending on how much
autonomy it has, takes up varying positions *vis-à-vis* its objective
other from which it is always different but never entirely separate." A page later he refers to mimesis as "the non-conceptual
affinity of a subjective creation with its objective and unposited
other" (*AT* 79–80). Habermas translates Adorno's multiple and
contextually complicated uses of the term *mimesis* into the prosaic
notion that "Imitation designates a relation between persons in
which the one accommodates to the other, identifies with the
other, empathizes with the other."[14] In this paraphrase, Habermas
ignores the distinction Adorno makes between the terms *mimesis*
and *imitation* while he offers a completely distorted view of how
the term *mimesis* actually operates in Adorno's writing. In his more
nuanced commentary on Adorno, Fredric Jameson notes that the
most enigmatic aspect of Adorno's use of the term *mimesis* lies not
in its content but in its overall status within his work. Though the
term is never clearly defined in *Dialectic of Enlightenment*, it

---

13 Brenkman, *Culture and Domination*, p. 48.
14 Habermas, *Communicative Action*, vol. I, p. 390.

appears "everywhere (as though we already knew what it was)"; and the later works refer "back to this volume as to its full-dress official philosophical presentation."[15] The function of this term in Adorno's writing recalls certain terms in poststructuralist discourses, such as the *big Other* in Lacan, *symbolic exchange* in Baudrillard, the *différend* in Lyotard, and *différance* in Derrida. I do not mean that these terms all mean the same thing or that they fail to mean anything, but that they tend to signify differently in different contexts; and while there are family resemblances between these different uses of the terms, there does not seem to be a unified global signification that would make the concept equivalent to itself in every context. Ideology, according to Adorno, "lies in the implicit identity of concept and thing" (*ND* 40). Any concept, insofar as it is stable and self-identical, tends to reduce what it signifies, even if what it signifies is an unstable social process, to the status of a thing; in other words, it operates according to the law of the commodity, which is to say that it has an abstract exchange value. As Jameson stresses, Adorno's philosophy points toward some notion of conceptual reification as the ultimate form of logical regularity.[16] It is against such reification that negative dialectics asserts itself. As Adorno stresses, "Thought need not be content with its own legality; without abandoning it, we can think against our thought, and if it were possible to define dialectics, this would be a definition worth suggesting" (*ND* 141). The concept of mimesis has just such a dialectical function in that, as both a concept and an anticoncept, it explodes the logical regularity of reified thought, which does not mean that it is necessary to identify mimesis with the irrational *per se* although it will assume that value in some contexts.

Habermas's understanding of mimesis as imitation and empathy resembles what Lacan would call an imaginary relation, namely, a relation between *persons* taken as real things, beyond ideology.[17] Habermas dismisses Adorno's concept of mimesis as an undertheorized version of his own theory of communicative

---

[15] F. Jameson, *Late Marxism: Adorno, or, The Persistence of the Dialectic* (London: Verso, 1990), p. 104.

[16] *Ibid.*, p. 81.

[17] See J. Lacan, *The Ego in Freud's Theory and in the Technique of Psychoanalysis*, book 2 of *The Seminar*, ed. J.-A. Miller, trans. S. Tomaselli (New York: Norton, 1988), p. 244.

rationality; but, as I have suggested, Habermas's theory presupposes that the subject is, in some originary sense, an autonomous whole (thus, from a Lacanian perspective, Habermas mistakes the imaginary ego for a real thing) and that its relation to other subjects depends on their common identity in the lifeworld constituted by language and culture. Habermas's reading of Adorno almost makes sense when Adorno suggests that the relationship in art between a subject and its objective other is determined by the degree of the subject's autonomy. In a footnote, Jameson speculates that for Adorno mimesis is a "substitute for the traditional subject–object relationship";[18] but "substitute" may not be a strong enough word for the concept that deconstructs the subject–object relationship by destabilizing the separation on which it is founded. If I may employ a poststructuralist rhetoric for a moment, the subject and the object may be different in the sense that they are articulated through a differential relation but not in the sense that they are metaphysically separate in terms of essence. The autonomous subject encounters the limit of its autonomy in the objective other insofar as that other turns out to be another subject. The absolute subject requires an absolute object, so that, when the object turns out to be a subject, the relation between subject and object is transformed into a sort of relationality without essence. There is no subject or object before the constitution of this relationality without essence as ground. I call this ground the *intersubject* and the relation it grounds *intersubjectivity*.

If aesthetic expression is, from one perspective, the non-subjective in the subject, it is also, from another, the "objectification of the non-objective." In effect, expression becomes a "second non-objective substance, one that speaks out of the artifact rather than out of the subject." It results in something "trans-subjective," though this dimension of the aesthetic process requires something like a subject as its condition. According to Adorno, "Art is expressive when a subjectively mediated, objective quality raises its voice to speak: sadness, strength, yearning." As with *suffering*, these affective terms should not be read as reducing expression to subjective feelings but rather as situating it in the context of "ordinary things and situations in which historical processes and functions have been sedimented, endowing them with the poten-

---

[18] Jameson, *Late Marxism*, p. 256, n. 14.

tial to speak" (*AT* 163). As I suggested earlier, suffering is intersubjective not in the sense that it reflects a moment of empathy between two autonomous subjects but in the sense that the subject as a historically situated social construction is constituted by antagonistic social relations. In particular, the subject of late capitalism is constituted by the contradiction between its democratic claim to freedom/autonomy *and* its determination by social relations of inequality according to race, class, gender, and a whole set of social distinctions that have become the *second nature* of capitalist ideology. Art as the expression of suffering determinately negates the autonomous subject as an ideological construction by disclosing the intersubjective ground of its formation.

Art does not express subjective feelings; rather, it materializes or makes visible the intersubjectivity of a socially constructed reality that would also include the historical formation – as opposed to the metaphysical constitution – of the autonomous subject. Expression is the voice of the intersubject, the determinate negation of the subject–object relationship. For Adorno, expression could not be anything but the expression of suffering because suffering is the non-objective, non-subjective experience of determinate negation. If the autonomous subject is the effect of reification, that is to say, of being-for-other, then the decomposition of that subject through expression constitutes being-in-itself as the transsubjective voice of the other, what Lacan would call the discourse of the Other, a sort of cultural unconscious. Intersubjective expression, by allowing art "to speak in itself," enables it to challenge its own status as being-for-other, a status that represents the domination of art by the interests of society. Such expression is what Lacan might call the moment of excess in speech, the moment when art says more than it knows. It is, according to Adorno, "the antithesis of 'expressing something'" (*AT* 164).

Expression in art does not communicate something in Habermas's sense of making a validity claim to subjective truthfulness. This does not mean, of course, that validity claims to objective truth, normative rightness, or subjective truthfulness cannot enter into the art work as its material. It only means that aesthetic expression cannot be reduced to a message conveyed by a medium. Samuel Beckett's famous remark about Joyce's writing in *Finnegans Wake* captures a quality that may belong to every true work of art: "His writing is not *about* something; *it is that something itself.*"[19] Aesthetic expression is being-in-itself, and at the same time it is the other as being-in-itself. Mimesis is the process in art by which the other becomes being-in-itself. Michael Cahn stresses that while Adorno understands mimesis as "adapting or correlating behavior," he does not follow the classical line of thought "which leads from imitation, via representation, to truth." He does not explain mimesis as the expression of the crisis of representation but relates it to the crisis of critique.[20] In Adorno's own words, mimesis represents "a stance toward reality that is different from the rigid juxtaposition of subject and object" and generates a kind of knowledge "not unlike the one that existed before the polarity of subject and object" (*AT* 162–63). Before that polarity, there was magic. Ironically, mimesis as the trace of magic could be viewed as something that art disavows in the process of adapting to what is most antithetical to its origins. The disavowal of magic is the sign of art's commitment to rationality. Yet art never completely rejects its origin and is able "to hold its own *qua* mimesis in the midst of rationality" by mimetically adapting itself to rationality. In this way, art responds "to the evils and irrationality of the rational bureaucratic world." These evils arise from the refusal of capitalist society to recognize the irrationality of its privileging of means-centered reason. Such a society disavows the fact that rationality, "viewed as the sum total of all practical means," must have as its goal "something other than a means, hence a non-rational quality." While society disavows such a thought as irrational, art "represents truth in the twofold sense of preserving the image of an end smothered completely by rationality and of exposing the irrationality and absurdity of the status quo" (*AT* 79).

As these references suggest, it is not quite accurate to say that art – or even mimesis as a dimension of art – can be reduced to the other of reason. Art has its own mode of rationality, and ironically it is the mimetic impulse behind art that brings it out. Although art as mimesis derives originally from sympathetic magic, it is also

[19] S. Beckett, "Dante ... Bruno. Vico ... Joyce," in *Our Exagmination Round his Factification for Incamination of Work in Progress*, by Samuel Beckett et al. (London: Faber and Faber, 1972; originally published in 1929), p. 14.
[20] M. Cahn, "Subversive Mimesis: Theodor W. Adorno and the Modern Impasse of Critique," in *Mimesis in Contemporary Theory*, vol. I, ed. M. Spariosu (Philadelphia: J. Benjamins, 1984), pp. 32–35.

inextricably implicated in the rationalization process that histori-cally works to destroy magic. Art is "part and parcel of the process of the disenchantment of the world, to use Max Weber's term" (*AT* 80). Art disavows magic and holds its own in the midst of rationality not by imitating but by assimilating its objective other with which it then has a *nonconceptual affinity*; it absorbs reason into itself as the immanent property of its form. Art exploits rationality as a means, but that means also becomes the essence of art insofar as art moves towards increased autonomization in a rationalized world. At the same time, the autonomy of art institutionally expresses the refusal of art as an ideology to recognize its own emplacement in the rational bureaucratic world of the commodity. Art does not merely respond to the evil and irrationality of such a world; in adapting to that world, it becomes a part of it and discloses through determinate negation the goal of rationality as "the sum total of all practical means." Art negates those means, on which it nevertheless depends, through mimesis. It discloses irrationality as the end of rationality by reproducing in its own history an infinite regress of means.

Capitalist society hides this irrationality by subsuming technical or instrumental reason within the myth of infinite progress. Art moves in the opposite direction. For example, modernism could be read as the triumph of reason in art through its commitment to technical innovation, while it also demonstrates the irrationality of technical reason as the infinite play of forms without center or determinate end. "The ground of modernism," writes Adorno, "is both the absence of a ground and the explicit normative rejection by modernism of a ground, even if there were one" (*AT* 34). Stated somewhat reductively, modernist art is absolutely rational in its insistence that *reason has no reason*. Postmodernism would be post-rational in taking the modernist critique of reason for granted; it employs the techniques of reason in art only to demonstrate directly what modernism demonstrates indirectly, which is that technical innovation has no progressive value. Reason becomes the absurd in high art and thrilling technique in popular culture. Today's art, including popular art, shows that the end of reason is something like an amusement park. The status quo is Disneyland.

In a sense, Habermas's reading of Adorno is on the mark. Reason would seem to be pure instrumentality for Adorno; and if art can be said to harbor another form of reason, it emerges from a self-subversive process that finally articulates the limits of rationality as an unresolved problem: "Art is rationality criticizing itself without being able to overcome itself" (*AT* 81). If society is completely dominated by instrumental reason, then in rejecting society by asserting its own negative autonomy art ironically works to justify society. Art legitimates society by endorsing the presumption in bourgeois ideology of a division between mind and body, between mental and physical labor, between culture and politics – in other words, between an ideal world of perfection and a real world of ugly imperfection. As Brenkman argues, culture is affirmative to the extent that the spiritual, intellectual, and aesthetic satisfactions associated with the inner world serve to justify the outer world in its current form.[21] Adorno interprets this Marcusian concept of affirmative culture as the risk of ideological abuse in art's distance or separation from society when it "betrays an attitude of non-intervention." Still, art's attitude toward society is profoundly ambivalent since, on the one hand, it subverts instrumental reason through its preservation of the mimetic impulse that destabilizes the subject–object relationship, and, on the other, it neutralizes its ability to oppose instrumental reason by destroying the social instrumentality of art. Mimesis criticizes instrumental reason by disclosing its terminal irrationality; but, as the price of this criticism, art itself affirms instrumental reason as the content of its form, its objective other. However, this contradiction within art only becomes aporetic if one imagines the separation between art and society as metaphysically absolute. Adorno's position is more flexible than the reading of Habermas would suggest. Art is neither pure affirmation nor pure critique. Art is not absolutely positive or negative because "society is not coextensive with ideology." Society in its totality can never be reduced to the negativity that *aesthetic form as critique* can be said to reveal. Even the most objectionable societies are capable of producing and reproducing human life and of sustaining some cultural formations that arise from collective human desires rather than manipulative social institutions. Art must take such social positivity into account even as it produces its own negative critique, at least until it becomes clear that the social process is

---

[21] Brenkman, *Culture and Domination*, p. 6.

headed for self-destruction. Ultimately, art's refusal of political judgment gives it no way of separating affirmation and critique (*AT* 321).

There is no question that Adorno's philosophy and social theory are pessimistic. They frequently *do* imply that the social process is headed for self-destruction. Still, as I have already suggested, it is possible to argue for a pessimistic view of the future of human culture and still remain faithful to a concept of communicative rationality. For just as Habermas's concept of reason does not transcend the philosophy of consciousness as thoroughly as he imagines, Adorno's critique of instrumental reason should be considered more flexible in *Aesthetic Theory* than it was in the *Dialectic of Enlightenment*. For one thing, in the later work, society is not coextensive with ideology for at least two reasons: (1) aesthetic phenomena that resist ideology are social to the very core of their autonomy; and (2) the autonomy of art is not a metaphysical absolute but a historical tendency. It is autonomy that makes it possible for art *both* to affirm the "well-rounded totality" of the world governed by instrumental reason *and* to reject this world and the legitimacy of instrumental reason as the essence of reason itself (*AT* 2). Art's affirmative and critical functions appear to be in irreconcilable contradiction; yet the autonomous work of art illustrates through its formal coherence the possibility of reconciliation. This promise of reconciliation, however, is not arrived at through the neutralization of contradiction but through its formal elaboration.

Art cannot separate affirmation from critique without, in effect, neutralizing the contradiction from which all of its force derives. Herein lies the distinction between autonomous art and the culture industry. The latter neutralizes the contradictions of art so that the "whole and the parts are alike; there is no antithesis and no connection." The culture industry wants art to imitate reality in such a way that it is no longer possible to distinguish one from the other: "Real life is becoming indistinguishable from the movies."[22] One does not have to accept Adorno's blanket dismissal of nearly all popular culture to recognize that his critique of the culture industry explains the effect that is produced when works of art have been emptied of their contradictory force through modes of

---

[22] Horkheimer and Adorno, *Dialectic*, p. 126.

reception that transform them into pure entertainment or prestige commodities. However strange it may seem, Disneyland and a curriculum founded on the *great books* concept have much in common. It is no accident that the latter idea has lent itself to a marketing strategy for making high culture turn a profit. From the Great Books of the Western World series to the commercial triumph of Allan Bloom's *The Closing of the American Mind*, the condition for marketing high culture is neutralizing its formal contradictions. Ironically, in surrendering its contradictions, art also surrenders its own form of rationality and succumbs to the irrational ends of instrumental reason.

Dialectical reason

As Adorno stresses, "art corrects the reason of the outside world by means of its own reason." The reason of art, however, is derived from its other: "Unity or synthesis in works of art springs from the violence perpetrated by reason against nature, but the same unity is responsible for reconciliation among the moments of works of art" (*AT* 424). Art can subvert its own origin: it can spring from instrumental reason and then transform that reason into the technical means for the formal reconciliation of instrumental reason with its other. It can do this because the rationality of art is dialectical. But even this formulation misses the mark by creating the impression that, for Adorno, there is something besides dialectical reason. The real difference between Adorno and Habermas, as Jameson suggests, is that Habermas has abandoned the concept of dialectical reason and substituted for it a theory of communicative rationality that offers no better explanation for the destructive effects of technical reason on the lifeworld than a normative theory of social pathologies. He constructs a Manichean concept of reason for which, in Jameson's words, "the only opposite number to Reason is the Irrational itself in all its demonic forms." To this extent, Habermas has abandoned the tradition of the Frankfurt school which accepted "Hegel's restoration of the dialectic as a superior mode of truth." This meant reordering the Kantian faculties so that *Vernunft*, or dialectical reason, subsumes *Verstand*, or understanding, a term which can be translated into twentieth-century philosophical discourse as analytical reason, or, after the Frankfurt school, instrumental reason. As far as Jameson is concerned, dialectical reason "has not yet come into being in any hegemonic form" because it "corresponds to a social organization that does not yet exist."[23] These remarks should be construed as saying not that dialectical reason is nonexistent but that it has been repressed by the privileging of one of its moments, instrumental reason, as the hegemonic form of reason itself.

In the present historical context, dialectical reason exists in the form of the determinate negation of instrumental reason. If the autonomy of art as an institution presupposes an affinity (that is, a mimetic relation) between art and instrumental rationality, it also makes possible the disclosure of the historical truth that instrumental reason cannot be itself without the other which negates it. Mimesis is the condition of instrumental reason. The human subject would not be able to manipulate and control objects without the power of discrimination; but discrimination, which refers to the way an object is experienced by a subject, presupposes the mimetic impulse as its epistemological ground. If this impulse "were extinguished altogether, it would be flatly incomprehensible that a subject can know an object" (*ND* 45). For Adorno, therefore, art and cognition are interdependent because they are both constituted by the dialectical relationship between mimesis and instrumental reason. The complexity of this relationship becomes apparent in the section of *Aesthetic Theory* to which I have already referred, "Mimesis and Rationality." Here I will briefly summarize the critical argument in that section and then elaborate on its implications.

Having defined mimesis as the nonconceptual affinity between the art work and its unposited other or the cognitive object, Adorno concludes that mimetic behavior attempts to pose a question about the *telos* of cognition, a *telos* which cognition "simultaneously hinders through its categories." Art "expands" cognition into the realm of teleological considerations where it was thought not to exist and, in this way, subverts cognition's claim to "uniqueness and univocality *vis-à-vis* knowledge." However, because art represents the secularization of its own origin in magic, it can be destroyed by superstition or the residue of magic in society. The latter refuses the rationality of art, while instrumental reason rejects art's historical connection with magic:

[23] Jameson, *Late Marxism*, p. 237.

The possibility and the greatness of art depend on how art handles this antinomy. Art cannot live up to its concept. Therefore each and every one of its works, including the most elevated, is smitten with imperfection, thus disavowing the ideal of perfection that all works of art must hanker after. Rigid but consistent enlightenment would discard art, just as sober and narrowly practical people do in fact discard it. The dilemma of art between regression to real magic and surrender of the mimetic impulse to thinglike rationality helps formulate art's law of motion; this dilemma must not be done away with.

Though mimesis and rationality are never completely reconciled, art comes into being historically as the impossible attempt to bring about such a reconciliation. The virtual impossibility of reconciliation is the condition of the image of reconciliation in art. As Adorno concludes, "It is only because literally no art work can succeed that the powers of art are set free; and it is here that art is akin to reconciliation" (*AT* 80–81).

Without the nonconceptual affinity of the aesthetic subject with the object of cognition, knowledge of the other would be impossible. This nonconceptual affinity is the intersubjective ground of human knowledge. Such a ground could be said to lie in language, but language understood not merely as the means of communication between autonomous human subjects but as the material condition of subjectivity itself. Before there can be subjects and objects, there must be language not as a finished system of communication but as a relation to the world as signifiable. Peter Dews, in a reading of Lacan from a Habermasian perspective, summarizes the Lacanian concept of intersubjectivity in this way: "if the mutual recognition of subjects precedes the cognition of objects, this is because no fixation of linguistic meaning, no act of naming, can be accomplished in isolation from the system of language as a whole, and therefore from the continuous intersubjective coordination of language use which sustains this system."[24] Dews presupposes that the subject of language as a function of the system, a subject which can recognize other subjects, somehow preexists any concrete use of language, although by positing the "continuous intersubjective coordination of language use" as the foundation of the system, he is also claiming the exact opposite. In adapting Lacan to Habermas, Dews

[24] P. Dews, *Logics of Disintegration: Post-Structuralist Thought and the Claims of Critical Theory* (London: Verso, 1987), p. 60.

posits an autonomous subject that somehow precedes *both* language as a system *and* speech as a concrete use of language. Implicitly, this subject would be self-conscious and conscious of others without the mediation of language since these forms of consciousness are the conditions of language. I would argue that a more careful reading of Lacan suggests rather different conclusions, which have a bearing on our understanding of Adorno. In *The Four Fundamental Concepts of Psycho-Analysis*, Lacan argues that a form of signifying relation must preexist signification proper as the ground of interhuman relations. Such a primordial signifying relation is "taken from whatever nature may offer as supports, supports that are arranged in themes of opposition. Nature provides ... signifiers, and these signifiers organize human relations in a creative way, providing them with structures and shaping them." Contrary to Dews's characterization, Lacan believes that the signifier must come before interhuman relations and the system of language itself. Like Levi-Strauss, Lacan understands language as something that must have arisen all at once – in the sense not that the systematic structure of communicative exchange was there from the beginning but that nature (although its concept did not yet exist) abruptly became signifiable. Natural signifiers did not operate according to the logic of equivalence by which one signifier corresponds to one signified within the framework of a relational system. On the contrary, it would make more sense to say that the signifier was indistinguishable from the signified and, as a consequence, the human was indistinguishable from nature. There is symbolization before there is any subject that knows itself as the one who symbolizes. As Lacan further remarks, "before any formation of the subject, of a subject who thinks," there must be "the level at which there is counting, things are counted, and in this counting he who counts is already included. It is only later that the subject has to recognize himself as such, recognize himself as he who counts."[25]

Historically, the intersubjective logic of the symbol is the trace of the origin of language in the "natural" signifier. Using a Derridean logic, however, it would be possible to argue that the symbol is itself a trace-structure, the postulated origin of which is nothing more than a myth, or an interpretation rooted in desire. Such a

[25] J. Lacan, *The Four Fundamental Concepts of Psycho-Analysis*, ed. J.-A. Miller, trans. A. Sheridan (New York: Norton, 1981), p. 20.

thought may underlie Horkheimer and Adorno's interpretation of the dialectic of enlightenment as, in effect, a concept that really has no origin. As Jameson notes, the originality of this concept lies in its exclusion of any first term, and in its specific description of enlightenment "as an 'always-already' process whose structure lies ... in its generation of the illusion that what preceded it (which was also a form of enlightenment) was that 'original' myth, the archaic union with nature, which it is the vocation of enlightenment 'proper' to annul."[26] It may be possible to infer the origin of mimesis in magical practices just as Lacan infers the origin of the symbol in the natural signifier; but this theory of origins does not matter as much as the fact that mimesis continues to exist and, as such, makes possible the mimetic adaptation of art to the historical process of rationalization. In *Aesthetic Theory*, Adorno refers to mimesis as a "memory trace," not the trace of magic but of itself in its ongoing differentiation from magic; the continued existence of mimesis in art "keeps alive the memory of ends-oriented reason" and proves that "to this day rationality has never been fully realized" (*AT* 190, 453).

So, to echo the subtitle of Jameson's *Late Marxism*, mimesis represents the persistence of dialectical reason as both the condition and determinate negation of instrumental reason. It is not that mimesis is identical to dialectical reason but that the interdependent relationship between mimesis and instrumental reason is the form of dialectical reason in the current historical context. By articulating a form of rationality that focuses on ends rather than means, art undermines the univocality of instrumental reason as the only form of knowledge. Mimesis reverses the tendency of cognition to block itself off categorically from its own *telos* through the privileging of means. (This reading is based on the German text of *Aesthetic Theory* which reads, "Denn worauf das mimetische Verhalten anspricht, ist das Telos der Erkenntnis, das sie durch ihre eigenen Kategorien zugleich blockiert."[27] In my view, the context suggests that the antecedent of *sie* is *Erkenntnis* while gender points to *Telos* as the antecedent of the relative pronoun *das*. So the official translation could be revised in such a way as to eliminate ambiguity: "For what mimetic behavior responds to is

[26] Jameson, *Late Marxism*, p. 100.
[27] T. Adorno, *Ästhetische Theorie*, ed. G. Adorno and R. Tiedemann (Frankfurt am Main: Suhrkamp, 1980), p. 87.

the *telos* of cognition, a *telos* which cognition simultaneously hinders through its own categories" [see *AT* 80].) In fact, rather than saying, as the translation does, that art expands cognition, Adorno's German suggests that art completes cognition or rather brings it back to that from which it has closed itself off (*"komplettiert Erkenntnis um das von ihr Ausgeschlossene"*) and thus encroaches upon or violates the character of univocal knowledge (*"beeinträchtigt ... den Erkenntnischarakter, ihre Eindeutigkeit"*).[28] Art returns cognition to itself by subverting the claim to unambivalent meaning that privileges information over interpretation. Yet for this reason, art is always threatened with destruction by a narrow concept of rationality that identifies art with superstition, or the mythological residue of the process of disenchantment. The crisis of art is the articulation of its essence, which lies in the contradiction between pure mimesis, or the social rationalization of magic, and pure reason, or the instrumental rationality of modern science and social theory. The latter constitutes itself by excluding the difficult question of ends.

Adorno makes the aesthetic judgment that the greatness of an art work depends on how it negotiates its own self-contradiction. More crucially, art "cannot live up to its concept" because the dialectical reason of art undermines conceptuality as a form of equivalence. All works of art aim at the ideal of perfection as the sign of their formal rationality; but art's nature is to transgress its nature by disclosing the content of form as a contradiction between, on the one hand, art's rejection of society and its reason and, on the other, art's reproduction of the social norm of reason in its formal, though negative, autonomy. Adorno recognizes that art is not blameless of commodity fetishism (though he is disinclined to recognize the operation of the pleasure principle in aesthetic experience). In my view, such fetishism becomes more dominant the more an individual work is reduced to the status of being a classic, which has the effect of neutralizing its internal contradictions. Nevertheless, the "fetish character of art works is a condition of their truth, including their social truth" (*AT* 323). If one recognizes the classic as a work of art that has been neutralized, one understands why Adorno privileges the modernist concept of the new in art. Art works that disrupt tradition in order to

---

[28] Adorno, *Ästhetische Theorie.*

reconstitute it (and this is how even a conservative modernist like T. S. Eliot would define great art) are also fetishes but of a different kind from the classics they may be destined to become, a fate from which they can be saved only by the same force that makes that fate inevitable, critical intervention. They are what Lambert Zuidervaart calls "defetishizing fetishes." Art defetishizes itself to the extent that it refuses to reconcile the contradiction between mimesis and rationality, even though its formal unity, and therefore its status as art, depends on the illusion of reconciliation. As Zuidervaart explains, "To be a determinate negation of society, an artwork must achieve its own unity, but achieving unity makes it illusory in two ways. First, the artwork's unity is usually feigned rather than fully achieved. Second, such unity covers up societal antagonisms, which include the artwork's opposition to society."[29] "Feigned" may not be the right word for what needs to be expressed in this context. I would prefer Adorno's notion that art is "smitten with imperfection" or that it is incomplete (the word translated as "imperfection," *Unvollkommenheit*, suggests not only defect but incompleteness[30]) in such a way that it fails to live up to its concept as a self-identical form.

Art as the absolute commodity should be a form of absolute self-equivalence, an absolute being-in-itself. Art posits this norm as its structural law but fails to live up to that law in its material realization. According to Adorno, "While no work of art is a total unity, every work of art pretends that it is and thus comes into conflict with itself" (*AT* 154). Every work of art tries to transcend the conditions of its own production, including the author as producer. The internal norm of art, however, guides its production through the mediation of the artist as a socially constructed subject. As a result, the art work never fully transcends the conditions of its production; there is always a trace in art of the subject and the social formation from which the subject derives. Consistent enlightenment would discard art because it fails to be fully rational as an object of knowledge; that is to say, there is too

[29] L. Zuidervaart, *Adorno's Aesthetic Theory: The Redemption of Illusion* (Cambridge, Massachusetts: MIT, 1987), pp. 88–91, 178–79. For a reading of Adorno that has a bearing on this aspect of the discussion, see A. Wellmer, *The Persistence of Modernity: Essays on Aesthetics, Ethics, and Postmodernism*, trans. David Midgley (Cambridge, Massachusetts: MIT, 1991), pp. 1–35.

[30] Adorno, *Ästhetische Theorie*, p. 87.

much of the subject in it. Practical people discard art because it does not speak their language: it contains too much of the object as the unposited other. Because art foregrounds the intersubjective dimension of human experience (or the relation to the world as signifiable before the intervention of language *as a system* constituting subjects and objects), it fails to meet the expectations of either common sense or cognitive reason. Consequently, *the formal unity of the art work, which is the ground of its identity as a cultural fetish, represents simultaneously the necessity and the impossibility of its autonomy.* Every work of art is an illusion because it is incomplete. It promises the completion or fulfillment of instrumental rationality by the means of an illusion. It brings that rationality back into relation with its other as a moment in the progress of dialectical reason. It posits reconciliation as the *telos* of dialectical reason, but it cannot realize that *telos* as long as art is constituted in opposition to society. Art is illusion because in a society dominated by instrumental or means-centered rationality, dialectical reason, or the rational subordination of means to ends, can only articulate itself as illusion. Between illusion and commodification lies the mimesis of reason and the reason of mimesis, the total form of dialectical reason to which both mimesis and instrumental reason are subordinated.

Appearance, apparition, and history

Every work of art is torn between pure illusion, its "real magic," and pure commodification, its "thinglike rationality." Mimesis and rationality may be irreconcilable as absolute concepts; but when they are yoked together in a dialectical process, they are complementary in projecting an image of reconciliation. This image is the promise of something that is not real, or, in Lacanian terms, a symptom. "Whereas in the real world all particulars are fungible," Adorno stresses, "art protests against fungibility by holding up images of what reality itself might be like, if it were emancipated from the patterns of identification imposed on it." Such an image is not real, but the promise it makes has an explosive impact on what is real: "On behalf of the unexchange-able, art must awaken a critical consciousness toward the world of exchangeable things." As a commodity, art is an appearance, a pure illusion. Still, the difference between art and Disneyland (that quintessential celebration of the culture industry) is that appearance in art tends to become apparition, a sort of preternatural appearance that rises above the consciousness of people, beyond the world of things as they understand it to be. Art rises above both the artist and the consumer of art because the image content of art is collective, or, as I would rather say, intersubjective. Art becomes an apparition, as opposed to mere appearance, when it exceeds both the intention of the artist (who is no more than a material condition of the aesthetic process) and the expectations of the consumers (who must now become critics). In such a moment, art makes visible what is inaccessible to everyday experience, namely, the "historical antagonism of subject and object." This is the "universal within the particular" or the "hidden principle of coherence of empirical life" (*AT* 122–24). In making this universal visible and concrete in the image, art reveals the fundamental historicity of the universal.

Art demystifies and reveals the historical nature of the opposition between subject and object, which grounds Western science and philosophy and justifies the inequitable social relationships of Western society. While ideology legitimates this opposition as a kind of second nature, art as apparition explodes that nature and discloses intersubjectivity as the principle of symbolic exchange, or the exchange of the unexchangeable, that must precede the formation of subjects and objects as their material condition or ground. Art brings the self-identity of things in an exchange society back toward the nonidentity of those social relationships that society has excluded from itself in order to produce its system of equivalences. This movement toward reconciliation is the apparition that explodes art's commodity form, but it is only as an image that this moment is able to endure. Only through its commodity form can art subvert the commodity form. As Adorno postulates, "To experience art means to become conscious of its immanent process at the moment when it stands still" (*AT* 125). Apparition in art is the explosion that promises a reconciliation of identity and nonidentity, of rationality and mimesis. In this moment, as Zuidervaart stresses, "possibility appears to be actual."[31] However, this actuality of the possible must necessarily be mediated by the image; and it is through such mediation that

---

[31] Zuidervaart, *Adorno's Aesthetic Theory*, p. 186.

collective human suffering, the intersubjective experience of history, comes to be expressed.

Adorno sums up the relation of art to history. As appearance or apparition, art "carries its negation in itself like a *telos*." Apparition as an abrupt and explosive appearance reveals the falseness of the aesthetic illusion. Yet these categories of aesthetic experience are essentially historical. The work of art is "not a being immune to change but an existent in the process of becoming." Historicism, as a rule, fails to grasp the true nature of art's historicity because it imagines that this nature lies in art's reference to what is outside of it, that is, to the actual events of history. Adorno, by contrast, argues that art's historicity lies in its "inner time"; and it is "the continuity of this inner time which gets blown up in the explosion of appearance." Because works of art are structured like monads, they store up historical content through their formal response to the historical context and not through their direct reference to it. Analyzing them means "becoming conscious of the immanent history stored up in them" (*AT* 126). Appearance as apparition (*Erscheinung*) gives the lie to aesthetic illusion (*Schein*) because it promises a historical actualization of the possible that the illusion only pretends to realize. It drives the illusion of art out into the open and makes apparent the failure of the individual work to live up to its concept. Still, art's self-negation entails a dialectical movement internal to the artistic process. Appearance as apparition explodes the aesthetic illusion, but the image limits the apparition by congealing its historical content. At the same time, the image can never be grasped in its total significance unless it can be brought back by critical intervention to the instant of apparition as the immanent process of art. This dialectic unfolds in real history. The force of an art work as the actuality of the possible is not the same in every context. When an art work first appears on the historical scene, it can have an explosive effect that is later blunted when it has been institutionalized and canonized as a masterpiece. The opposite effect is also possible. Through a defamiliarizing critical intervention, the work of art can once again produce an unexpected apparitional effect, although this effect will then enter the historical process on its own and may become subject to another neutralization. A work may even have a delayed apparitional effect, one that was not visible when it first appeared but that has an enormous impact on a later generation approaching it with different modes of knowledge and political values. (Classics of children's literature, like *Alice's Adventures in Wonderland* and *Through the Looking-Glass*, as well as some feminist classics, like *The Yellow Wallpaper*, could be said to have this effect.) As such, the work of art is something in the process of becoming; and it must be kept in mind that the historical record of its impact on readers, viewers, and listeners is always incomplete.

Yet it would be an error to see Adorno as a reader-response theoretician in any sense. While he rejects a naive historicism that limits the truth or meaning of an art work to the historical context from which it emerged, he does not suggest that art's meaning depends on the reader as an autonomous subject. The inner time of art is its internal historicity as an objective thing in the world. Art cannot be said to reflect a context; rather, as a segment of objective time within history, it reflects itself as a historical form. In Adorno's thinking, a reductive relationship between the art work as text and the historical background as context betrays both history and art because such a relationship takes for granted an unproblematic view of art's autonomy. If historicism assumes that the art work is a transparent window onto the historical context, that it is a standpoint towards, or a position determined by, its relation to real history (*"seiner Stellung in der realen Geschichte nach"*[32]), it must also assume that in some sense art transcends the historical context in order to be able to look into it from the outside or to reflect it. Art is a *windowless* monad not because it is outside of history but because it is itself an existent historical thing in the process of becoming. It offers no view to the outside. The explosion of appearance, its sudden apparition, causes the continuity of art's inner time to jump or spring. It separates the monad from the temporal frame that determines it.

In this context, Adorno's thinking about art closely resembles Benjamin's concept of historical materialism. The historical materialist approaches history "only where he encounters it as a monad." Such a formation or historical symptom effectively "blasts a specific era out of the homogeneous course of history – blasting a specific life out of the era or a specific work out of the lifework." The traditional historian views history through the logic of causality as "a sequence of events like the beads of a

---

[32] Adorno, *Ästhetische Theorie*, p. 132.

rosary." The historical materialist "grasps the constellation which his own era has formed with a definite earlier one. Thus he establishes a conception of the present as the 'time of the now' which is shot through with chips of Messianic time."[33] While dropping the apocalyptic rhetoric, Adorno has transferred Benjamin's concept of historical materialism to the aesthetic realm. Apparition in the work of art is the moment of such a historical explosion or rupture in which the inner time of art enters into a constellation with a definite past and, to push the Benjaminian logic further, a definite future (or the actuality of the possible); and it is the constellation itself that brings about the explosion or apparition. Because art has the structure of a monad, it is autonomous; and that autonomy is its historical form. Still, art does not transcend history but is the means by which history engages in self-reflection without transcending itself. The work of art is the objective materialization of the historical process, the ideological form of which it is able to rupture by negating itself.

Art's negative truth

According to Adorno, "The truth content of art works, as a negation of their being, is mediated through them, but they do not communicate it in any way whatsoever." Art does not convey its truth as the specific content of its representations, or as an encoded message that can be reached through the simple act of decoding. Art's truth lies in the dialectical relationship between its content and its form. Art does not *communicate* truth because it is not the transparent expression of the autonomous subject that would be able to convey its message through the aesthetic medium according to the normative criterion of truthfulness, as Habermas would have it. The truth of art does not lie in its meaning but rather in the nonexistent to which this existent points. In the art work, the nonexistent is "a constellation of existents." The utopian dimension of art emerges through its failure to live up to its concept. Art as apparition is the constellation of existents that destroys the illusion of wholeness and thereby redeems illusion itself, not by making the nonexistent transparent as the negation of society but by negating itself, by positing the nonexistent as the negation of art

---

[33] Benjamin, *Illuminations*, p. 263.

and its historical content (those unresolved social antagonisms that appear in art as problems of aesthetic form). Art negates itself by revealing its failure to live up to its promise: "the promise of happiness, a promise that is constantly being broken" (*AT* 193, 196). Criticizing Adorno's assumption that "art can testify for the possibility of the possible," Zuidervaart concludes that, in order to realize its truth, "art must transcend itself in cooperation with a philosophy intent on redeeming illusion."[34] To qualify this formulation, I would argue that (1) for Adorno, art does not transcend itself in the metaphysical sense but rather negates itself; (2) it does not articulate the possibility of the possible but the actuality of the possible as a dimension of human thought, as the expression of human suffering; and (3) it is not subsumed under, or redeemed by, philosophy but rather philosophy and art are distinct moments within the process of dialectical reason.

According to Adorno, art requires explication as a moment within the aesthetic experience itself. "Comprehension," he says, "takes the form of a confrontation between historically given categories and moments of aesthetic theory, on the one hand, and artistic experience, on the other. Theory and experience correct each other reciprocally" (*AT* 484). Adorno further insists that aesthetics must be dialectical in conformity with the model of dialectical philosophy which "holds that fact and concept are not diametrically opposed but are mediated by each other" (*AT* 471). Adorno's aesthetic theory presupposes that the category of the autonomous work of art and all the categories that make the analysis of such a work possible are historically given. Peter Bürger has relied on Adorno's insight to develop his theory of the emergence of the category *art as an institution* during the period of the historical avant-garde. He then claims that Adorno employs the concept of the autonomous work of art without fully taking into account its historical implications: "the autonomy of art is a category of bourgeois society that both reveals and obscures an actual historical development. All discussion of this category must be judged by the extent to which it succeeds in showing and explaining logically and historically the contradictoriness inherent in the thing itself."[35] Presumably, what the concept of the

---

[34] Zuidervaart, *Adorno's Aesthetic Theory*, p. 212.
[35] P. Bürger, *Theory of the Avant-Garde*, trans. M. Shaw (Minneapolis: University of Minnesota Press, 1984), p. 36.

autonomous work of art reveals and obscures is the emergence of art as an institution that was posited and then challenged by the historical avant-garde.

Still, even if Adorno does not formally produce a theory of *art as an institution*, he implicitly theorizes such a category through the elaboration of his own concept of aesthetic autonomy. No theorist has done more than Adorno to demonstrate the contradictoriness inherent in the latter concept. On the one hand, autonomy is nothing less than the ideological form of the art work; and, on the other, it is precisely this form that art negates in the process of becoming the absolute commodity that redeems its own illusion. It does not matter whether Adorno accepts Bürger's contention that the category *art as an institution* only becomes available to aesthetic theory with the historical avant-garde. The historical process by which art becomes autonomous clearly involves its institutionalization. The exact moment when this process results in the social recognition of art as an institution can be debated, but this recognition in itself does not bring to an end the historical process from which it emerges. Art as an institution may be a category of bourgeois culture, but that culture is not self-contained or without internal dynamism. As Bürger concludes, the historical avant-garde failed in its mission to destroy art as an institution and to reintegrate it with the praxis of life; however, it does not follow from this failure that such an institution has therefore transcended the historical process. Adorno's focus on the individual work of art suggests that the aesthetic experience, which results in the form of the windowless monad, cannot be reduced categorically to any absolute concept, including the concept of art itself. For this reason, aesthetic theory must be dialectical since the "name of dialectics says no more, to begin with, than that objects do not go into their concepts without leaving a remainder, that they come to contradict the traditional norm of adequacy" (*ND* 5).

Dialectically speaking, the fact of aesthetic experience in the individual work of art and the concept of art as an institution mediate one another and reciprocally correct one another. As Jameson stresses, Adorno seems relatively unconcerned with defending or theoretically grounding the fact of aesthetic experience.[36] He takes such experience itself as an irreducibly given,

---

[36] Jameson, *Late Marxism*, p. 238.

although the significance of this given depends on its dialectical relation to the conceptual framework or configuration transforming it into an object of knowledge. The difference between philosophy and art does not correspond directly to the difference between concept and experience. Although philosophy is compelled to operate with concepts, it is unable, by the very nature of the concept, to limit itself to pure conceptuality: "To refer to nonconceptualities ... is characteristic of the concept, and so is the contrary: that as the abstract unit of the noumena subsumed thereunder it will depart from the noumenal." In other words, the relationship between conceptuality and nonconceptuality, and between identity and nonidentity, is dialectical; but this dialectic does not lead toward the Hegelian resolution of contradiction in the unity of identity and nonidentity. The concept is a unit of the noumena that has separated itself from its own origin in the noumenal: like Lacanian metalanguage, it can never be a form of identity because it can never reconcile its articulations of the Real, or the noumenal, with its own origin in the Real. In philosophy, negative dialectics has the task of negating the illusion of conceptual completeness or wholeness understood as the unity of the concept and the thing conceived: "To change this direction of conceptuality, to give it a turn toward nonidentity is the hinge of negative dialectics ... Reflection upon its own meaning is the way out of the concept's seeming being-in-itself as a unit of meaning [*aus dem Schein des Ansichseins des Begriffs als einer Einheit des Sinns*]" (*ND* 12).[37] As the German indicates, the concept's being-in-itself is a semblance or illusion (*Schein*). This suggests that both art and philosophy find their common ground in the process of determinate negation as a form of self-reflection which articulates the relation between identity and nonidentity as a permanent tension or contradiction.

Philosophy uses concepts to negate the illusion of conceptual equivalence. Art destroys the illusion of its autonomy by bringing to bear on its claim to formal completeness the historical truth of its incompleteness. Art as experience cannot fully enter into the concept of the autonomous work, while the concepts of philosophy cannot fully master the nonconceptualities that they articulate. Adorno recognizes that, although the aesthetic moment "is ...

[37] T. W. Adorno, *Negative Dialektik* (Frankfurt am Main: Suhrkamp, 1970), p. 22.

not accidental to philosophy," it is still necessary for philosophy to rid itself of aestheticism by bringing the aesthetic back to the real through the deployment of "cogent insights." In spite of his use of the German verb *aufheben*, which carries Hegelian connotations, Adorno does not suggest that philosophy and art are reconciled at some higher level of the dialectic. On the contrary, philosophy's "affinity to art" lies in a mimetic impulse that has nothing to do with imitating art in the sense of copying or trying to become a work of art. Rather, the philosophical concept must adapt itself to its other in such a way as to assume, like art, a stance toward reality that cannot be reduced exclusively to subject–object relations. Both art and philosophy remain faithful to their own substantial properties through the mediation of their opposites: art by resisting the conceptuality of meaning; philosophy by voiding itself of empirical content (*ND* 15). Art resists meaning insofar as meaning "synthesizes the various intentions of a work into a whole" (*AT* 217). Stated differently, in negating its own illusion, art negates what it cannot avoid as a coherent form: "the hypnotic suggestion of meaning amid the general loss of meaning" (*AT* 222). By refusing to accept the illusion of meaning, art expresses the yearning for authentic meaning, a meaning that art, as the absolute commodity or thing, can never realize. The philosophical concept, on the contrary, negates yearning as the residue of empirical desire, although it can never abandon yearning as the nonconceptual remainder of its own self-negation. Philosophy, like art, "keeps alive the category of meaning in determinate negation" (*AT* 225). Neither art nor philosophy can ever be reduced to the purely aesthetic or the purely conceptual. As Jameson observes, if Adorno's social philosophy always comes back to the aesthetic (or rather, I would say, to the concept of mimesis as the nonidentity of both art and philosophy), it can also be said that his aesthetic theory leads us back to history as the absent cause.[38]

"Truth content," writes Adorno, "is the crystallization, in art works, of history" (*AT* 193). Art and philosophy not only do not transcend history; they also never escape being the symptoms of the historical process. They are precisely the medium through which historical experience deposits its memory-trace within the culture of technical rationality that works to efface history from

[38] Jameson, *Late Marxism*, p. 239.

the public mind. In that sense, art and philosophy become the symptoms of the political unconscious by means of which history survives as the absent cause. As Jameson has long since reminded us, "History is what hurts." As a narrative category, it is the "experience of Necessity" as the "inexorable *form* of events."[39] Still, history need not become another version of Hegelian *Geist*, some transhistorical subject that promises full self-realization as its end. For Adorno, neither art nor philosophy is utopian if by "utopian" one means that they are oriented toward the future as the site of a reconciliation that can be anticipated and planned for, or if one means that they are linked to an ideal past in which man and nature were united before the historical process of rationalization. It seems to me that the whole point of the *Dialectic of Enlightenment*, even if it went to an extreme in its level of historical generalization, was to destroy any trace of the Marxist nostalgia for a pre-capitalist past. Adorno never really challenges the specificity of the Marxist critique of the capitalist mode of production and carefully grounds his understanding of the autonomy of art in that critique. Even at its most abstract moments, *Aesthetic Theory* always understands itself and the concept of art it theorizes as historically situated. Nevertheless, by positing instrumental reason as a form of rationality embracing both capitalism and what precedes it, Adorno insists that the horizon of Marxist critique is not the horizon of history itself.

Dialectic of Enlightenment historicizes the historical consciousness of Marxism by implying that instrumental reason in the interest of self-preservation – insofar as it lays claim to being a second nature – is an ideological concept that even Marxism has not managed to get beyond. The narrative of infinite technical progress, the ultimate myth of global capitalism, is not the inexorable form of events but the ideological representation of real history. Even Marxism participates in the myth of global capitalism when it identifies itself as the predictive science of historical continuity (the inevitable progress toward communism) rather than as an intervention in *the time of the now* with the intent of exploding continuity. To slightly revise Jameson's interpretation, history as a narrative category does not locate the experience of necessity in the success of a narrative that lives up to its concept

[39] F. Jameson, *The Political Unconscious: Narrative as a Socially Symbolic Act* (Ithaca: Cornell University Press, 1981), p. 102.

insofar as its end seems to be contained within its means. This subsumption of ends by means is the utopia of capitalism and state socialism where the ideology of science and technical means continues to supersede the more humane values of enlightenment, including the value of democracy. Instrumental or means-centered reason is the form of rationality that takes itself as its own end: it comes to rest in itself, so to speak. Negative dialectics, on the other hand, "will not come to rest in itself, as if it were total. This is its form of hope" (*ND* 406). The determinate negation of instrumental reason and its myths brings forth the experience of necessity not as the true narrative that all other narratives have distorted but as the limit of any narrative, the point at which every narrative fails to enter fully into its own concept as a self-contained whole. The inexorable form of events speaks to the impossibility of formal closure, the impossibility of absolute truth as the end of history's many detours. The inexorable form of events is the form of dialectical reason.

History hurts whenever the narrative representations that give meaning to everyday life suggest their own incompleteness by alluding to something other, something that is neither a subject nor an object but rather the relation without essence which I have called, after Lacan, intersubjectivity. The intersubject as a relation both precedes and exceeds the formation of subject and object as binary positions. Intersubjectivity subverts the illusion of the subject's absolute autonomy through the language of suffering. It subverts the distance between subject and object through mimetic adaptation. Although suffering arises from the experience of narrative failure (or broken promises), it is the only true hope that historical materialism can grant itself (and thus suffering can also produce pleasure, or *jouissance*). When the subject of a narrative confronts the other in itself or the self as other, when it fails to achieve narrative closure and the resolution of all contradictions, it becomes the voice of the intersubject which makes itself heard with all the force of collective suffering. The historical truth of Adorno's *Aesthetic Theory* lies in this realization. This truth is neither the message of art nor the ideal essence to which all works of art conform. The truth of art is neither art's autonomy nor its social character. The truth of art has nothing to do with art. It is what art expresses through its silence, through what it does not say in the midst of what it says.

In Adorno's philosophy, art can never be subordinated to philosophy; and philosophy is in no danger of becoming a work of art. This does not mean, of course, that one cannot argue for the aesthetic value of *Aesthetic Theory*. It means simply that the method of negative dialectics calls into question any metaphysical concept of the essence of art or the essence of philosophy on the basis of which it would be possible to construct relations of subordination and theories of negative contamination (a subject to which I will return in the last chapter of this work). Adorno's theory of art is not a theory of essence but a historical investigation of how it is that art can articulate what is not art. Insofar as art is a form of determinate negation, it is a form of dialectical thought. According to Adorno, if such thought "is to be true – if it is to be true today, in any case – it must also be a thinking against itself." Truth is never absolute. Truth springs abruptly from the confrontation of dialectical thought with a shifting and undecidable historical context – in the sense that history is always subject to revision and reinterpretation – and then abruptly disappears into its own memory-trace. The truth of art as a form of thought is what escapes art's own concept. As Adorno concludes, "If thought is not measured by the extremity that eludes the concept, it is from the outset in the nature of the musical accompaniment with which the SS liked to drown out the screams of its victims" (*ND* 365).

Art's dilemma, its horrifying contradiction, is revealed by the thought of what it may have made possible for human beings to tolerate or endure, of what it may have drowned out of human consciousness. Still, art is only a form of thought, which, in and of itself, cannot guarantee the liberation of humankind. This is not to endorse the idea of a metaphysical difference between thought and social practice, however. As the example of art profoundly demonstrates, human thought can be considered a form of social practice subject to all the uncertainties and ambivalences that characterize human actions of every sort. The distinction between thought and action, between theory and practice, is worth maintaining and even defending (as Adorno is inclined to do) in the interest of human intervention in the historical process; but such a distinction is the tool of practice, not a transcendent metaphysical difference. Within the framework of human praxis, the concept of liberation would never emerge without thought; and without the experiential framework of human praxis, thought would have nothing to work with, no basis on which to construct its concepts. As a form of thought, art is neither inherently good nor inherently evil. As the absolute commodity, it articulates the moment in the history of instrumental reason when all the means available to it are mobilized in the material realization of the irrationality of reason, of the irrationality of the means of reason when reason is divorced from the ambivalent and always uncertain question of ends.

Dialectical reason survives in the contradictions of art and philosophy not as the metaphysical guarantee of this or that utopian end of history but rather as the inexorable form of events, the inexorable divisions of time, that demand the thought of an end without ever making that thought the moral guarantee of valid human action in the present. The end of history, both its conclusion and its moral purpose, is what thought can never define absolutely and can never stop contemplating. This end is nothing in itself, a Nowhere or literal utopia that Lacan calls the Thing. To define this Thing destroys thought and the viability of the human praxis within which thought operates. Art's historical truth is revealed by the persistence with which it aims at transcending history and moving toward the absolute meaning of the end of history only to fail and thus display the other of art, the *time of the now* that demands the decision to act with the knowledge of the absolute risk that human action requires. In a sense, every work of art has only one message: either act or do not act. Art itself never chooses.

3

❖❖

Sexual nations: history and the division of hope in *The Crying Game*

❖❖

> So perhaps there is hope for our divisions yet.
> Neil Jordan, Introduction to *The Crying Game*

The culture industry

When I began writing this essay, Neil Jordan's film, *The Crying Game*, was still in release at theaters throughout the United States. One could argue that to make such a film the object of a critique whose method in some sense derives from Adorno's *Aesthetic Theory* undermines the spirit of Adorno, who once described the culture industry as a form of mass deception. This thought carries even more weight if one keeps in mind that the success of *The Crying Game* is in part the result of an ingenious advertising ploy. I remember hearing about this film on National Public Radio shortly before its release. The reviewer faithfully explained that he could not reveal the plot of *The Crying Game* because it contained a number of unexpected reversals. The point, he seemed to suggest, is that you never really know what the film is about; with each reversal, it changes directions so dramatically as to call into question the meaning of what has happened up to that point. Beyond this observation, the reviewer revealed nothing except that the film involved the Irish Republican Army, Northern Ireland, and a hostage.

For the next few months, before I saw the film, I was fascinated to see how it compelled silence from spectators and reviewers alike on what soon came to be known as the secret of *The Crying Game*. Already a few skeptical critics were saying that the film's secret was just a gimmick, but even they refused to give the secret away. And finally one could not help asking, so what? Obviously, the secret was a gimmick, but knowing this did not stop me or anyone else from wanting to see the film in order to find out what the secret was all about. As Horkheimer and Adorno argue in *Dialectic of Enlightenment*, advertising works best when it can compel the consumer to buy a product that even the consumer knows is just a gimmick.[1]

The Crying Game can certainly be seen as a triumph of advertising. According to an article in *The Wall Street Journal*, Miramax paid between 1.5 and 2.5 million dollars for the US rights to the film and another 5 million dollars in marketing costs. By the time of the Academy Awards in early April 1993, the film had grossed about 60 million dollars for Miramax and was expected to earn more money both in the theaters and on video. The financial success of *The Crying Game* is probably the major reason behind the purchase of Miramax Films by Disney for as much as 60 million dollars.[2] Of course, these numbers merely suggest that at one level *The Crying Game* simply represents business as usual in the film industry; and the only thing that would distinguish it from a film like *Batman* would be the economy with which the former was able to produce such enormous profits. Still, whatever one may think of *Batman* (and simply dismissing it as a product of the culture industry without subjecting it to an immanent analysis may be to miss Adorno's point about the culture industry and art altogether), *The Crying Game* has done something unique. Although any successful Hollywood film could be said to inaugurate its marketing strategy by anticipating in its internal structure possible audiences and the various appeals that can be made to them through advertising, rarely has a film become its own self-advertisement in the way that *The Crying Game* did.

Warner Brothers sold the first *Batman* by disseminating the ambiguous Batman logo all over America through a series of Batman products, by using the press and media to anticipate a

[1] Horkheimer and Adorno, *Dialectic*, p. 167.
[2] T. R. King and R. Turner, "Disney Agrees to Buy the Distributor of 'Crying Game' at Possibly $60 Million," *The Wall Street Journal*, Southwest Edition (May 3, 1993), B7.

success that would justify the film's enormous production costs (including the cost of its star, Jack Nicholson), and by distributing a trailer that was a masterpiece of high-tech seduction. The trailer was arguably better than the film in terms of timing and originality of style. It used the techniques of music videos to create the impression of breathtaking speed and almost horrific darkness. The trailer and all of the other advertising seemed to promise something utterly deep, an apocalyptic drama. At least it sent these signals to prepare any future audiences for what they would see. As Horkheimer and Adorno stress, the culture industry never encourages independent thinking and designs it products so that they can prescribe the consumer's reaction to them by means of signals. The film itself, when it finally appeared, would have been a disappointment if anyone in the audience really expected Hollywood films to live up to their advertising. It might make more sense to say that the film was not a surprise. All the signals in the trailer seemed to be in the film, except for that sense of thrilling anticipation that the trailer conveyed so effectively to its audiences. And yet, in a way, the thrill was there. Having waited impatiently to see *Batman* made *Batman* a thrill to see; and if one had learned how to recognize the signals of its mysterious depth, it hardly mattered whether the film managed to get beneath the surface of its own images. While there is no reason to prejudge the results of an immanent analysis of such a film, it should be recognized that nothing in the film or in the advertising that preceded its release invites the audience to engage in such an analysis. On the contrary, every step in marketing a film like *Batman* works toward eliminating any need for reflection.

According to Horkheimer and Adorno, "The culture industry perpetually cheats its consumers of what it perpetually promises."[3] It cheats them not because the individual work fails to live up to its promise (since, as Adorno demonstrates in *Aesthetic Theory*, no work of art lives up to its promise) but by seducing the consumer away from any analytical reflection on art's failure to live up to its promise. The culture industry, as Jameson stresses, is neither art nor culture but rather business as such, the place in which "the tendential convergence between monopoly and instrumentalization can be observed more clearly than in other

---

[3] Horkheimer and Adorno, *Dialectic*, pp. 137–39.

kinds of commodity exchange."[4] As Jameson suggests, business constantly aims at eliminating the need for reflection in the reception of its products so that these products can be reduced to a form of exchangeable value. Reflection raises difficult questions about ends that make cultural products less predictable in their value and thus less subject to rational control aimed at maximum profitability. The point is not that a film like *Batman* could not be subjected to an immanent analysis as a work of art that would produce quite different results than would an analysis of the business that produces and tries to control its effects as a commodity. Every work of art, including canonized art, is a commodity, as Adorno knew even when he wrote *Dialectic of Enlightenment* with Horkheimer; but art aims at the status of absolute commodity by subverting the illusion it produces. True art always invites reflection on its negative truth; and all art is true to the extent that reflection has dialectically disclosed its commodity form. Without such reflection, art never reveals its truth as the crystallization of history.

As a product, *The Crying Game*, unlike *Batman*, virtually sold itself. Everyone who saw the film became an advertisement for it insofar as they participated in the game of either revealing or not revealing its secrets. A spectator may or may not have liked the film or thought it of any particular value; but by reflecting on the film's structure to the extent that it demands such a response, he or she would have been required to decide whether something in the experience of seeing the film would or would not be destroyed if its plot were revealed. Even those people who revealed the film's secrets in order to show that the whole game of *The Crying Game* was nothing but a cheap gimmick still participated in the game by recognizing that the film required some form of reflective judgment, that it was necessary to respond to it one way or the other. The difference between *The Crying Game* and a film like *Batman*, therefore, is not that the former has internalized its identity as a commodity (which would be true of both films). Rather, it has internalized the act of reflection on its commodity status that everything in an advertising campaign like the one for *Batman* tries to block from entering into the product.

This does not mean that *The Crying Game* has somehow tran-

---

[4] Jameson, *Late Marxism*, p. 108.

scended the culture industry. Rather, it has formally disclosed the contradiction between its status as a commodity and the material that it has shaped and adapted to the commodity form – the contradiction between the culture industry as a business and art as a form of mimesis. I would not disagree with reader-response critics like Janice Radway who suggest that readers and spectators play an active part in determining their responses to art-forms, whether the latter are identified as "cheap romances" or "classics." Just as women can read popular romances through "combative and compensatory" oppositional strategies,[5] one can easily imagine spectators of *Batman* or *The Terminator* who could experience these films as negative criticisms of contemporary society.

However, it would be naive to assume that the culture industry plays no role in determining how these works are consumed or that these works have no objective form that would limit the possibilities for subjective interpretation. Ironically, it is the objectivity of art that makes it intersubjective. Because the subject comes up against the limits of its own autonomy in the work of art, it must adapt to that work in a way that reveals the intersubjectivity of aesthetic experience. By the same token, art is never merely the objective expression of the artist but mimetically articulates the intersubjective conditions that have entered into the formation of the artistic subject. In effect, the autonomous work of art is unthinkable outside the subject–object relationship which it nevertheless calls into question by disclosing the intersubjective grounds of that relationship and the limits of art's negative autonomy. A film like *The Crying Game* differs from the usual product of the culture industry in two ways. First, it does not efface its relationship to that industry but dramatizes it by transforming its status as a commodity into the content of its aesthetic form. Second, it situates the historical fact of its commodity form in a contextual framework that includes other dimensions of history that both adapt themselves to, and resist identification with, the commodity form. These objectively self-reflective dimensions of the film force the spectator to assume a critical attitude that subverts the work's stability as a commodity by constantly raising the question of ends. A film like *Batman* only requires the spectator to take it or leave it. The question as to whether it has

---

[5] J. Radway, *Reading the Romance: Women, Patriarchy, and Popular Culture* (Chapel Hill: University of North Carolina Press, 1984), p. 211.

satisfied a self-reflective norm (rather than an extrinsic norm prescribed by the culture industry itself) simply does not make much sense, unless the spectator takes it out of the context of the culture industry and submits it to an immanent analysis. With *The Crying Game*, on the other hand, even though the question can never be answered, it is posed from the beginning, even within the culture industry: what is art for? What is the use of it?

The symptom

Before I undertake an immanent analysis of *The Crying Game* (which, if it does not answer these questions, at least contextualizes them), I need to clarify briefly how I understand the relationship of such a procedure to Adorno's *Aesthetic Theory*. Peter Uwe Hohendahl makes two points about Adorno's theory of reading and interpretation that I find useful in this context. First, he says, "Close reading is for Adorno, strange as this may sound, a contextual reading." This practical insight follows directly from Adorno's concept of the work of art as a windowless monad, which, though historical in itself, never simply reflects a history that is outside of itself. Hohendahl's second point, though it follows from the first, is more difficult to grasp: "When we talk about Adorno's approach we have to realize that he refuses to offer an objectified scientific method that can be abstracted from the individual act of understanding and then applied to various works."[6] It could be argued that Adorno's approach to philosophical reading rejects the notion of normative methodology because this would presuppose a transcendent and universal set of values that we have already associated with the concept of cultural tradition espoused by Gadamer and, from a different perspective, by Habermas. Adorno certainly recognizes that individual art works strive to realize a dynamic and self-generated concept of normativity, but such a concept or norm is highly unstable because it is the structural manifestation of contextual forces rather than of transcendent universals. Adorno counters the tradition-oriented history-of-ideas approach with the idea of shedding "light on all art from the perspective of the most recent artistic phenomena." Deep down, he suggests, traditionalists who

---

[6] Hohendahl, *Reappraisals*, pp. 86–87.

posit universal norms wish that "there are no changes and that everything stays the same." Since "authentic modern works are criticisms of past ones," Adorno concludes that "Aesthetics becomes normative by articulating these criticisms" (*AT* 492). In other words, normativity for Adorno represents the critical dimension of art, the way art as a dialectical process continually calls itself into question with the production of each significant work.

As Hohendahl insists, these concepts of normativity and close reading have nothing in common with the ideology of New Criticism as an academic practice (which should not be confused with the best work of individual practitioners of this method who often exceed the ideological norm). First, New Criticism takes for granted the existence of certain universal norms and values that remain constant, though often implicit, throughout the history of artistic forms and techniques. Even T. S. Eliot, who privileges innovation in art, posits "a conformity between the old and the new" as the condition for true innovation in the ideal order of existing monuments.[7] The nonidentity of each new work of art contains in itself the identity of the ideal order of which it is a coherent expression. Second, New Criticism takes a completely unproblematic view of the autonomy of art as an essence that transcends history. Since this autonomy is rooted in universal norms, it invites a New Critical procedure that respects organic unity and meaning. The validity of criticism would lie in the coherence and consistency of its results. Every new work of art, no matter how anomalous it may appear to be, should produce a comparable effect through a resolution of tensions. Adorno's theory of the windowless monad presupposes that each work of art is in some way incommensurable in relation to the history of art. Such incommensurability calls into question the presumption of universal norms by positing a normativity beyond the universal. This normativity is more like an explosion than a stable ground. It does not reflect the universal but rather bears the imprint of the particular, of history itself. "Truth content in art works," writes Adorno, "is the materialization of the most advanced consciousness, including the productive critique of the status quo both in art and outside of it. It is a kind of unconscious

[7] T. S. Eliot, "Tradition and the Individual Talent," in *Selected Essays* (New York: Harcourt, Brace, 1950), p. 5.

historiography, one that sides with what has been vanquished" (*AT* 274).

By advanced consciousness, Adorno does not mean a consciousness that is further along the line of evolutionary progress but a consciousness that has exceeded the normativity of tradition. Such a consciousness punctures the illusion of traditional values to reveal what Jameson would call the political unconscious, or the trace of real history, of what has been excluded from traditional narratives and cultural forms. Such a consciousness is not rooted, finally, in the autonomous subject but rather in the historical context. It is the immanent response of art to history. Consequently, it is impossible to derive an "objectified scientific method" from the "individual act of understanding" because every act of understanding constitutes itself as an articulation of its own historical context, which cannot be taken for granted as a stable construction. Every act of understanding, every immanent analysis of the aesthetic monad, is a negotiation between the critical subject as situated construct and the work as symptom of history, between a subject and the intersubjective process. There can be family resemblances between interpretive acts but no methodological identity. Each interpretation expresses its own unconscious historiography. Consequently, I am not presenting this reading as a model to be followed in every case since different works with different histories call for different strategies of reading.

A work of art like *The Crying Game* is both a commodity of the culture industry and a symptom of history. On the one hand, as a commodity to be consumed, it must at some level ask for an uncritical reception. On the other, the nature of its self-advertisement, of its introjection of the culture industry that frames it, makes the experience of viewing it reflective to the extent that one begins to expect the opposite of what one would normally expect. I do not mean that the film is unpredictable in the style of many so-called *art films* but rather that it teaches us to expect or predict disappointment. It is precisely the articulation of disappointment that both discloses and determinately negates the film's commodity form. To state it somewhat paradoxically, the film negates its commodity form through the self-conscious articulation of that form. By insisting that it is a commodity, it unravels the illusion of autonomy crucial to the nonreflective consumption of commodities. In the process of this unraveling, the film takes on a symptomatic relation to history not as its representation or resolution but rather as the historical truth of the commodity form itself, its broken promise. The film expresses the historical context not as the object of its representations but as the failure of those representations to reflect the outside as an object. *The Crying Game* fails as a historical metaphor while it succeeds as a metonymic symptom (the *sinthome*, in Lacanian terms), a knot of threads that have not been cut away from the historical fabric of which they are a part and to which they point as the unfinalized totality that can never be contained or reflected in the part.

In a sense, the meaning of *The Crying Game* is the disappointment of art in its own response to the contradictions of history. Once this meaning is grasped, the reaction of critics like Stanley Kaufmann begins to make sense as a symptomatic response in its own right. In a review that more or less dismisses the film's structure as a series of tricks, he comments that "the whole film seems to assume a sympathy for the IRA that even a good many Irish people, north and south, do not share."[8] Curiously, Kaufmann faults the film for not being politically correct and repeats what has by now become a familiar expression of public outrage directed at organizations like the Irish Republican Army that employ violence to achieve political goals. Without dismissing this indignation, one should keep in mind that the use of the term *terrorism* to describe this violence has the effect of eliminating critical thought rather than expressing it. It seems unlikely that *The Crying Game*, at the time of its release, was a favorite among the active members of the IRA, for it hardly presents a flattering picture of that organization or of its members. Still, the response of those members might not be that different from Kaufmann's response: disappointment. The film does not do justice to the IRA, they might say, because it does not shed light on the historical context in which the IRA operates. It provides no information on the conflict in Northern Ireland that has its origins in the Irish revolution earlier in this century and has only recently, after more than twenty years of confrontation, shown some signs of coming to a resolution. It fails to take into account the historical impact of the British presence in Ireland that has lasted for centuries. As a

---

[8] S. Kaufmann, "The Haunted and the Hunted," *The New Republic* (December 14, 1992), 29.

representative bourgeois critic, Kaufmann would dismiss the film as a neutralization of the reality of terrorism, while the so-called terrorists might fault the film as a neutralization of the history of imperialism. I would argue that both criticisms are valid responses to the film as a commodity but wholly inadequate as analyses of the film's immanent historical content.

"Neutralization is the social price art pays for its autonomy," writes Adorno (*AT* 323). What enables a work like *The Crying Game* to be something more than the expression of a political ideology, whether of the left or of the right, is that it is the expression of an aesthetic ideology. It is an aesthetic commodity. Yet, as a commodity, it requires that the spectator reflect on his or her own expectations of such a work and on the fundamental disappointment that lies at the root of the aesthetic experience. Nothing, however, requires the spectator to reflect on the work to the extent of engaging in an immanent analysis of its historical content. On the contrary, the forces of the culture industry work at substituting an ideological response for an analytical one. For example, when the lead actor in the film, Stephen Rea, was interviewed on a morning news program in the United States, he was asked about the film's political content and meaning. His response was the predictable denial that the film has any political meaning or, rather, the implied claim that politics is only the background to a story about love, loyalty, and the ambivalence of human nature. While at some level this statement is perfectly true, at another it is contradicted by the fact that the question itself has to be posed repeatedly by sources as uncritical as television interviewers and film journalists. *The Crying Game* is a profoundly political film not because it has a political message or expresses a political ideology but because it systematically fails to represent and resolve the historical contradictions that nevertheless negatively determine its aesthetic form. It resists the neutralizing tendency of reception that Adorno refers to by refusing to identify itself with any ideology beyond its own self-concept as a work of art, even while it displays and to some extent subverts that concept by insisting that art is ultimately an illusion. Perhaps critics like Stanley Kaufmann are not off the mark when they see the film as a series of tricks that hardly do justice to the historical context they try to represent. The film's failure to represent that context as a coherent totality is the condition of its immanent historical truth as the symptom of social contradictions.

Cinematic sutures

In his introduction to the original screenplay of *The Crying Game*, Neil Jordan stresses that the story ends with "a kind of happiness" even though it involves "the separation of a prison cell and other more profound separations, of racial, national, and sexual identity" (*NJR* xii–xiii). The two tracking shots that frame the film further suggest that divisions can be overcome without destroying the differences that constitute them. The original screenplay merely notes for the opening shot that *"we see a carnival in the distance – with a Ferris Wheel turning round and round"* (*NJR* 179).[9] In and of itself, the carnival is a traditional figure for human society as a sort of masquerade or play; and, after one has seen the film a few times, the Ferris wheel inevitably starts connoting a Joycean sense of the circularity of history. The masquerade concept takes on more symbolic value as the film progresses through its reversals, not only its major reversals but the more subtle disclosures that anticipate, without fully revealing, the climactic ones. In each case, what is disclosed is the instability of what appeared to be a stable identity (of race, nationality, gender, or sexuality). At the same time, there is the sense that nothing really changes, that in the world opened up by each reversal or revelation the same incongruity of human relations and events repeats itself.

The opening shot of the film also contains something that is not described in the original screenplay. Looking through the arches of a bridge in a slow tracking shot to the left, with the view occasionally broken by the pylons as the credits appear on the screen, the spectator sees the carnival on the other side of the bridge and across a river. This shot produces an image of space divided and connected by the same physical structure. The camera also lures the spectator with another illusion. As it tracks across the bridge at a low angle, it creates the impression that the bridge is moving while the carnival remains stationary in the distance. This shot suggests two meanings and produces a third crucial effect. First, the carnival signifies the finite store of symbolic forms as the raw material of human history, which remains more or less impervious to time not because it is self-identical and universal

[9] References to the screenplay are to this text, though in my general discussion I am referring to the film itself.

but because it possesses the nonidentity of the mask. This material is both *real* and the means by which we represent the Real. The second meaning, which involves the bridge, says that both divisions and the hope of overcoming or resolving division constitute the movement of human history as a narrative form. The camera produces the illusion of motion which foregrounds the *real* fact that a bridge is the materialization and resolution of interlocking and opposing forces. It is an interpretation of those forces, a kind of suture that figures the cinematic process itself (as I will argue in a moment). Like a bridge, history simultaneously interprets and materially constitutes the forces of the real world. It is both a representation and the social construction of the thing it represents. To draw analogies with Benjamin's philosophy of history, the historicist would see the bridge as motionless, complete, and permanent – the concrete representation of the history of the victors. The historical materialist would see the bridge as something dynamic and in motion; and it is his or her task, like that of the camera in the shot I have described, "to brush history against the grain."[10] The bridge is never seen as a whole in the distance but from different angles that suggest not a totality but an incomplete process.

The other effect of this shot is to foreground the instability of the suture that constructs a subject-position for the spectator. As the camera tracks across the span of the bridge, the spectator seeks a point of stability in the distant carnival; in fact, the spinning Ferris wheel creates a center for the eye that curiously recalls the credits to Hitchcock's *Vertigo*, another film about mistaken identities. (I admit that this is a stretch, but consider the structural similarity between the two films. Both fall neatly into two parts. In the second half of both films, the central character feels responsible for the death of someone and in the process of working through that guilt and loss discovers the real identity of the dead person through a shocking revelation about a living one. In both cases, one could argue that the main character should have known the truth about *the other* long before the revelation itself. And finally, the endings are different but symmetrical: in *Vertigo*, the other really dies the second time around, while in *The Crying Game* another's life is redeemed through a symbolic death.) As Christian

[10] Benjamin, *Illuminations*, p. 257.

Metz has theorized, the spectator identifies with the camera as the substitute for the individual gaze: it functions "as a pure act of perception ... as the condition of possibility of the perceived and hence as a kind of transcendental subject, which comes before every *there is.*"[11] Ironically, the shot in question here, whose object is the carnival as spectacle, implies the instability of any subjective identifications that the spectator may project onto the scene of diegetic reality in the film. In other words, the transcendental subject is, strictly speaking, an illusion or a simulacrum; and the real position of the spectator lies in the unstable and moving space hollowed out by the eye of the camera. Though the film invites the projection of the spectator's own imaginary identity or social mask, the spectator's *real* subject-position, the location of the barred subject, resides in the space of narrative potential, a kind of hole, that will undermine or at least challenge the imaginary. As Stephen Heath elaborates, the cinematic suture is the process which binds the spectator as subject to cinematic spacing through "its framings, its cuts, its intermittences." It is that aspect of cinema which operates like a language, which possesses what Derrida would call iterability, or the possibility of repetition with a difference as the ground and internal limit of intentionality. Through the effect of suture, the spectator, though "immobile in front of the screen," can experience the film as the articulation of his or her social fantasy; and the film actually regulates that movement of fantasy and captures the spectator-subject through the "shifting and placing of desire, energy, contradiction, in a perpetual retotalization of the imaginary."[12] The suture is what makes cinema into a kind of writing that reverses the direction of intentionality by identifying the spectator as the simulacrum of its origin of meaning.

The Crying Game, in this opening shot, situates the spectator in a contradictory relation to his or her own desire. As an ego (the transcendental subject as imaginary identificaton), the subject necessarily seeks a stable center in the carnival, which will become, as the narrative takes off, the scene of disguise and deception. In the same cinematic gesture, however, the subject's

[11] C. Metz, *Psychoanalysis and Cinema: The Imaginary Signifier*, trans. C. Britton, A. Williams, B. Brewster, and A. Guzzetti (London: Macmillan, 1982), p. 49.
[12] S. Heath, *Questions of Cinema* (Bloomington: Indiana University Press, 1981), pp. 52–53.

desire is captured by the lack or hole configured by the moving camera. Throughout the film, the subject's quest for its place in the Other subverts the space of its fantasy, the fiction by which it projects itself onto the world. To some extent, this effect is true of all films, since it articulates the structural gap between the speaking subject and the subject as spoken, between enunciation and statement. In *The Crying Game*, however, this gap is exploited to drive a wedge between the subject and the ego, between desire and identity. The subject moves, while the ego collapses before the disappointments of desire. Again, the tracking shot of the bridge figures this process in the contrast between the carnival world of illusory identities and the bridge as the constructed resolution of a field of differential forces. The bridge functions like the cinematographic apparatus itself, which, according to Jean-Louis Baudry, "both selects the minimal difference and represses it in projection, so that meaning can be constituted: it is at once direction, continuity, movement."[13] In other words, the cinematic suture is a bridge.

The final shot of *The Crying Game* corresponds to the opening shot. The scene is the visiting room of a British prison. Fergus Hennessy sits behind a glass screen through which he tells his "special friend," Dil, the story of the scorpion and the frog. As he speaks, the camera slowly tracks to the right and reveals several long rows of tables, each row with male prisoners on one side and mostly female visitors on the other. Hands are touching and lips are moving, but the only thing the spectator can hear is the sound of Lyle Lovett singing "Stand by Your Man." Obviously, this song complements the music to the opening credits, Percy Sledge's version of "When a Man Loves a Woman." In *The Crying Game*, both songs are ironic since the film thoroughly undermines the concept of gender as a natural category bound to a normative sexual identity. The songs demonstrate the force of popular culture to produce gender as another symbolic suture like the one that undergirds cinematic perception itself.

The scene preceding the final tracking shot drives this logic home. Dil speculates as to why Fergus is doing time for her and wishes that he would explain the reason why; but Fergus only

---

[13] J.-L. Baudry, "Ideological Effects of the Basic Cinematographic Apparatus," trans. A. Williams, in *Apparatus: Cinematic Apparatus, Selected Writings*, ed. T. H. K. Cha (New York: Tanam Press, 1980), p. 29.

responds, "As the man said, it's in my nature" (*NJR* 267). He then explains the meaning of "nature" by telling the story of the scorpion and the frog (to which I will return later). In this context, doing time means not only serving a prison sentence but surrendering personal freedom in order to achieve the freedom of the other, sacrificing self-interest to the interest of the other; it is a means by which socially symbolic divisions can be overcome. Of course, as the camera pulls back, both the glass separating Fergus from Dil and the tables separating the other prisoners from their visitors are still there; nothing has been overcome. The scene represents not the transcendence of difference and division; on the contrary, the prison space emphasizes the rigidity of the divisions and the obstacles they pose to the impulses of desire. Resistance to these divisions appears impossible. Yet the impossibility of resistance, the irrevocable nature of the divisions in question – and in the case of Fergus and Dil, these would include the divisions of racial, national, and sexual identity – create the conditions of hope that are realized by the act of doing time. The bridge over the river, the prisoner doing time for someone else – these images signify the hope that emerges from the historical truth of division. It is not that hope makes the divisions of human society endurable but that hope articulates these divisions as forms of consciousness through the recognition that change is possible but only through the sacrifice of time. There is no hope without the consciousness of division, without the subject's awareness of the other as absolutely separate and yet near, as absolutely nonidentical and yet the condition of identity. Hope is the suture-effect by which the subaltern subject finds its place in history.

Hope is divided in itself, and this division constitutes the perspective of historical materialism. One could put it this way: historicism (as a form of idealism that would include not only Hegel's philosophy of history but all the rationalist historiographies derived from Hegel, including some variants of Marxism) tries to efface divisions by insisting that all differences ultimately express one totality and absolute truth. By contrast, historical materialism insists on the fact, even the necessity, of division as the expression of hope. In cultural terms, historicism leads not to hope but to nostalgia for a cultural identity that never was or will be. Materialism, on the contrary, refuses nostalgia by insisting on the unbridgeable gap between the present, the past, and the future. The past and the future exist as the divisions of the present, and hope is not the dream of escape but the painful awareness that social change necessarily involves temporal sacrifice and the postponement of desire. The bridge is never complete and the process of doing time never finished. The only way art can register hope that is neither nostalgia nor propaganda is through the articulation of its broken promise. In effect, hope has the structure of the suture, neither a complete connection nor a complete separation.

Context and contradiction

Since hope expresses suffering through determinate negation, one could eliminate the consciousness of suffering by eliminating hope, which would also mean neutralizing the contradictions that give rise to art. For Adorno, to eliminate suffering completely would be to eliminate art in any meaningful sense: "Surely it would be better for art to vanish altogether than to forget suffering, which is art's expression and which gives substance to its form. Suffering, not positivity, is the humane content of art" (*AT* 369). Yet, if art expresses hope through the language of suffering, it does not express the opposite when that language is silenced. When art forgets suffering, it retreats into the commodity form; and the goal of the culture industry would be to enforce this retreat in each of its products. In this way, the culture industry participates in the ideology of the modern bourgeois state which also tries to eliminate hope and the dangerous divisions it introduces into the social fabric. The modern state eliminates hope by fostering in its people the conviction that the status quo is not an interpretation and a social construction of reality but its true and absolute form. If change is possible, it must be change within the system and not change of the system. The modern democratic state typically seeks to minimize the use of violence as a means of controlling unruly popular desires, since overt repression only enhances despair or the negative form of hope. Though the state will apply force to those who threaten it, it primarily uses force to secure and protect its monopoly of force and justifies itself with the claim that this monopoly guarantees the existence of democracy. At the same time, it disseminates the ideology that appropriate change can only take place through official, state-approved means and that any attempt to bypass the state and its authorized institutions in order to achieve change challenges not only the state but democracy itself. If change cannot be brought about through the official channels of the state, then it is not appropriate change. The modern state sees itself as the rational expression of the will of the people and denies the existence of internal conflicts of interest arising from irresolvable social contradictions (that is to say, irresolvable within the framework of the state's own system).

The conflict in Northern Ireland since the late sixties is the historical context which negatively determines the content of *The Crying Game*. These events have also been the occasion of a conflict of interpretations that illustrates the politics of social representation more dramatically than most ideological debates. The label one chooses to identify this sequence of events, especially since 1971 – a "civil war," "a nationalist war of liberation," "an anticolonial struggle against imperialism," or a "sectarian conflict" – largely determines how one will respond to the brutal realities of the conflict, from the death of innocent Catholics and Protestants in Northern Ireland itself to the brutal bombing campaigns in England. For example, Conor Cruise O'Brien, the former minister for posts and telegraphs who was instrumental in keeping Provisional Sinn Fein off the Irish airwaves in 1976, has been one of the most outspoken critics of the republican organizations and of his own government's quasi-tolerance of them. In an article entitled "Ireland: The Shirt of Nessus," he claims that republicans on both sides of the border are as sectarian as their Protestant counterparts; in fact, his rhetoric lays the blame for the conflict *primarily* on Catholic republicanism. When IRA gunmen "systematically pick off Protestant farmers and shopkeepers in the border areas," they do not interpret what they do as a form of "sectarian civil war," but rather as a means of "breaking the connection with England, by killing the people who form that connection." O'Brien realizes that the Protestant establishment of Northern Ireland is sectarian; but at least, he implies, they have the virtue of being honest about it. Still, when it comes to the sectarian civil war, there is little doubt in his mind that historically its motives arise out of the latent meaning of Catholic republican ideology although an actual civil war between Catholics and Protestants – or, if one insists, between republicans and unionists – did not become reality until 1971 when the Provisional IRA became "the heirs to the ideology in its purest, perfected and most deadly form."[14]

In this essay, O'Brien makes the argument that from its origins in the late eighteenth century to the present, the nationalist movement in Ireland has been linked to the sectarian cause of Irish Catholicism. In *The Field Day Anthology*, one of the contributors comments on the central difficulty O'Brien has in making this case since republicanism as a source of insurrectionary ideas derives from the secular ideologies of the Enlightenment. Furthermore, the physical-force movements in Ireland have always had strong Protestant affiliations while they were condemned by the Catholic church.[15] Gerry Adams, the President of Sinn Fein and former Westminster MP for West Belfast, flatly contradicts O'Brien's interpretation of the conflict. He insists that republicanism is strictly anti-sectarian, despite the claim of those like O'Brien "who seek to equate republicanism with a certain tradition of Catholic nationalism." He identifies republicanism as a struggle of the dispossessed for equality and notes that those who have benefited from the dispossession of others naturally regard any attempt to rectify that situation as an attack on their own privileges.[16] Whatever one may think of Adams (and it goes without saying that O'Brien would consider him the front man for a terrorist organization), one has only to look back at the 1916 Proclamation of the Republic or The Democratic Programme of the First Dáil in 1919 to see that at least the aspirations of the republican movement have not been strictly sectarian. The 1916 Proclamation promised "religious and civil liberty, equal rights and equal opportunities" to all citizens of the republic; and the Democratic Programme declared that "all right to private property must be subordinated to the public right and welfare" and guaranteed "the right of every citizen to an adequate share of the produce of the Nation's labour."[17] Of course, neither the Free State of 1922 nor the Republic of 1949 ever lived up to these aspirations; but a distinction needs to be made between an Irish

[14] C. C. O'Brien, *Passion and Cunning: Essays on Nationalism, Terrorism and Revolution* (New York: Simon and Schuster, 1988), p. 218.

[15] S. Deane (ed.), *The Field Day Anthology of Irish Writing*, 3 vols. (Derry: Field Day Publications, 1991), vol. III, p. 595.

[16] G. Adams, *The Politics of Irish Freedom* (Wolfeboro, New Hampshire: Brandon, 1987), p. 113.

[17] Deane (ed.), *Field Day Anthology*, vol. III, pp. 733–34.

Republic that legislatively espouses a Catholic morality (a situation that may be changing even as I write) and a sectarian state that institutionalizes racism. As J. J. Lee has recently argued, "the Proclamation of the Ulster Provisional Government in 1913 adopted a concept of 'Ulsterman' that defined Catholics out of existence." Lee admits that nationalist thought contained some elements of racism but stresses that these were not as central to Irish nationalist ideology as they were to Unionism. While Ulster Protestants regarded Catholics as "not only different but inferior," the Catholics, for the most part, regarded the Protestants as simply different.[18]

Tom Nairn, in *The Break-Up of Britain*, argued some time ago that the real problem in Northern Ireland is the absence of Ulster nationalism. In his view, the key to events in that state has always been in the hands of the Protestants. By resisting the Civil Rights Movement in the sixties, they reinvigorated the roots of Catholic nationalism and the tradition of physical violence. By assaulting the Catholic areas of Belfast in 1969, they forced the British government to send in the army. The Protestant identification with, and dependence on, the British army created the conditions for the IRA's reemergence as an effective force. After the dissolution of the old Northern Irish State in 1972, which the Protestants considered a betrayal, they expanded their own secret armies into a much larger force. Above all, according to Nairn, the Protestants "decisively destroyed the only serious effort at a new, more democratic and inter-communal solution to the question in 1974" by means of a general strike. With the failure of the new constitution and the Sunningdale Agreement, they "demonstrated, finally, where the centre of political gravity lies in any farther developments." For Nairn, any historical solution to the conflict in Northern Ireland must necessarily evolve from the development of a genuine Ulster nationalism. This, he believes, first reared its head in the 1974 general strike which "defied, and defeated, three bourgeois governments and the British Army." It was "the most successful *political* action carried out by any European working class since the World War," and it "relegated the claims of the I.R.A. forever to that historical archive from

---

[18] J. J. Lee, *Ireland, 1912–1985: Politics and Society* (Cambridge: Cambridge University Press, 1989), pp. 5, 9–10.

which they should never have re-emerged."[19] Recent events would suggest that Nairn spoke too soon; and, up to the present time, Ulster nationalism has not gained momentum, while the republican organizations might just prove themselves capable of achieving the political recognition they have always claimed to be the goal of the violence. Nairn clearly underestimated the historical commitment of the Ulster Protestant workers to racist rather than nationalist ideology. He rejects the "pseudo-marxist theory of 'anti-imperialist' struggle in Ireland" and argues that the Ulster Protestant territories should be grouped with other economically developed societies that claim the right to self-determination, societies like Israel and Scotland.[20] Still, these comparisons seem forced in many ways. The state of Israel owes its existence in part to the intervention of European imperialist interests in the Middle East (interests which denied self-determination to the Palestinians and other Arab nations after World War I); and today Israel faces the challenge of negotiating its own settlement with those who were displaced by the process. Similarly, Scottish nationalism is of a completely different character from Northern Irish loyalism.

According to Nairn, the historical justification of Ulster nationalism is not cultural or religious, but social and economic. Even in their relationship to Britain, the Protestants of Northern Ireland were "too strong to suffer the normal fates" of minorities. They allied themselves with the "English imperialist and nationalist right wing" and blackmailed the liberals and socialists with "the threat of 'something worse.'" By something worse, Nairn means that Ulster Protestants, once they take up the mantle of national self-determination, have the strength to produce their own version of "the nationalist 'final solution' at least over the four or six counties of the partition." Even if one agrees with Nairn that "all nationalism is both healthy and morbid," "both progress and regress,"[21] it is difficult to understand why he has to privilege the nationalist cause of a sectarian society committed to a racist program simply because it has, *in his opinion*, the power virtually to exterminate its enemies.

In *The Politics of Irish Freedom*, Gerry Adams explains the policies

---

[19] T. Nairn, *The Break-Up of Britain: Crisis and Neo-Nationalism*, 2nd edn. (London: NLB, 1981), pp. 240–41, 242.

[20] *Ibid.*, pp. 230, 248–49.

[21] *Ibid.*, pp. 238, 347.

of the Provisional IRA and Sinn Fein with an argument that sounds more rational than one would expect after listening to defenders of state power like O'Brien or the might-makes-right version of Marxism that Nairn endorses. He insists that since 1920–22, the six counties of Northern Ireland have been in a "colonial situation." The twenty-six counties in the south, by contrast, are governed by a "neo-colonial state" in which the former occupying powers have been replaced by business interests. The latter have reshaped the old system for their own purposes without significantly altering the social relations that prevailed under the empire. While Nairn may be technically correct in suggesting that Protestant control of the economic means of production in Northern Ireland should have been the material base on which their national identity was constructed, he ignores the actual history of the region, *the history of what was constructed*: a sectarian state designed to defend both Protestant privilege and British interests. The struggle for national identity took a completely different form from what Nairn believes it should have taken and no amount of theorizing is going to send the facts of history shuffling off to the archives. As Adams further stresses, the partition as a division of both territory and people virtually subverted the principles of national sovereignty and self-determination in the Irish case. Still, while the people were partitioned, the economic control "remained securely in the hands of its previous owners," the capitalist classes of both Ireland and Great Britain. The failure of the New Ireland Forum in 1984, the signing of the Hillsborough treaty in 1985, and the events that have followed from the "Downing Street Declaration" of December 15, 1993 make it clear that Britain will pursue any policy that supports the economic and political interests of the United Kingdom in both Northern Ireland and the Republic. After the Hillsborough treaty, the Republic recognized the legitimacy of Northern Ireland, with, in Adams' words, "the Dublin government acting as the new guarantor of partition."[22] O'Brien believes that this treaty creates the impression of a weakened United Kingdom which can no longer prevent the Ulster Protestant community from resorting to Holy War as the solution to its problems. But he also believes that, technically speaking, the treaty could work if it were used to enlist

---

[22] Adams, *Politics*, pp. 39–40, 105.

the power of both states to suspend civil rights for the purpose of crushing the IRA.[23]

I have lingered over this background not because I want to defend the IRA (which should be subjected to a critique that takes into account both the ethical and political efficacy of its tactics and ideology) but because I want to foreground the contradictions that become visible in those representations of the conflict which presuppose a viewpoint transcending the historical context. Whether they appeal to moral, political, or scientific absolutes, most of the interpretations I have cited fail to take into account their own historical determination by the conflict itself. Yet both Conor Cruise O'Brien and Tom Nairn admit that the configuration of historical forces in this situation is such that there may not be any solution to the problem. According to O'Brien, the concept of problem and solution does not provide an answer to the complexity of the *conflict* in Northern Ireland, "which is likely to continue as long as the island of Ireland contains both a large Ulster Protestant community, and a significant and determined minority of Irish Republicans, with a hold on the Catholic community."[24] For Nairn, by contrast, the best that can be hoped for without the formation of Ulster nationalism is a war of attrition that finally results in a stalemate through the exhaustion of both sides. He concludes that "Not all real historical situations have 'solutions' in the sense that radical or progressive thinkers have to hope for."[25] Finally, Gerry Adams can only defend the IRA from O'Brien, who would destroy it, and Nairn, who would send it back to the archives, by pointing to the fact of its continuing existence. He insists that, despite the message of anti-terrorist propaganda in Britain and throughout the West, the IRA could not exist and operate without the consent of "a sufficient number of people" who make it physically possible for the members of the IRA to survive and who create a political infrastructure as the basis of armed struggle.[26]

In the last analysis, the historical contradiction at the center of this debate may be the one between hope and security. Both Ireland and the United Kingdom recognize, in the words of the Anglo-Irish Agreement, "the major interest of both their countries

---

[23] O'Brien, *Passion and Cunning*, pp. 206, 225.   [24] *Ibid.*, p. 211.
[25] Nairn, *Break-Up*, p. 241.   [26] Adams, *Politics*, p. 63.

and, above all, of the people of Northern Ireland in diminishing the divisions there and achieving lasting peace and stability."[27] But the question remains as to whether the divisions in question can be diminished without the recognition of their determination by socio-historical contradictions. The latter require the transformation of the social system if not some form of cultural revolution. Is the statement I have quoted an expression of hope or an ideological strategy for achieving state security? In either case, hope does not guarantee that the end-result of violence will be the resolution of division rather than futile self-destruction; and security, as it is defined by the state with its monopoly of violence, does not guarantee that it is anything more than the enforcement of the status quo. The Anglo-Irish Treaty, *as a text*, is as ambivalent as the conflict it tries to resolve; and this textual ambiguity participates in the same social process that assumes a different form in works of art: "Their reality ... lies in the fact that they are answers to questions brought before them from outside. The tension in art therefore has meaning only in relation to the tension outside." *The Crying Game*, as Jordan's introduction to the original screenplay makes clear, is about irresolvable divisions in a world where violence is the normal way of solving problems and resolving conflicts. The film expresses human suffering not by seducing the audience into sympathizing with the IRA but by capturing in aesthetic form the ambivalence of the historical context to which it responds. According to Adorno, "The unresolved antagonisms of reality reappear in art in the guise of immanent problems of artistic form" (*AT* 8). This means that aesthetic forms are not so much representations of the historical context as they are interventions in it. Through its reversals and the self-conscious disclosure of its commodity form, *The Crying Game* responds to the question posed by the recent history of Northern Ireland: is there something beyond the division of hope?

Aesthetic politics

What makes *The Crying Game* offensive to the bourgeois critic like Stanley Kaufmann (and one can imagine the response of someone like O'Brien) is not that it idealizes the IRA but that it historicizes

---

[27] Deane (ed.), *Field Day Anthology*, vol. III, p. 803.

the terrorist through the means of indirect or symbolic representation. It presents an image of the IRA from a viewpoint that is normally denied representation and does so through a style that is able to escape the censorship of both the state and the culture industry. As David Lloyd theorizes,

Control of narratives is a crucial function of the state apparatus since its political and legal frameworks can only gain consent and legitimacy if the tale they tell monopolizes the field of probabilities. The state does not simply legislate and police against particular infringements, it determines the forms within which representation can take place. Access to representation is accordingly as much a question of aesthetics as of power or numbers, and not to be represented often as intrinsically a function of formal as of material causes.[28]

There is of course a long history of direct state censorship in Ireland, but I think Lloyd wants to articulate a concept of the state apparatus that embraces the relationship between the state as a system of laws and institutions and something like the culture industry. In other words, his concept of the state apparatus is what Gramsci would call the *historical bloc*, a concept which describes the reciprocal relations between structure and superstructure within the system of hegemony.[29] In *Anomalous States*, Lloyd produces "an analysis of the developing state apparatus in Ireland which is at one and the same time the analysis of the hegemonic role of culture in the formation of citizen-subjects."[30] In this period of late capitalism, particularly with the movement towards European unity (the Maastricht Treaty received a two-thirds vote in favor from the Republic of Ireland), the power of the culture industry could be said to surpass in many ways the power of any individual state. It contributes to the formation of the citizen-subjects not only of Ireland but of Europe and even, if one keeps in mind some of the recent arguments of Fredric Jameson, of the world. In the introduction to *The Geopolitical Aesthetic*, Jameson suggests that the older categories of culture or ideology critique, as they developed from Marx to Althusser, will not work in a context that has witnessed the replacement of national cultures by the global economic system that distributes, along

[28] D. Lloyd, *Anomalous States: Irish Writing and the Post-Colonial Moment* (Durham: Duke University Press, 1993), p. 6.

[29] Gramsci, *Reader*, p. 193.

[30] Lloyd, *Anomalous States*, p. 7.

with other cultural and economic commodities, mass-produced images of the older traditions which it has destroyed. Jameson supplements his earlier concept of the political unconscious with the "geopolitical unconscious ... which now attempts to refashion national allegory into a conceptual instrument for grasping our new being in the world."[31]

The implications of this last remark become clear if we look at an ordinary commercial product of Hollywood like *Patriot Games* to see how national history can be redeployed by the global culture industry in order to define the legitimate citizen-subjects of the new world order. With the end of the Cold War, Hollywood films have had to show some ingenuity in coming up with the sort of villains who can support the Manichean ideology that has been transferred from the American/European political unconscious to the geopolitical unconscious. The villains of *Patriot Games* are Irish terrorists; and while they formally turn their backs on the IRA early in the film, they are still represented as the logical outcome of nationalist politics insofar as it unleashes a kind of violence that always risks becoming an end in itself. In spite of the national identity of the main character and the American flag prominently displayed in the advertising, the film is not really about American patriotism (in fact, the term "patriot game" alludes to an Irish republican ballad[32]); rather, it makes a distinction between two forms of violence that define the limits of the new global community, patriotism and terrorism. Patriotism is the legitimate violence of the legitimate state; and terrorism is illegitimate violence which, though it may hide behind various ideological claims and political causes, is ultimately unmotivated and malignant.

For having saved the lives of British royals, the hero of the film becomes a new breed of global patriot not because he is particularly committed to royalty, a connection which seems to embarrass him as a good American, but because he is committed to the status quo and global security. The Irish terrorists, by contrast, show virtually no ability to distinguish between political and criminal violence; and when the more moderate terrorists are killed by their evil comrade so that he can pursue vengeance for its own sake,

---

[31] F. Jameson, *The Geopolitical Aesthetic: Cinema and Space in the World System* (Bloomington: Indiana University Press, 1992), p. 3.

[32] R. Kearney, *Transitions: Narratives in Modern Irish Culture* (Manchester: Manchester University Press, 1988), p. 234.

they are not represented as victims deserving the sympathy of the audience. If the film makes some token effort at distinguishing the real IRA from a supposedly lunatic fringe, it still sends a message that any form of nationalist violence not recognized by the states that constitute the new global community (from which are excluded such "outlaw" states as Iraq, Iran, and Libya) is terrorism. The other side of the coin is that any state recognized as legitimate by the global community may use any degree of violence in order to pacify those terrorist elements that refuse to submit to the new world system. The most chilling moment in *Patriot Games* is the scene in a high-tech, anti-terrorist war room at the CIA where the hero and his former colleagues watch the termination of a terrorist encampment on a monitor through the medium of live infrared video images. This sequence emphasizes the cold impersonality with which the state can destroy its enemies as if they were mere points of light on a video screen and makes no effort to hide the fact that vengeance can play a role in the process. The hero is invited to watch because his family was nearly killed by the terrorists. Still, the film never leaves the spectator with the impression of ambivalence. It is the unquestionable evil of terrorism as a threat to the civilized world that absolutely justifies any violent means the state may use to eliminate it.

The Crying Game is not innocent of this Manichean ideology; otherwise, it would never have escaped the censorship of the culture industry. Yet while it assimilates or adapts itself to this new global ideology, it also recontextualizes that ideology in such a way as to make it unfamiliar and ambivalent. In the film, the ideological view of terrorism could be said to determine the characterization of Jude, the Irish woman, although one has to examine several levels of overdetermination before the full complexity of her symptomatic construction can even be hinted at. If Jude repeatedly demonstrates the malice and deception which the state attributes to the terrorist, she is also a version of Kathleen Ni Houlihan, or Mother Ireland, who repeatedly calls on her sons to sacrifice their lives in order to liberate her from the shackles of British domination. Since Jude is the only *real* woman in the film, it is impossible not to see her as the symptom of misogyny, the object of hatred and ambivalence that would seem to confuse women, in this case, with the national identity itself. Near the film's end, when she comes to execute Fergus for what she perceives to be his betrayal of Ireland, she is brutally executed by the woman who has taken her place (Ireland's place) in Fergus's life, a woman who is not a woman and who is not Irish. The nonidentity of the transvestite kills the self-identity of the symbol of Irish nationality. Jude champions identity throughout the film by trying to keep Fergus from betraying his Irish nationality and, whether she knows it or not, his masculinity. She blocks his desire to communicate with the other, whether the other is the British soldier held hostage or the black transvestite.

Several scenes in the film suggest that Jude symbolizes the fusion of the political and the aesthetic. In particular, they show that her physical image changes as she becomes more defined politically. When she appears in Fergus's room in London during the film's second half, she looks completely different from the person she was in the first half. Her makeup and dress are far more self-consciously stylized; and her hair has been changed to a darker color. She tells Fergus that she gave up being a blond because she needed "a tougher look" (*NJR* 239). Later, as she dresses for the suicide mission she has blackmailed Fergus into going on, she sits in front of a paneled vanity mirror that gives back three images of herself from slightly different angles as she puts on her makeup. The shot conveys the idea that Jude's identity is an illusion, a kind of nationalist drag. It also marks her as the *femme fatale* in the *noir* atmosphere of this part of the film: in more than one sense, she prepares to witness a killing. Finally, in the scene where she confronts Fergus with Dil at the Metro, she comments on Dil's use of heavy makeup, which elicits Dil's reponse that a "girl has to have a bit of glamour" (*NJR* 243). While Dil understands glamour as a masquerade that arises from the ambivalence of identity, Jude uses makeup in order to express what she imagines to be her true essence. She hides behind the "tougher look" that ironically expresses who she really is. At the same time, everything about her new look underscores the fact that her gender is not ambivalent. She embodies in her physical appearance the message she brings to Fergus, the message that Dil translates when she asks: "She own you, Jimmy?" (*NJR* 249). Jude owns Fergus (Jimmy) insofar as she symbolizes both his identity and his destiny as an Irish subject. When he initially tries to resist her commands, he discovers the power she has over him. She sticks a gun in his face and becomes the phallic mother, or, in this case, Mother Ireland herself in the guise of the terrorist who threatens her son with castration so that he can become the man he is supposed to be. She tells Fergus to keep his mind on the job; and when she gives him back his phallic identity in the form of an assassin's gun, she reminds him to forget about the other woman.

David Lloyd associates such feminization of the national identity with the aestheticization of Irish politics in general. This takes place through the production, or rather repetition, of the racial archetype "in the ever more commodified and familiar images of Irish nationalism," which include the image of Mother Ireland or Kathleen Ni Houlihan. The latter figure virtually articulates the relationship between an Irish national identity and the Irish ground that naturalizes such identity as "racy of the soil," a phrase found in the slogan of the *Nation*, the political organ of Young Ireland in the 1840s. This identity supposedly "precedes difference and conflict" and reproduces itself as "the ultimate unity that aesthetic works both prefigure and prepare."[33] In other words, by taking its own self-concept and symbolic identity as a metaphysical essence, the nationalist movement begins to understand itself as if it were an autonomous work of art. It fails to recognize that the image it projects of the resolution of social divisions and historical contradictions is an illusion, not in the sense that it is false but in the sense that it is incomplete, that its truth does not lie in the object it constructs but in the process of determinate negation which enables it to subvert the subject–object relationship. Historically, Irish nationalism arises as a dialogical response to British imperialism; it is an attempt to subjectify the object of British domination, to construct a subject-position for the subaltern which gives him or her the power to question the identity of the master or dominant subject.[34] Ireland's *original* identity is the racial archetype that the state of the future, the republic, will express without contradiction or remainder; in other words, the national identity should find its political reflection in the postcolonial state. The founding of the state brings to a conclusion the aesthetic project of cultural nationalism by giving concrete historical expression to the sym-

[33] Lloyd, *Anomalous States*, p. 17.
[34] D. Lloyd, *Nationalism and Minor Literature: James Clarence Mangan and the Emergence of Irish Cultural Nationalism* (Berkeley: University of California Press, 1987), p. 77.

bols of national identity. This conclusion, however, presupposes that the state is the *telos* of the historical process, the expression of its metaphysical tendency. As Lloyd notes in his reading of Yeats's "Easter 1916," "The founding of any nation state is necessarily an act of violence irrupting as an absolute discontinuity in the course of history, an utter transformation by way of a singularly trans-formative utterance, and its legitimacy is established not in itself but in the subsequent rememoration it invokes." The "terrible beauty" of Easter 1916 lies in the historical disjunction between the dream of cultural nationalism and the concrete reality of state formation which led Yeats to wonder if the deaths in question were worth it after all.[35]

Yeats was prophetic in expressing the ambivalence that would eventually erupt into the Irish civil war and that would continue to haunt the official state of Ireland with the various campaigns of the IRA and the emergence of the Provisional IRA in Northern Ireland. In effect, to clarify Lloyd's statement, while the goal of cultural nationalism is symbolic, the state itself is necessarily allegorical, which suggests that whatever meaning it has is not derived from some metaphysical essence but has to be constructed through repeated acts of historical recollection. The division of labor between masculine and feminine representations is there-fore transformed by the "terrible beauty" of state formation. As Lloyd stresses, the phrase "terrible beauty" sutures together the two fundamental aesthetic categories, the sublime and the beauti-ful, with their gender connotations. The sublime is "the masculine domain of production and transcendence evoked in response to the terror of death and the potential dissolution of the self"; the beautiful is "the feminine sphere of reproduction, both literally and in the sense of the harmonious reproduction of harmonious forms." Before the revolution, the beauty of Mother Ireland represents the fulfillment of her promise that any young man who dies for her will be remembered forever. At the end of Yeats's *Cathleen ni Houlihan*, for example, the old woman is transformed into a young girl, presumably in anticipation of the blood sacrifice of the young men she has sent forth to redeem the nation. The sublime terror of death brings back youth; masculine violence nourishes feminine beauty. The men who die for Ireland live

---

[35] Lloyd, *Anomalous States*, p. 72. See W. B. Yeats, *The Poems*, ed. R. Finneran (New York: Macmillan, 1983), p. 181, l. 7.

forever in the memory of their motherland. As Lloyd concludes, this version of nationalist myth is sublime because it enables revolutionary subjects "to transcend death even in death by identifying with the greater life of the nation they are producing." But when the nation-state is achieved, it closes such a "horizon of transcendence, as it spells an end to the developmental desire of cultural nationalism, absorbing terror into the heretofore feminine sphere of rememorative reproduction."[36]

To state it differently, in Ireland the postcolonial nation-state that finally emerges from the War of Independence cannot possibly live up to its own concept; so its birth becomes the occasion of civil war while its history is punctuated by acts of violence that have symbolic as well as real effects. In either case, these acts work to delegitimate the actual state in the name of what Sean O'Faolain once called the "Symbolical Living Republic first declared during the 1916 Rebellion and set up as a *de jure* ... underground government during the troubles."[37] Ironically, the official postcolonial state ruthlessly appeals to the same myth in order to justify itself and to distinguish the legitimate violence that founded it from the illegitimate violence that threatens its authority. The terror of death and blood sacrifice that was once separate from the beauty of a reborn national identity is now indistinguishable from it. The national identity is itself a source of terror. Whether it is the state claiming its monopoly of violence or the revolutionary claiming his or her right to use violence against an oppressive state, the symbol of the nation has become the image of a beautiful woman with a gun. (This image assumes commodity form on the posters advertising *The Crying Game*. It is a distorted and highly aestheticized image of Miranda Richardson's Jude, as she appears in the second half of the film, holding a smoking gun next to her face. The image conveys the eroticism of violence even as it insists upon what contemporary feminist film critics would call a disavowal of castration.) In *The Crying Game*, this woman no longer appears as a maternal figure calling on the young men of Ireland to do their duty. When Jude surprises Fergus in his room, she conveys her intentions bluntly by putting her hand on his crotch and saying, "Fuck me, Fergus." When he removes her hand, she sarcastically responds, "Am I to take it that's a no?" As

---

[36] Lloyd, *Anomalous States*, pp. 72–73.
[37] Quoted in Kearney, *Transitions*, p. 219.

the scene unfolds, it becomes clear that Jude possesses the phallus. Indeed, as Dil later suspects, she owns Fergus and lets him know it when she suddenly reveals her gun. Although Fergus refuses to become a man for Jude (that is, to repossess the phallus that she offers him), he cannot ignore her threats: "Maybe you don't care whether you die or not. But consider the girl, Fergus. The wee black chick." Jude threatens to kill the racial other if Fergus does not come back to the real ground of his identity as an Irishman and commit himself to the blood sacrifice that will transform him "utterly" into the racial archetype of the nation. In death, he will enjoy a permanent erection as the phallus of the motherland. According to Jude, Fergus has become useful to the cause because he "vanished quite effectively" and became "Mister Nobody," or the castrated subject (*NJR* 239–40). His nonidentity makes him the perfect choice to make a suicidal hit; and when he dies, he will return to the mother as the source of his true identity. This woman will not take no for an answer.

Historically, because the Irish Free State achieved its freedom through the division of Ireland, it remained, even after it became a Republic in 1949, associated with that division. If love of the motherland inspires the cause of nationalism before the revolution, that love becomes inextricably bound to terror after the foundation of the state. Richard Kearney poses this question about the relation between the 1916 republican movement and the movement today: "Is it possible that the guiding motivation of militant Republicanism was, and still is to some extent, less the appropriation of the socio-economic means of production, than an exigency of sacrifice to a mythological Ireland: an ancestral deity who would respond to the martyrdom of her sons by rising from her ancient slumber to avenge them?"[38] In his 1913 article, "The Coming Revolution," Patrick Pearse proclaimed that "bloodshed is a cleansing and a sanctifying thing, and the nation which regards it as the final horror has lost its manhood." Though this statement would seem to support Kearney's viewpoint, one should take into account the context in which Pearse was writing. "The Coming Revolution," which appeared after the passage of the Home Rule Bill of 1913, stresses the fact that Home Rule in and of itself will not be the end of Ireland's struggle for independence.

---

[38] Kearney, *Transitions*, p. 211.

There remains the complicated task of building the nation itself, which is not going "to be achieved without stress and trial, without suffering and bloodshed; at any rate, it is not going to be achieved without *work*." Pearse was not the last colonial revolutionary to produce a political rationale for armed struggle: "Ireland unarmed will attain just as much freedom as it is convenient for England to give her; Ireland armed will attain ultimately just as much freedom as she wants."[39] The events after the passage of the Home Rule Bill – the formation of the Ulster Defence Force and the Ulster provisional government (which was set up by the Ulster Union Council), the Curragh Mutiny, and the postponement of implementation of home rule after the onset of World War I – suggest that Pearse was not completely mistaken in his forecast.[40] After 1914, the British knew not only that Ulster would resist unification with the South but that the British army would not fight the Protestant forces in the North.[41] The goal of Irish home rule, much less the goal of an Irish republic, would never be achieved without the use of force.

Though Pearse may have been fascinated by death, as various historians have claimed, he made a more serious political error when he miscalculated what Ireland could achieve by violence; and this points to a common problem in anticolonial struggles that distinguishes them from the political conflicts of the postcolonial era. The goals of anticolonial nationalist movements have tended to be unrealistic because, as Neil Lazarus argues, in such a movement no one pauses "long enough to give its ideal of 'freedom' a content." In Africa during the 1950s and 1960s, "the radical anticolonial writers tended to romanticize the resistance movement and to underestimate ... the dissensions within it. Their heavy emphasis on fraternalism blinded them to the fact that within the movement there were groups and individuals working with quite different, and often incompatible, aspirations for the future."[42] Similarly, the Irish intellectuals who made the decision

[39] Deane (ed.), *Field Day Anthology*, vol. II, pp. 557–58.
[40] T. P. Coogan, *The IRA: A History* (Niwot, Colorado: Roberts Rinehart, 1994), pp. 8–9.
[41] I. S. Lustick, *Unsettled States, Disputed Lands: Britain and Ireland, France and Algeria, Israel and the West Bank–Gaza* (Ithaca: Cornell University Press, 1993), pp. 194–217.
[42] N. Lazarus, *Resistance in Postcolonial African Fiction* (New Haven: Yale University Press, 1990), p. 5.

to sacrifice their lives in the Easter Rising had committed themselves to a national ideal that did not reflect a true consensus
among the people or the future leaders of the state. As I stressed
before, the socialist values in the 1916 Proclamation and the
Democratic Programme of the First Dáil did not survive in the
government that emerged out of the civil war. It may be that the
revolutionaries of 1916 believed in the mystical value of blood
sacrifice, as Kearney speculates; but they also believed that some
practical political goals could be achieved through the use of force.
Despite their tactical and ideological errors, they possessed a form
of hope that no one in Ireland after the civil war could reproduce in
exactly the same form.

The postcolonial Irish revolutionary can keep the dream of a
resurrected Kathleen Ni Houlihan alive only by undergoing a
profound disillusionment with the state itself. In other words, the
love of the motherland that inspired the founders of the Irish state
between 1916 and 1922 is transformed into the terror that seeks to
undermine the state as it actually exists in both the North and the
South after that period. The new revolutionary cannot avoid the
question as to whether any state can live up to the republican
concept after the failure of the first revolution. However, this
disillusionment does not mean that myths have triumphed over
political thought, since the republican concept of 1916 was not
altogether based on myth. It was the product of enlightenment
thinking and had the practical aim of achieving social and
economic justice through the formation of an egalitarian democratic state. According to Kearney, "It is because the IRA *cannot*
achieve military victory (and is at times even suicidal) that it can
assume a sacrificial mystique."[43] In other words, the disavowal of
castration or political impotence animates the cult of blood
sacrifice to Mother Ireland as the woman with a phallus. Still, it
does not follow that because the IRA cannot achieve military
victory it uses terror and violence merely to sustain a tradition of
blood sacrifice. The problem may lie in trying to separate the IRA's
strategy of violence and sacrifice from the goal of social revolution.
The most hopeless situations arising from apparently irreconcilable divisions (like those produced by the history of the political
and economic oppression of the Catholic minority in Northern

[43] Kearney, *Transitions*, p. 231.

111

Ireland) require the reinvention of hope. To hope when victory is no longer certain makes possible the fusion of love and terror. The risk is that hope will succumb to fatalism or the illusion that freedom and self-fulfillment can only be achieved through submission to death itself.

Misogyny, racism, and the death drive

In the first half of *The Crying Game*, erotic love and terrorist violence take the form of an unreconciled tension in the relationship between Jody and Jude. After the credits, the camera offers a high-angle shot of a carnival booth and then slowly zooms in for a two shot of Jody, the black soldier in the British army, and Jude, the blond Irish "girl." Though the word "girl" in the screenplay may seem innocent enough, it still links Jude with the rejuvenated Kathleen Ni Houlihan at the end of Yeats's play. Jody has just won a teddy bear which he gives to the woman. Presumably, since stuffed animals are the most common transitional objects of small children, this gesture suggests that Jude is a maternal figure, though, as Jody realizes, she shows no sentimental interest in the bear. Then, when Jody goes into the toilet, he keeps holding Jude's hand and remarks, "Don't run off, Jude." She replies, "You don't know me, do you?" (*NJR* 179).

In truth, neither Jude nor Jody knows each other, though they both wear complicated masks and have similar names which suggestively echo the name of Judas. Just as Judas exploited the love of Christ by betraying him with a kiss, Jude and Jody also commit acts of sexual betrayal in this opening sequence. Jude, of course, uses her sexuality to deliver Jody over to the IRA. Jody, by the same token, is deceiving Jude about his true sexual identity and is betraying the man/woman he loves, Dil. In other words, both Jude and Jody presuppose that the other's identity is transparent, when in fact neither of them grasps the true identity of the other. Later, after they leave the carnival, Jude lays down under the bridge and tells her soldier to come and get her. Perhaps Jody imagines that Jude will become the bridge between himself, a member of the British army, and the rest of Ireland; but this scene also repeats the myth of the sexual conquest of Ireland by England. The phallus is the symbolic bridge that both constitutes and expresses sexual and social difference; but as a symbol it is also ambivalent or subject to displacement. As Jody struggles to penetrate the woman beneath him, a gun is put to his head; and he realizes that the phallus is not where he thought it was.

After he is taken to the farmhouse, Jody appears to be paralyzed and virtually lifeless; in effect, he has been symbolically castrated. With his head hooded he no longer has the power of the gaze, while Fergus Hennessy seems to glory in such power as he plays with a flashlight that looks almost like a film projector. Fergus puts the light on Jude and then on Jody. He tells Jude to poke the hostage in order to determine that he is still alive; but when she prods him and lifts the hood, he "*suddenly moves like lightning*" and "*pins her to the ground.*" As Jordan notes in the screenplay, "*He writhes on top of her in a grotesque parody of love.*" The scene is quite violent on the screen, and Jody clearly wants to regain the phallus that has been taken away from him by overpowering the woman who represents the Irish nation. When she calls him a "fucking animal," there is no question that she means for the phrase to carry racial implications (*NJR* 183). As Jody comments later, Northern Ireland is "the only place in the world they call you nigger to your face" (*NJR* 191). In other ways, Jude's attitude toward the black man seems more ambivalent. After all, she shares symbolic space with Jody as the object of Fergus's gaze and the possible object of his desire; and, like Jody, she may want the phallus for herself. When Fergus asks her if Jody went all the way with her, she responds that there are some things she will not do for her country. After Jody throws himself on top of her, Fergus takes her outside where she says to him, "And you know what, Fergus? One of you made me want it." "Which one?" he says, and then they embrace; but Jude never answers his question (*NJR* 184). By seducing Jody without giving him everything, Jude empowers herself as a revolutionary; and by holding back from Fergus the truth about her desire (the answer to the question, *which one do you want?*), she already displaces Fergus as the phallic subject, the one who knows. These moves anticipate her reincarnation in the film's second half.

If Jude is a racist, it seems that Jody is a misogynist. He shows almost no anger toward the men who hold him captive, while his feelings about Jude are virulent. At first, this emotional response seems justified, since it is Jude's sexual masquerade, after all, which has deprived him of his freedom. When Jody fears being left alone with Jude for a while, he tells Fergus that she is dangerous. As it turns out, this danger does not lie in her sexual attraction, since, as Jody stresses, he never really liked her because she is not his type. Fergus wonders why Jody came on to her in the first place; and the best answer Jody can give, besides calling her a bitch, is that he was lonely and wondering what he was doing in Ireland. With Jude he thought that somehow "Maybe I'll get to understand" (*NJR* 190). Only later in the film can the spectator fully appreciate the ambivalence of these words. Jody, a British soldier in Ireland, reaches out not only to the Irish other that he has been sent to control and dominate but to his sexual other, not insofar as he is a man and she is a woman but in that he is a homosexual or a bisexual for whom this woman may not be the preferred object of desire. When he says, "Maybe I'll get to understand," he suggests that he wants to understand Ireland and women, nationality and sexual difference. Jody's relation to gender is further complicated by the fact that the man he loves, Dil, constructs himself as a woman. So it is not gender as a social construction that constitutes Jody's other but the Real of sexual difference. Later, after Jude hits him with a pistol, Jody again warns Fergus that women are trouble. Then he qualifies his judgment: "Some kinds of women are." The exception to the rule, of course, is the woman who is not a woman, Dil. Given Jody's obvious distrust of women, Fergus wonders about Dil, and Jody explains that he loves her "Whatever she is" (*NJR* 199). He suggests not only that Dil is not a woman but that she cannot be defined by any categorical signifier. In this scene, the film conveys the force of Jody's feelings through an extreme close-up of his mouth, which literally fills the screen.

Insofar as Jude embodies the national identity, she represents the transcendence of the divisions that threaten the nation from within – divisions of class, race, gender, and sexuality. In practical terms, she cannot allow herself or the nation she symbolizes to be contaminated by difference. She perceives Jody in terms of racial difference and confines him to that category in order to erase the division within her own identity that might undermine its transcendent unity. In other words, the unity of the nation requires the eradication of any internal ambivalence through the enforcement of an absolute external division or exclusion. Jude embodies the violence required by the imaginary construction of a national identity that in the postcolonial era must even transcend the authority of the state itself. In spite of its claim to representing the nation, the state, as history repeatedly demonstrates, is a hegemonic compromise between different interests, both inside and outside the national territory. Internally, the Irish state claims to represent the whole people while it enforces socio-economic and sexual inequality. As a revolutionary nationalist, Jude operates as the mirror image of both the Irish and the British states. She refuses any divisions that threaten her autonomy, even while she insists on the absolute division between the Irish and any other race, between a unified Ireland and any other nation. While Jody also fears difference, he is fascinated by it, which explains why he loves a man who constructs himself as a woman and why he allows himself to get involved with a *real* woman like Jude. Jody's misogyny derives less from his hatred of women *per se* than from his fear of unambivalent sexual identity that calls into question the complicated structure of his own desire. Jody fears Jude because he believes what Fergus comes to believe after he meets her again in London: namely, that she is a manifestation of the death drive. If the state that was supposed to redeem the national martyrs has failed, then the only way to achieve the true *Symbolical Living Republic* is through death. Death itself becomes the goal of the nationalist struggle.

This does not mean, and Neil Jordan does not say, that the struggle in Northern Ireland can be reduced to, and dismissed as, a suicidal death wish on the part of a republican minority. It means that the symbolic ideal at the heart of the conflict of interpretations I described earlier is an expression of the death drive, its symptom. When Conor Cruise O'Brien appeals to the absolute authority of the state and the unquestioned legitimacy of its monopoly of violence, he appeals, whether he knows it or not, to the same imaginary construction, the same symbolic ideal, that he attributes to the republicans. Just as the formerly colonized nation-state, by refusing to recognize the internal divisions on which it is founded, tries to destroy the hope that would challenge its authority, Jude also bypasses hope and promotes commitment to death as an end in itself. Not as a character but as a symbol, she eradicates the division within herself that would give ground to hope as the possibility not of destroying division or of transcending it but of speaking through it. There can be no hope without the opening of the subject to its own incompleteness, to those internal divisions that signify the dialectical relationship between identity and nonidentity, self and other. Hope is intersubjective; it forces the subject to recognize the ground of its symbolic construction in the impossibility of its desire. The subject cannot exist without the other who calls out to the "totally other" from which the subject derives.

This analysis does not respond fully to the problem of misogyny in *The Crying Game*, which constitutes one of the boundaries or limits determining its unconscious historiography. Still, before that limit can be articulated, it must be analyzed as an expression of the mimetic or intersubjective relationship which is the social content shaped by the immanent form of this work of art. *The Crying Game* consists of two stories, one of friendship and the other of love, that are bound together by a difference or division that both parts strive to overcome without reaching any absolute reconciliation. The story of friendship unfolds between Fergus and Jody and repeats a topos of postcolonial Irish literature. In the introduction to the screenplay, Jordan himself mentions Frank O'Connor's short story, "Guests of the Nation," and Brendan Behan's play, *The Hostage*, as the precursors of his film; and his understanding of their similar themes suggests that all three works fall into the category of what Jameson would call national allegory: "The attraction of such a theme for Irish writers," writes Jordan, "the friendship that develops between two protagonists in a conflict, that grows paradoxically deeper than any of their other allegiances, lies in the broader history of Anglo-Irish relationships: two cultures in need of each other, yet at war with each other." Jordan identifies *The Crying Game* with the traditions of modern Irish literature by foregrounding something which underlies the relationships between men in the two earlier works: "an erotic possibility, a sense of mutual need and identification that could have provided salvation for their protagonists." Jordan claims that he avoids O'Connor's and Behan's tragic endings by bringing this "erotic thread to the surface" (*NJR* xii).

In my view, both O'Connor's and Behan's works are more ironic than tragic, and Behan's play approaches farce until the end when the British soldier held hostage is killed by the government forces coming to rescue him. The first half of *The Crying Game* changes the tone of *The Hostage* and wants to avoid both tragedy and farce by constructing the sense of melancholy that Benjamin attributed to the allegorical mode of German *Trauerspiel*. By contrast with symbolic tragedies like *King Lear* (at least from the romantic perspective), in which "destruction is idealized and the transfigured face of nature is fleetingly revealed in the light of redemption," the allegorical *Trauerspiel* confronts the the observer "with the *facies hippocratica* of history as a petrified, primordial landscape." Unlike Yeats's "Easter 1916," which captures the terrible beauty of death as a symbolic act of redemption, postcolonial Irish literature tends to allegorize death as the trace of history itself in a fallen nature, the ruin of time. In effect, the postcolonial revolutionary finds hope, if he or she can find it, only through a direct confrontation with what Joyce called the "nightmare of history." The first half of *The Crying Game* ends with Jody's death but not in a way that is tragic. Fergus is supposed to execute Jody but cannot bring himself to do it after Jody runs away from him; yet, with a brutally ironic turn in the plot, Jody is killed anyway when he is hit by a Saracen tank and then run over by another. Fergus's scream in that moment (the composition of the shot vaguely resembles Edvard Munch's "The Scream") suggests less the sense of personal responsibility and guilt than sheer horror before the reality of historical violence without any redemptive logic.

As he runs away, the camera cuts to the farmhouse where the violence of the state is displayed in an apocalyptic form. In a stunning low-angle shot, the spectator looks up through the glass roof of the greenhouse at a hovering helicopter while bullets are flying into the building from all directions. Within seconds, the farm buildings burst into flames; and even though the spectator sees Peter and Jude trying to escape from the farmhouse just before the fire breaks out, he or she is left with the impression that no one could have survived. In this scene, the state has no face and does not have to confront its victims as human beings. It is nothing more than the organized use of raw force. After a last shot of the burning farmhouse, the camera abruptly cuts to what appears to be a barren landscape with a broken-down car in the foreground and an isolated box-shaped dwelling in the background. An old man on a bicycle passes the rusting car from which Fergus emerges. Although there is no physical connection between the two places, the contrast between the almost pastoral landscape at the farm and the barren landscape where Fergus meets the old man, Tommy, emphasizes a purely negative image of historical transience. As Benjamin says of *Trauerspiel*, "In the process of decay, and in it alone, the events of history shrivel up and become absorbed in the setting."[44] These abrupt cuts and shifts articulate the sudden transformation of Fergus's historical viewpoint. The logic of revolutionary self-sacrifice that made sense to him up to the point of Jody's death has turned his world into a wasteland; the promise of social liberation has revealed its darker truth as the death drive. Fergus repeats a version of postcolonial history as he travels from the green countryside (the nativist pastoral), through the wasteland of disenchantment and historical violence, to the postimperial metropolis (London as the multicultural and multi-sexual hybrid).

Nature, nation, and mimetic identification

Before he can make this journey, however, Fergus has to confront his failure as a revolutionary. This realization results from his relationship with Jody, especially from his failure to keep that relationship objective and impersonal. It is surely no coincidence that most of the scenes between Fergus and Jody take place inside a greenhouse. When Kathleen Ni Houlihan calls on her sons to sacrifice themselves for Ireland, she also calls them back to the earth from which they came. In Seamus Heaney's poetry, as David Lloyd reads it, there is "an explicit affirmation of a sexual structure in the worker's or the writer's relation to a land or place already given as feminine."[45] If the regeneration of Ireland's national identity requires death and blood sacrifice in order to nourish the feminine earth, there may be something beyond national and sexual identity in a relationship that grows in the artificial environment of a greenhouse. Before he goes into the greenhouse, Fergus is intellectually and erotically bound to Jude as the symbol of motherland. In the greenhouse, another erotic thread starts to surface. Claiming that he has seen Fergus's face, Jody describes him as "about five ten with the killer smile and the baby face." He calls Fergus "the handsome one" (*NJR* 185).

Jody fights for his life with the only weapon available to him: language as a form of seduction. He has to use language in order to

44 Benjamin, *German Tragic Drama*, pp. 166, 179.
45 Lloyd, *Anomalous States*, p. 20.

make Fergus see him as another human being, another subject, that is, a desiring subject with which Fergus can identify as the desire of the Other. First, he convinces Fergus to remove the hood that hides his face; then, he does his best to make Fergus identify with him through conversation and story-telling. Rhetorically, Jody tries to drive a wedge between Fergus's self-identity as an ego (or an individual with a history of his own) and his social identification with the other members of the IRA. The initial key to this strategy is Jody's appropriation of the word "nature." Jody points out that the IRA cannot just let him go free. Fergus wants to know why, and Jody says that it is not in "your" nature. However, he soon qualifies himself by explaining that he is not talking about Fergus but about "his people." When Fergus angrily asks, "What the fuck do you know about my people?", Jody replies emotionally, "Only that you're all tough undeluded motherfuckers. And that it's not in your nature to let me go" (*NJR* 188–89). In the actual film, I cannot decide whether the word Jody uses is "deluded" or "undeluded." Both terms work in their own way. The members of the Provisional IRA as postcolonial revolutionaries are surely undeluded in the sense that they no longer accept the conviction of the 1916 revolutionaries that the foundation of the nation-state in and of itself will bring about the material reality of the symbolic republic. On the other hand, they are surely deluded in sacrificing their lives for a symbolic republic that may be nothing more than an imaginary construction camouflaging the death drive.

Later Jody comes back to the idea of "nature" when he tells Fergus the story of the scorpion and the frog. Briefly summarizing, a scorpion convinces a frog to carry him across a river with the argument that it would not be in his interest to sting the frog as they would both drown. Nevertheless, the scorpion does sting the frog; and as they drown, the frog asks the scorpion why he did it: "Scorpion replies, 'I can't help it, it's in my nature.'" Ironically, Jody uses story-telling as an artifice in order to convince Fergus that *by nature* he has more in common with Jody than with his nationalist comrades in the IRA. He once again induces Fergus to take the hood off, this time with the claim that it is in Fergus's nature to be kind. This scene, with the support of the background music, suggests a breakdown in Fergus's ideological armor. When Jody says, "I was right about you," Fergus responds with confused emotion, "Don't be so sure" (*NJR* 196–97). It never occurs to

Fergus that the allegorical meaning of the fable suggests that if he is the frog, the other man must be the scorpion. Jody may not want to hurt his captor, but his desire for life could and eventually does put Fergus's life in jeopardy. Jody knows that Fergus may *have* to kill him; so he tries to transform Fergus's revolutionary anger into compassion for the enemy – his desire *for* the Other into identification with the Other's desire. Jody creates a bond with Fergus that causes the suffering of the one to be assimilated by the other; at the same time, this *com*passion hints at a subliminal eroticism. Jody seduces Fergus by planting emotional seeds and nurturing erotic feelings that will make it difficult for Fergus to see Jody as a thing, although they may make it possible for him to identify Jody with *the* Thing, or the lack in the Other.

Gradually, the two men begin to share their experiences and their histories. They are both soldiers, both working-class men, and both members of ethnic minorities. As Lewis P. Curtis shows in *Anglo-Saxons and Celts*, British ideologues in the nineteenth century took it for granted that the Irish were ethnically distinct and inferior.[46] Although the Irish are European, they share the historical experience of British colonization with other former subjects of the empire, such as an immigrant from Antigua like Jody. Jody's manipulation of Fergus's "nature" actually appeals to his historical situation as a displaced postcolonial subject who must construct his identity out of the hybrid cultural text which is the legacy of colonialism. Jody's appeal, whether he knows it or not, presupposes that Fergus shares some of his own experience of alterity, of living in a culture which both constitutes and negates his identity. In a sense, the difference between Jody and Fergus as colonized subjects takes the symptomatic form of their respective passions for cricket and hurling. In Ireland, the use of a Gaelic sport like hurling to express the national spirit goes back to the formation of the Gaelic Athletic Association in 1884, which "inculcated among its members an uncompromising hostility to foreign games."[47] In African-Caribbean culture, cricket takes on a different function; since the sport originated in England, it as-

---

[46] L. P. Curtis, Jr., *Anglo-Saxons and Celts: A Study of Anti-Irish Prejudice in Victorian England* (Bridgeport, Connecticut: University of Bridgeport Press, 1968), pp. 36–65.

[47] F. S. L. Lyons, *Ireland Since the Famine*, rev. edn. (London: Collins/Fontana, 1973), p. 226.

sumes value for colonized subjects insofar as it enables them both to *abrogate* the culture of colonization and to *appropriate* it for their own purposes.[48]

Both Jody and Fergus believe that their sport is the "best game in the world." Still, Jody's passion for cricket is the symptom of his complex historical background as a British soldier from Tottenham who was born in Antigua where "cricket's the black man's game." As he tells Fergus, "The kids play it from the age of two. My daddy had me throwing googlies from the age of five. Then we moved to Tottenham and it was something different ... Toffs' game there. But not at home." And then Jody adds, "So when you come to shoot me, Paddy, remember, you're getting rid of a shit-hot bowler." In these statements, Jody discloses one dimension of this film's unconscious historical truth. This dialogue takes place immediately after Jody has complained about the racism in Northern Ireland. Fergus laughs and advises him not to take it personally, but Jody responds by imitating a Belfast accent: "'Go back to your banana tree, nigger.' No use telling them I came from Tottenham" (*NJR* 191–92). Yet the truth, as we immediately learn, is that Jody's nation of origin is Antigua; and this formerly colonized island in the Caribbean differs from other Caribbean islands, according to Jamaica Kincaid, in being "deliciously hot and dry" because it is "a place that suffers constantly from drought." Kincaid observes that, while the weather in Antigua creates hardship for the people who live there, it is popular with tourists who can enjoy a tropical climate without having to endure the rain. Of course, Jody does not mention these things to Fergus and may not even remember that much about Antigua; but the disjunction between the reality of a place characterized by dryness and drought and the stereotype of the Caribbean black man amidst the banana trees on a tropical island is a symptom of the cultural unconscious that determines this cinematic text from the outside. Kincaid, for example, describes the headmistress of a school for girls in Antigua under colonial rule: "This woman was twenty-six years old, not too long out of university, from Northern Ireland, and she told these girls over and over again to stop

[48] For the use of these terms in postcolonial theory, see B. Ashcroft, G. Griffiths, and H. Tiffin, *The Empire Writes Back: Theory and Practice in Post-Colonial Literatures* (London: Routledge, 1989), pp. 38–39.

behaving as if they were monkeys just out of trees."[49] In this sentence, we get a glimpse of how Northern Ireland would look from the viewpoint of someone with Jody's historical experience. Similarly, when Jody calls Fergus "Paddy," a term with a long history as a form of anti-Irish stereotyping,[50] he disturbs the cultural unconscious that determines Fergus's identity; and though Fergus sternly refuses the name, he merely proves Jody's implicit point that racial slurs are always personal.

Jody's passion for cricket makes such a deep impression on Fergus that, in the second half of the film, on the three occasions when he dreams or fantasizes about Jody, he imagines Jody as wearing cricket whites. Kincaid sarcastically notes that in Antigua cricket is more culture than sport. Her sarcasm derives from the fact that cricket has become part of the official culture of Antigua, promoted by the Minister of Culture without any reference to its political uses in the historical colonial context. According to Kincaid, this kind of promotion forgets the real meaning of "cultural things": "For is it not that people make them up as they go along, make them up as they need them?"[51] Kincaid refers to something that is historically true. In the West Indies under British colonial rule, cricket became something the people needed, namely, a symbolic form of resistance to imperialism, as has been powerfully documented by Trinidadian C. L. R. James in *Beyond a Boundary*. Simon Gikandi sums up the political significance of this work: "Taking cricket as a synecdoche of colonial culture, James writes about how West Indians have adopted this symbol of the English upper class and reverted it into an expression of popular will, a mode of communicating an emerging national consciousness."[52] In other words, West Indians abrogated the class content of cricket and appropriated the game as a symbolic expression of their desire to destroy the boundaries of race and class that have so violently determined the history of their nations. Although men were organized into the Trinidad cricket clubs according to the color of their skin, once they walked onto the field of play the game provided the legal opportunity for expressing their opposition to, and hatred of, social inequality and domination. In telling his life

[49] Jamaica Kincaid, *A Small Place* (New York: Plume, 1989), pp. 4, 29.
[50] Curtis, *Anglo-Saxons*, pp. 49–65.   [51] Kincaid, *Small Place*, p. 49.
[52] S. Gikandi, *Writing in Limbo: Modernism and Caribbean Literature* (Ithaca: Cornell University Press, 1992), p. 43.

through the history of West Indian cricket, James creates a figure for the colonized subject's resistance to the cultural imperialism that shapes his or her identity:

I haven't the slightest doubt that the clash of race, caste and class did not retard but stimulated West Indian cricket. I am equally certain that in those years social and political passions, denied normal outlets, expressed themselves so fiercely in cricket (and other games) precisely because they were games. The British tradition soaked deep into me was that when you entered the sporting arena you left behind you the sordid compromises of everyday existence. Yet for us to do that we would have had to divest ourselves of our skins... The class and racial rivalries were too intense... Thus the cricket field was a stage on which selected individuals played representative roles which were charged with social significance.[53]

If, as James indicates, cricket can be appropriated and used to construct a subject in opposition to the process of colonization, then it represents the possibility of a postcolonial identity that is not rooted in some essentialist theory of the nation but plainly accepts the hybridity of culture as the material from which liberating narratives can be written. It is not necessary to go back to Africa or to force the Gaelic language on a population that no longer has any compelling reason to speak it. As Gikandi stresses, cricket can be used as an instrument of decolonization when the cricket players reimagine the playing field as "the site of struggle rather than the place where the colonized reproduce the colonizer's world view."[54] In *The Crying Game*, Fergus may not grasp these messages and Jody may not consciously intend them (nor need Jordan consciously intend them though they are implicit in what he does as a filmmaker). Nevertheless, an idea of decolonization finds its material expression in the relationship between Jody and Fergus: the idea that decolonization has to be more than the violent destruction of difference in the interest of a univocal national identity, that it involves going *beyond a boundary* through the act of symbolic exchange between self and other or between identity and difference, and that as a historical process decolonization must recognize as its ground the intersubjectivity that finally calls into question any absolute concept of national or racial essence. Such a relationship challenges the dialectical relation between the master and the slave in Hegel's *Phenomenology* by

[53] C. L. R. James, *Beyond a Boundary* (New York: Pantheon, 1983), p. 72.
[54] Gikandi, *Writing in Limbo*, p. 53.

implicitly revising the Hegelian scenario along the lines of what Patrick Taylor calls the "narrative of liberation." If the primal struggle between master and slave is a struggle for dominance, it also opens up the possibility of a secondary struggle for "true universality and mutual recognition": "The secondary struggle for recognition must recommence the primary struggle so that the master is compelled by the slave to recognize their mutual freedom." The secondary struggle, however, is not immanently related to the primary one; it can only be brought to pass through the construction of an alternative interpretation of historical reality, or a liberating narrative.[55]

James is trying to create such a narrative by writing the history of cricket in the West Indies; and unconsciously Jody appeals to the same logic. This logic is an alternative to the logic of Irish nationalism with its identity thinking and its nativist ideology. Perhaps nothing expresses the process of decolonization better than the laughter that Fergus and Jody share to the annoyance of Peter and the violent anger of Jude. Peter and Jude reproduce the identity of the imperialist power they oppose by interpreting their relationship to Jody as an act of domination pure and simple. When Jody expresses his bond with Fergus by defending him as a good soldier, he gets whacked by Jude with a pistol. She cannot allow the object of her power to become *a subject with a voice*. After Jude leaves, however, the extreme close-up of Jody's mouth as he speaks suggests that his voice has already developed beyond her control, at least for Fergus. The two men do not imitate one another; they adapt to one another and shape their identities in such a way that the intersubjective ground of the mimetic impulse, as Adorno understands it, is brought into play. They change one another and open up new possibilities for the meaning of freedom.

Two crucial scenes foreground the act of symbolic exchange that subverts the self-identity of the two men and destabilizes the block against mimetic identification. In both scenes, there is more going on beneath the surface than Fergus knows (or than the spectators know on the first viewing), although Jody must know more than he says. After he explains to Fergus that in truth Jude is not his type, he asks Fergus to approach him so that he can show him something. Holding a gun to Jody's face, while following his

[55] P. Taylor, *The Narrative of Liberation: Perspectives on Afro-Caribbean Literature, Popular Culture, and Politics* (Ithaca: Cornell University Press, 1989), p. 84.

directions, Fergus takes a wallet out of Jody's pocket. There are some subtle visual effects at this point in the film. As Fergus approaches Jody, the camera captures Jody's face and upper torso on the left side of the screen; then Fergus enters the frame from the right as the camera slowly turns counterclockwise to include Fergus's head within the same frame as Jody's but at an oblique angle that defamiliarizes normal perception. This tilt shot brings into focus the moment of mimetic identification between the two men. At the same time, the angle and disruptive movements of the camera as a cinematic eye/I force the spectator as subject to recognize his or her own position outside the cinematic frame as mediator of this symbolic exchange. The narrative drive of the film almost stops as "the spectator's identification with the characters" becomes secondary to a more "preliminary identification with the (invisible) seeing agency of the film itself as discourse, as the agency that *puts forward* the story and shows it to us."[56] In effect, the film's sutures are made visible. These are the identifications which bind the spectator to the camera as the subject of the gaze and to the characters as subjects of the desire of the Other, a collective desire, which is the animating force behind the film's narrative reality. The constructed nature of the image, the momentary foregrounding of what Metz would call the *cinematic signifier*,[57] calls into question any natural identity or gaze. The looks exchanged between these characters, and the look of the spectator outside the frame, do not reflect identity but rather construct it as the desire of the Other. This Other is the overdetermined locus of culture and history. The image in this case assumes the explosive force of what Adorno would call the apparition, as it makes visible the contradictory relation between *real* historical events and *imaginary* cultural identities. The soft lighting used in this and all of the daylight scenes between Jody and Fergus in the greenhouse enhances the impression of intimacy by giving the faces of the two men the soft, glowing look that one might associate with the faces of young lovers in the movies.

When Fergus opens Jody's wallet, the first thing he sees is a picture of Jody in his cricket whites; but Jody directs him to the picture of himself and Dil, who, as the screenplay stresses, is *"a beautiful black woman"* (*NJR* 190). At this point, the explosion of the

---

[56] Metz, *Psychoanalysis and Cinema*, p. 96.
[57] *Ibid.*, p. 34.

image resolves into the predictable homosocial bond between two men based on the symbolic exchange of a woman or, at least, the image of a woman. In a sense, the photograph of Dil and Jody together restabilizes the sutures of sexual identity that have been momentarily exposed and thus brought into crisis. It also makes possible, though not necessary, the restabilization of the spectator's projected identity in the film (though the subject of the film's discursive gaze must remain radically unstable as the effect of the cinematic process). Jody emphatically insists that Dil belongs to him; but clearly he wants to win Fergus's admiration for her beauty as a lure to gain his intimacy. It is immediately after this moment that Jody explains what he was doing with Jude as well as his reactions to racism and love of cricket.

Then the second crucial scene takes place. Fergus leads Jody out of the greenhouse to piss, but there are some complications. Jody is alarmed when he realizes that Fergus does not intend to untie his hands; and he has no choice but to insist that Fergus take his penis out for him. Fergus's homosexual panic comically reveals itself in his embarrassed facial expressions when he has to touch Jody's penis. Jody finds Fergus's embarrassment amusing; and one necessarily connects this incident with the earlier scene in which Jody pisses while holding Jude's hand. Both gestures suggest strategies for the disavowal of castration by identifying with the phallus as the signifier not only of desire but of autonomy and power. In the scene with Fergus, Jody momentarily dominates the man who holds him captive. When they get back to the greenhouse, Jody thanks Fergus and starts to laugh. In a spirit of camaraderie, Fergus interjects, "The pleasure was all mine" and begins to laugh himself (*NJR* 194). Though Fergus is joking, he says something true; in taking pleasure from Jody's sense of humor, he has allowed the other to relate to him as a real subject in such a way as to call into question the determining force of the master–slave relationship.

Subjectivity and narrative displacement

Retrospectively, it seems obvious that everything Jody does or says in the first half of the film has the purpose of trying to undermine the psychological ability of his captor to kill him. (Obviously, the meaning of these events changes after Fergus learns that Jody is a homosexual or at least a bisexual, though the terms *homosexual, heterosexual,* and *bisexual* are deconstructed in the film's second half.) Exercising far greater control over Fergus than Fergus knows, Jody intentionally pulls the erotic strings in this homosocial relationship, strings which Fergus is too blind or repressed to recognize. Though Jody is the captive, he effectively becomes the teacher of his captor. Like the celebrated Caribbean cricket players who played "representative roles" in the struggle against cultural imperialism, Jody plays a representative role in showing Fergus the interimplication of the social, sexual, and racial divisions that bind the two of them to specific identities. It is not that the struggle of the Irish republican movement against British imperialism or Northern Irish racism is inherently wrong but that the commitment of Irish nationalism to a myth of national identity that endorses the same ideology of racial exclusion and class inequality as the force it opposes fails to create a true alternative to the master narrative of European imperialism. This alternative narrative of liberation must avoid becoming another Manichean allegory in which the divisions between love and hate, self and other, man and woman, master and slave, are always construed as unbridgeable metaphysical oppositions. Jody unconsciously teaches Fergus that the real divisions between human beings are symbolic and that hope depends on the subject's learning to adapt itself to the other who makes visible the symbolic gap, or hole in the Real, from which the subject itself derives.

Fergus is seduced by Jody's love of Dil even though he does not know what it means. As Jody contemplates his death, he asks Fergus to go to London and find her in order to tell her that Jody was thinking of her before he died. He gives Fergus her picture and directions just before Peter comes in to give Fergus the execution order. While Fergus mistakenly thinks that Dil is a woman, he correctly understands that the relation between Dil and Jody points toward a completely different construction of human identity from what he has experienced in his relationship with Jude, the more conventional object of his heterosexual desire. As the phallic mother, Jude demands Fergus's submission to sexual and national identities from which he may not deviate without losing her love. In other words, the love between Jude and Fergus is not the articulation of desire for the impossible object but another version of the master–slave relationship. Jody's relation to Dil seems to promise something different, although Fergus will not discover the meaning of that difference until he goes to London.

Jody's final lesson to Fergus concerns the power of narrative. After Jody learns that he is going to be executed, he asks Fergus to tell him a story; but Fergus finds himself almost speechless:

FERGUS: Like the one about the frog?
JODY: And the scorpion. No. Tell me anything.
FERGUS: When I was a child…
JODY: Yeah?
FERGUS: I thought as a child. But when I became a man I put away childish things…
JODY: What does that mean?
FERGUS: Nothing.   (*NJR* 202)

Jody wants to hear something that will give him hope, a liberating narrative, even if in this context it must be an illusion. He has told Jude that Fergus believes in the future; but the truth is that Fergus cannot imagine a future that expresses hope of any sort. Disenchanted with postcolonial Ireland and the failed promise of the nationalist revolution, he has lost the ability to construct a future that promises anything more than perpetual conflict and finally death. Ironically, for lack of any story to tell, he quotes the Bible and, specifically, the King James translation of 1 Corinthians 13: 11. Fergus uses one of primary texts of British imperialist culture in order to communicate his loss of hope. The passage he quotes from speaks of the failure of prophecies, the failure of language, and the failure of knowledge:

For we know in part, and we prophesy in part. But when that which is perfect is come, then that which is in part shall be done away. When I was a child, I spoke as a child, I understood as a child, I thought as a child: but when I became a man, I put away childish things. For now we see through a glass, darkly; but then face to face: now I know in part; but then shall I know even as also I am known.   (1 Cor. 13: 9–12)

Fergus tells the story of a perfection that is the end of the world and the end of all divisions. This dream of perfection signifies the resurrection and life after death that the New Testament promises, but for an Irish revolutionary it also anticipates the promise of the symbolic republic. When the child becomes a man, he will put away the thoughts of a child that have divided the child against himself and made him see darkly. Allegorically, the division between man and that which transcends man will be lifted. I use the word "man" because it is appropriate to this profoundly patriarchal vision of human history. Jody takes small comfort from Fergus's words because he wants some promise of life, whereas Fergus can only express his disenchantment with life by contrast with the *Symbolical Living Republic*. Unlike Fergus, Jody does not desire the end of the world as the final justification of somebody's version of universal history.

Both Jody and Fergus play the crying game that articulates the bizarre conditions necessary to achieving either love or hope in a world so radically divided by interests. Fergus decides that the only story he can tell means nothing, while Jody just wants to hear something or anything that promises hope. "Not a lot of use, are you, Fergus?" he finally says. "Me? No, I'm not good for much" (*NJR* 202). In a sense, Fergus spends the rest of the film trying to figure out what his use-value really is. Neil Jordan dramatizes this emotional climax through a series of reverse angle shots that slowly zoom in for extreme close-ups of the two men as they speak. In this way, he visually conveys the intersubjectivity of suffering which, in the film's second half, is shown to be indistinguishable from the erotic bond, indeed from a kind of pleasure. The next day Fergus discovers that he cannot kill Jody but has to take responsibility for his death anyway. Then he crosses the division of his own being in quest of the other who both is and is not himself.

Critics like Stanley Kaufmann have faulted the film for its incoherence, and to some extent they are right. The shots between the destruction of the farmhouse and Fergus at the construction site in London take slightly over a minute. The actual join of the film's two parts, the shot of the ferry crossing the sea, only lasts a few brief seconds. Jordan may even intentionally give the appearance of a rough cut to these displacements as if to force the audience to recognize the join for what it is. It draws attention to the film's system of suture, or, to quote Stephen Heath again, "the dual process of multiplication and projection, the conjunction of the spectator as subject with the film – which conjunction is always the terrain of any specific ideological operation of a film."[58] In this

---

[58] Heath, *Questions*, p. 109.

case, the spectator becomes aware that the position he or she took
for granted in viewing the film's first half in relative stability (but
not, as I argued earlier, without moments of narrative disruption)
has come unraveled and thus requires a repositioning of the
spectator. The film forces on the spectator a Brechtian awareness
of the cinematic signifier as a constructed object. Henceforth, and
in every subsequent viewing of the film, the spectator must
confront the instability of her or his own construction *vis-à-vis* the
system of sutures that both gives the film its narrative continuity
and disrupts that continuity through the displacement of the
cinematic signifiers. After this displacement, of course, the spectator can easily enough reconstruct her or his identity as a projection
onto the narrative movement of the film; but something has been
called into question, something like the ideology of mastery that
Judith Roof criticizes in most of contemporary film theory. As Roof
argues, even though spectators identify with the camera's gaze as
a form of visual mastery, they may shift identification "even with
the camera, sometimes seeing from outside it ... sometimes
looking against what it seems to privilege in its framing and
editing, often in collision rather than collusion with it in one way
or another."[59] While Roof effectively challenges Metz and
Baudry's presupposition of the camera's gaze as transcendental
subject, she devotes less attention than she should to the way that
editing as a system of sutures can force spectators to confront the
spectacle of their own desires. In my view, *The Crying Game* is not a
film that foregrounds the cinematic signifier but rather subordinates discourse to narrative, form to content. Still, as much as any
film, it illustrates the inseparability of these two dimensions of the
aesthetic process. The spectator is neither the repository nor the
origin of desire; rather, as subject, he or she is constituted as a
function of desire, or rather of desires.

An Adornian concept of the cinematic art work does not reject
the spectator as one determining ground of the filmic experience
but situates the spectator as part of the context which the aesthetic
monad objectifies. The camera position in and of itself certainly
does not govern the desires of the spectator; but the film *as a whole
that is not-whole* (in the Lacanian sense of *pas tout*, not everything)
articulates through its system of sutures the possibilities of desire

[59] J. Roof, *A Lure of Knowledge: Lesbian Sexuality and Theory* (New York: Columbia
University Press, 1991), p. 43.

within a given historical context. There is no way of predicting the form of the spectator's desire, but at the same time such desire cannot be separated from the construction of the film as a cultural symptom, that is, as a signifier. As Lacan writes, "The subjection of the subject to the signifier ... is really a circle, in as much as the assertion that is established in it [the subject] ... refers only to its own anticipation in the composition of the signifier."[60] I take this to mean that the relation between subject and signifier is dialectical, that while the subject is subjected to the signifier – in the sense that it is constrained by the limits of the material formation, or, in the case of cinema, by the apparatus – it cannot be reduced to that signifier. By the same token, the signifier is nothing in itself without the subject and the dialectic of desire. The suture names the relation or system of relations by which the subject appears, in Heath's terms, as a "join in the chain"; it refers to the division/constitution of the subject through its imaginary identification with itself as a whole ego "in the fiction of the sign."[61] This identification and the desire to which it lends a support need not follow a predetermined path; but identificatory desire is not completely free either. I am suggesting that the rough cuts in the middle of *The Crying Game*, which mark the discontinuity between the first and second halves of the film, clear the path for the displacements of desire that not only make up the content of the rest of the film but require the spectator to reconsider everything up to that point in light of what comes later.

Before crossing the water, Fergus tells Tommy that he needs to lose himself for a while. If Fergus's identity has been shattered by the events at the farmhouse, he has not yet figured out where this situation has deposited him. In going to England, he leaves behind his favorite pub, the Rock, in order to find Jody's favorite pub, the Metro. He goes from the rock of national identity (which recalls Yeats's line in "Easter 1916" about how national self-sacrifice can turn the human heart into a stone[62]) to the metropolis that may be located in the heart of the empire but has succumbed to the hybrid culture of its postcolonial history. As a subject, Fergus has been

---

[60] Translation revised. See J. Lacan, *"Ecrits": A Selection*, trans. A. Sheridan (New York: Norton, 1977), p. 305, and *Ecrits* (Paris: Seuil, 1966), p. 806.

[61] Heath, *Questions*, p. 106.

[62] Yeats, *Poems*, p. 181, ll. 57–58.

forced to recognize the internal divisions that subvert the imaginary gaze of the motherland. It is not that he has become a good subject of the empire but that his mimetic relation to Jody has fractured his national identity so that it no longer mirrors the structure of imperialist ideology. Fergus has not ceased to be Irish by crossing the sea to England, but he has opened himself to the hybridity of postcolonial culture that calls into question not only the absoluteness of national divisions but the absoluteness of any identity that is rooted in a binary opposition: man/woman, nature/culture, black/white, homosexual/heterosexual. In the first half of the film, these categories remain in force even though Jody tries to challenge their grip on Fergus's mind. In the film's second half, Fergus – unconsciously perhaps, but no less actively – struggles to find his way beyond these binarisms toward a changed relation to cultural difference, although he also resists recognizing the interrelatedness of the binary structures. In other words, the second half of the film comments on and rewrites the first half, even as the rules and values of the first half remain in force as a weight on the progress the second half charts.

The gaze, the mirror, and the masquerade

The first scene in the second half of the film suggests the possibility of rebirth. Fergus, who has assumed a working-class identity, breaks through the wall of the building he is helping to renovate. This sequence begins with a point of view shot as Fergus knocks some bricks out of the wall to reveal men playing on a cricket field directly opposite the building. Initially, the screen is almost entirely black with a small glimpse of green; then the opening widens as the bricks are removed. The second shot is taken at about a 120 degree angle in relation to the first and shows Fergus inside the opening removing the bricks with an electric chisel. The third shot returns to the initial point of view shot. The fourth shot, at about the same angle as the second shot, is a medium close-up of Fergus as he notices the players on the field. The fifth shot is a closer point of view shot of the players, this time from outside the hole. The last shot is a close-up reaction shot of Fergus. This sequence captures Fergus's gaze as it moves from darkness to light, from enclosure to the open field. It suggests that in some sense he is about to be reborn. Wearing his work overalls, he is covered with dust as he looks through the hole in the wall at the cricket match in progress.

This scene indicates not only that Fergus now identifies himself with Jody and is trying to see the world, in some sense, through Jody's eyes; but it also repeats the narrative point of departure of C. L. R. James's *Beyond a Boundary*. The first section of that work, entitled "A Window to the World," describes James as a boy of six gazing out his window at the cricket field behind his family's house in Trinidad. Since his cultural inheritance included puritanism as well as cricket, James thought that predestination may have played a role in locating his family home in the exact location from which he would be forced to confront a figure of what would become his life's work.[63] According to Simon Gikandi, in James's writing, the cricket field is a metaphor and a metonym. As a metaphor, it "functions as the inherited space of representation in which colonial peoples express their English identity"; while, as a metonym, it is "a site in which original, colonial meanings, and the identities of colonial subjects, are displaced; it is a place where the sign and the signified no longer correspond."[64] In other words, as both metonym and metaphor, cricket constitutes a space that cannot be reduced to any absolute identification with nature or culture or, from a different perspective, with nation or empire. Insofar as James sees cricket as his inheritance by predestination, he can hardly distinguish the sport from nature or even providence. His relation to it is not only not a matter of choice; it is the starting point of any attempt at self-representation he may undertake. At the same time, cricket is a game, the rules of which are arbitrary; but, more important, the meanings one may attribute to the game cannot be governed by any single metaphorical identification. Cricket operates very much like the English language with which James also associates it from the beginning, since the room in which he watched the cricket matches as a boy also contained the books through which he learned the language that, as a man, he finally uses to write his life in the guise of a history of West Indian cricket.

In other words, as a historical signifier, cricket articulates the space between determination and freedom. It is both and neither; and it represents not the transcendence of history but the radical

[63] James, *Beyond a Boundary*, p. 17.
[64] Gikandi, *Writing in Limbo*, p. 46.

ambivalence of historical representations. Whereas Fergus has
associated hurling with an Irish essence that transcends historical
determinations, he now gazes at the cricket match as the signifier
of hope because its meaning is subject to historical displacement.
This gaze, in many ways, constructs the tone of the film's second
half, which escapes the predominant melancholy of the first half.
Because Fergus implicitly questions his identity as either an
imperial or a national subject, he opens himself to something new.
After confronting history's deathmask in the "petrified, primordial landscape" of Northern Ireland, he finds himself in the
position of Benjamin's allegorist. The fragments of history are now
"unconditionally in his power"; the historical object is "quite
incapable of emanating any meaning or significance of its own;
such significance as it has, it acquires from the allegorist."[65]
Nonetheless, the allegorist is not a metaphysically autonomous
subject who simply informs the world with his private meanings
but a subject in process, the subject in displacement from itself, the
one who learns how to read the historical signifiers in their excess
of signification. This subject of allegory is itself a fragment or
symptom of history, a signifier without a signified. His or her
power over meaning resembles that of Humpty Dumpty; it is
absolute but groundless.

The first place Fergus visits in his confused quest for meaning is
Millie's Unisex Hair Salon where he expects to find Dil. After the
cricket game, "Unisex" is the first signifier to point toward the
identity of nonidentity that Fergus unknowingly seeks. By contrast with the characters at the farmhouse in Northern Ireland, Dil
demonstrates a rather loose relation to national identity. She asks
Fergus if he is American or English until he deceptively affirms
that he is Scottish. (An unidentified reader of the present essay in
manuscript comments that Dil's guess is "the sort of 'stupid'
mistake all too naively attributed to women/blacks/queers,
whereas it could easily be read as the sort of barbed teasing Dil
engages in, to see by subtle indirection just how naively these
incomprehending blockheads estimate the naiveté they attribute
to him/her." This reader further speculates that it is at least
possible that Dil only pretends not to recognize Fergus's national
identity, that in truth she "has put together the connections,

---

[65] Benjamin, *German Tragic Drama*, p. 152.

'kidnaps' Fergus, and is waiting for Jude to show up, knowing that Jody's death has been at the hands of one or more of these people and fully intending vengeance on them." These compelling though inconclusive speculations suggest that Dil is another version of the *femme fatale*, a counterpart to Jude, despite her sexual ambiguity.) Although the original screenplay says nothing about her history, as a mulatto she probably comes from African-Caribbean ancestry like Jody. Still, she betrays no particular interest in racial identity; nor does anyone around her, not even Dave. The only person in the second half of the film who even remarks on her color is Jude.

After following Dil into the Metro, Fergus cannot stop looking at her. The emphasis on looking and mirrors in this scene suggests that Dil largely exists for Fergus, initially, as an imaginary object, a function of his fantasy. She is the object of exchange between men, a symptom of the erotic bond between Fergus and Jody. However, when Fergus glances over at Dil sitting on the other side of the bar, he discovers that she is already looking at him. She comments on his look to Col, the bartender. The next shot is a view of Dil's face in the mirror behind the bar, looking directly into the camera. Then the camera cuts to the object of her gaze, namely Fergus's reflection in the mirror. He surreptitiously steals a glance at her mirror image (by looking directly into the camera) only to discover again that she is already looking at him. He turns away embarrassed. Dil comments on this look, and Col affirms the accuracy of her perception. The point is that while Fergus may want to subject Dil to his fantasy, from the moment he meets her she confronts his gaze with her gaze, by which she insists on what lies beyond the fanstasy, the real other. After he follows her home and watches her perform for Dave through the window, he returns to his room: "*Fergus, in bed. Fade to black as we see Jody as a bowler, running in slow motion, toward the camera. He releases the ball; we see Fergus in bed, breathing heavily.*" These directions, which the film follows to the letter, suggest that Fergus's attraction to Dil tries to recapture or reproduce his homosocial bond with Jody; it involves a transference. The next day at work, before he goes back to the Metro, Fergus watches another cricket game and, trying to be more like Jody, imitates the batsman hitting a ball. Ironically, this act gives his British contractor, Tristram Deveroux, the opportunity to label him with the name "Pat": "So Pat's a cricket fan, eh?" (*NJR* 213).

Unlike Dil, Deveroux sees no ambiguity in the class or in the national/racial identity of his employee.

Fergus returns to the Metro, and Col is presumably on the verge of telling him the truth about Dil's sexual identity when she appears on the stage to suggest something far more complicated than anything Col could have said. She lip-syncs a recording by a female artist of Dave Berry's "The Crying Game." As the directions in the screenplay comment, *"She mouths the words so perfectly and the voice on the song is so feminine that there is no way of knowing who is doing the singing."* In effect, Dil so completely adapts herself to the voice of another that it becomes her voice. This act in and of itself is a figure for the intersubjectivity of mimesis. It is not that Dil has imitated another but rather that she takes something from the other, something that is not her, and adapts it to her identity, finding her own voice in the voice of the other. While she lip-syncs, she also interprets the words through a series of physical gestures with her body and, in particular, with her hands. The screenplay suggests that *"she is drawing moonbeams with her hands"* (*NJR* 215). These gestures point toward the significance of the mimetic act as the means by which the subject comes to know itself through the mediation of the other. Though the lyrics to "The Crying Game" are pedestrian, they express the intersubjective ground of human suffering, the real content of most popular love songs and the source of the pleasure they give. Curiously, the use of the song throughout the film, including in the final credits, suggests that works of popular culture can be adapted to different contexts, including different sexualities. When Dil lip-syncs the song, the voice is feminine; but later in her apartment she plays Dave Berry's version. In the final credits, the voice is that of Boy George which, in my view, seems to evade specific gender identification. Of course, these judgments are subjective; but the whole point of the film is to undermine the presuppositions about sexual identity that enter ordinary perceptions as something objective.

In other words, sexual identity always involves the masquerade of social convention, not because sexuality is purely social, since biology surely provides some impetus to sexual behavior, but because without the masquerade, without language as the discourse of the other, the fact of biological sex would never be able to *realize* itself on the plane where symbolic interhuman relationships take place. The point of the song ("Why there are heartaches,

/ Why there are tears, / And what to do / To stop feeling blue / When love disappears") is that the human demand for love can never be satisfied with the momentary extinction of the body's sexual needs. The symbolic network of language and cultural values that frames human sexuality posits the formation of desire as, in Lacan's phrase, the difference between need and demand. The song that Dil lip-syncs articulates the human demand for love as the call to the other that would bridge the incommensurable difference between subjects.

This difference cannot be reduced to sexual difference in the decidable sense that determines the binarism man/woman. As Fergus eventually discovers, Dil has the body of a man, which has the immediate effect of blocking Fergus's desire (but, as psychoanalysis teaches us, this blocking or repression also restarts desire). Afterwards, when Fergus admits to Dil that he liked her as a woman, she reminds him, "You can always pretend" (*NJR* 237). This remark underscores the fact that Fergus still approaches Dil as the conventional object of desire, what Lacan would call the *objet a*. He has not yet come to terms with the undecidable difference that lies beyond the *objet a*, the difference that cannot be governed by any structure of value, including the conventional structure of sexual difference. The question remains, however, as to whether Dil is also *pretending to be a woman* when she lip-syncs "The Crying Game." I would argue that pretending and performing are two different acts, and that Dil identifies what she does as a performance. When Dil steps onto the stage, she is not a man pretending to be a woman; rather, she acts out or performs the truth of her sexuality. She is a biological male who adapts herself to, or adopts and integrates with her biological sex, specific behaviors that are associated with the feminine gender. I use the term "gender" here to refer to the cultural construction of sexual difference and not to any concept of sexual essence.

Deconstructing the sexual difference

At the same time, it is necessary to underscore the irreducibility of sexuality to gender relations. In *Epistemology of the Closet*, Eve Kosofsky Sedgwick argues for the inadequacy of any binarism as a representation of human sexuality and underscores the historicity of the current map of sexual identities: "What *was* new from the turn of the century was the world-mapping by which every given person, just as he or she was necessarily assignable to a male or female gender, was now considered necessarily assignable as well to a homo- or a hetero-sexuality." Although Sedgwick does not use Lacanian terms, she suggests that there is a sexual Real beyond the categorical signifiers of sexuality, that there is something in excess of the meaning and values associated with the binary terms, man/woman, homosexual/heterosexual. Within the symbolic dimension of what we may call culture, the law of gender and the law of sexuality are compulsory to the extent that the binary logics they represent are normative for a given historical context. Still, for Sedgwick, this constructivist view of gender and sexuality finally raises its own set of problems through its binary opposition to an essentialist view. Even "the most scrupulously gay-affirmative thinkers" may not be able to separate these terms "from the essentially gay-genocidal nexuses of thought through which they have developed." Any restrictive commitment to the constructivist/essentialist opposition necessarily reproduces the binary opposition between culture and nature. The history of the debates that have surrounded the latter opposition suggests that culture is something that can be changed while nature is fixed. In the area of sexual identity, the concept of culture implies that human beings are responsible for the object-choices that energize their desires and therefore can be held accountable to social norms that would privilege *legitimate* over *illegitimate* forms of sexual behavior.[66]

In *The Crying Game*, Dil does not require the illusion that she is not a man in order to be the kind of woman she is. After she reveals her body to Fergus, it can be deduced that it was this full revelation that she desired all along but had to postpone until she thought Fergus understood the truth about her sexuality. When Fergus reacts with horror, she remarks that things never work out as one expects. Still, Fergus, who is known to Dil as Jimmy, is not the man he claims to be, which makes it ironic that he should become nauseated by the discovery of Dil's anatomical sex. Later, Jimmy/Fergus leaves Dil a note in which he apologizes for hitting her; and when she appears at his work site the next day, he recognizes that she is "something else" (*NJR* 234), something irreducible to the sexual categories that govern his expectations. While Fergus

[66] E. K. Sedgwick, *Epistemology of the Closet* (Berkeley: University of California Press, 1990), pp. 2, 40–41.

admits that he still cares for Dil, he stresses, as he walks her home from Millie's, that he liked her better as a female. Dil advises him to pretend, but she does not require this fantasy for herself and makes it clear that Jody knew the truth about her sexual identity. In order to hide her from Jude and Peter, Fergus decides to make her into a man by dressing her in Jody's cricket whites; and she agrees to this transformation. What becomes clear from this act is not that gender can be taken on and off like so many articles of clothing but that gender as a signifier imperfectly articulates Dil's *real* sexuality which cannot be reduced to the logic of the binary opposition. Her real sexuality is the Thing itself, *das Ding*.

As the film draws to its climax, Dil tells Fergus that she cannot help being what she is. Though she has tried to give him everything she thinks he wants, she realizes that he is not telling her the truth about himself. This moment in her room can be juxtaposed with the moment of her performance in the Metro; and the message is the same in both instances: this is what I am, not a man, not a woman, but this. This may be called a homosexual, a gay man, a queer, a queen, an invert, or a pervert; but each one of these labels carries its own connotations and ideological restrictions and misses the Real that is the masquerade of sexuality itself. Dil's performance, her act in all of its specificity, deconstructs the divisions of gender-identity and sexual orientation, which is not to say that she does away with them or somehow resolves the antagonism between these social positions.

It may be, as Sedgwick claims, that deconstruction has fetishized the idea of difference to the extent that it no longer has any meaningful application to real historical experiences of cultural division.[67] Yet she describes her own critical strategy in *Epistemology of the Closet* as deconstructive. She demonstrates, for example, that binary sexual categories like heterosexual/homosexual actually operate out of a complicated set of relationships. Though they appear symmetrical, one term, "homosexuality," is actually subordinated to the other, "heterosexuality," as the social norm of a heterosexist society. However, the meaning of the ontologically valorized term, "heterosexuality," requires both the inclusion and the exclusion of the other term, insofar as its meaning depends on its negative determination of the other from

---

[67] Sedgwick, *Epistemology of the Closet*, p. 23.

which it must absolutely distinguish itself. Since the ontologically valorized term logically constitutes the other that it excludes, it is always possible to reverse the relationship of priority and claim that the other term, "homosexuality," also logically constitutes its binary opposite at some moment in their relationship. In effect, as a concept homosexuality is both internal and external to the concept of heterosexuality, and vice versa.[68]

In *The Crying Game*, this pattern of relations operates on more than one level. In the film's first half, Fergus is identified as a heterosexual both by his relationship with Jude and by the homosocial bond he develops with Jody. This bond is virtually sealed by the symbolic exchange of Dil, whom Fergus believes to be a woman. As Sedgwick emphasizes in her earlier study, *Between Men*, modern homosocial desire is characterized by homophobia which involves the stigmatization and disavowal of homosexuality. In effect, there is an asymmetry between masculine and feminine bonding which suggests that for women there is no contradiction between homosocial and homosexual relationships, while for men these relationships are radically discontinuous as one is defined as the negation of the other. Furthermore, she concludes that, given the example of the Greeks, the presence or absence of such a homosocial/homosexual continuum in society is not constituted by innate human nature but by cultural determinations.[69] Jody complicates the male bond he creates between himself and Fergus by concealing from Fergus the fact he, Jody, is gay and that the woman he symbolically shares with Fergus is a biological male. In effect, Jody has already deconstructed male homosociality which he carefully exploits in an effort to save his own life. Still, the fact that he must conceal his sexual identity dramatizes the subordination of homosexuality to the heterosexual norm. After Jody has died, it is the repressed homoeroticism within homosocial desire that compels Fergus to leave Ireland and seek out the object of Jody's desire. He seeks what he imagines to be the truth of Jody's fantasy but finds what turns out to be his own truth. Dil's revelation is the truth that explodes Fergus's fantasy.

That Fergus's erotic attraction to Dil harbors homoerotic desire would seem to be the meaning of the sexual act performed in

---

[68] Sedgwick, *Epistemology of the Closet*, pp. 9–10.
[69] E. K. Sedgwick, *Between Men: English Literature and Male Homosocial Desire* (New York: Columbia University Press, 1985), pp. 1, 4–5.

Dil's apartment when Fergus goes there for the first time. The moment Fergus enters the room his eye falls on Jody's picture. Later he wants to know all about the man in the picture; but Dil refuses to tell him anything except that he was different. When they start to make love, Fergus places his hand under her dress, but she pulls it away. Fergus, somewhat jealous, wonders if she treated Jody in the same way; so Dil decides to show him how she kissed Jody and performs fellatio on him until he has an orgasm. In the screenplay, the scene is described in this way: *"Fergus stares at the picture of Jody. Jody's eyes seem to burn through him. Dil raises her head and kisses his mouth. There are tears in his eyes"* (*NJR* 225). In the film, when Fergus is on the verge of orgasm, the camera cuts to the picture of Jody in his cricket whites, which appears to be the object of Fergus's gaze. That image dissolves into a repeat of the scene of Jody as a bowler. The implication is that Fergus has in some sense *realized* his homoerotic desire for Jody through the mediation of the woman Jody loved, Dil. The heterosexuality of his attraction to Dil not only depends on but virtually interprets the homosexuality of his attraction to Jody. Fergus's heterosexual desire takes on meaning through both the inclusion and the exclusion, the displacement and the disavowal, of his homosexual desire. This process reaches a crisis when Fergus discovers that Dil is biologically male and brutally rejects her as a sexual object. He realizes something that destroys the structure of his fantasy: namely, to use the Lacanian phrase, *the Woman does not exist*.

Nevertheless, Dil's revelation destabilizes not only the hetero-sexual/homosexual dyad but the politics of gender relations based on the dyadic structure. This may be the reason why the revelation scene has such an impact on audiences. Although I can only speak speculatively, it seems to me that the effect of the scene depends on the fact that heterosexual men and women in the audience unconsciously identify with what they presume to be Fergus's *normal or heterosexual* desire. (As feminist film theorists in the wake of Laura Mulvey have argued, the cinematic apparatus, in its most conventional forms, produces a masculinization and a heterosexualization of the spectator-position that require some sort of identificatory leap as the condition of pleasure by other subjects with different gender- and sexual-identities. Still, as Roof argues, despite the normalizing tendency of the cinematic apparatus, it can challenge the normative structure of desire and allow for a multiplicity of spectator-positions.[70]) When Fergus first sees Dil's picture, he tells Jody that she could be anyone's type; and the reaction of the film's predominantly heterosexual audiences to the revelation scene verifies this judgment. Just before he finds out that Dil is a man, Fergus asks her if Jody ever told her that she was beautiful. "All the time," she says. "Even now" (*NJR* 228). Dil may be beautiful; but, in my own case, when I saw the film a second time, I decided that the physical structure of her face worked as male or female although her dress and sense of style express what Jordan describes in the screenplay as an exaggeration of the feminine (*NJR* 222).

Yet it would be a mistake to identify Dil with the conventional movie cross-dresser like the character played by Dustin Hoffman in *Tootsie*. In that film, whatever one may think of Dustin Hoffman's imitation of a woman, the whole comic effect hinges on the fact that the audience never forgets that Dorothy Michaels is really Michael Dorsey. In *The Crying Game*, one can surmise that Dil is a gay man by noting the language she and Jody use to describe sexual relationships. Jody refers to Dil as his "special friend"; and when Fergus takes her out for the first time, she asks him if he has or wants a "special friend" (*NJR* 198, 221). Nevertheless, the film presupposes that a significant portion of the audience, like Fergus, will not automatically recognize this language or any other signs of gay lifestyle. This is not to suggest that such ignorance is innocent; on the contrary, it points toward the sexual politics that underpins political relationships of every sort in this film. Once the truth has been *outed*, two things become apparent. First, just as Fergus admits to Dil that he should have known the truth about her, it becomes clear that the audience should have known as well. Second, the truth does not reside in the fact of Dil's having a penis. At the end of *Tootsie*, Dorothy Michaels is revealed to the cast and audience of a daytime sitcom as the man Michael Dorsey. By contrast, though Dil is biologically male and culturally

[70] Roof, *Lure of Knowledge*, p. 51. In addition, see L. Mulvey, *Visual and Other Pleasures* (Bloomington: Indiana University Press, 1989); E. A. Kaplan, *Women and Film: Both Sides of the Camera* (New York: Methuen, 1983); T. de Lauretis, "Oedipus Interruptus," *Wide Angle* 7 (1985), 34–40; M. A. Doane, "Film and the Masquerade: Theorizing the Female Spectator," in *Issues in Feminist Film Criticism*, ed. Patricia Erens (Bloomington: Indiana University Press, 1990), pp. 41–57.

female, her *real* identity is neither one nor the other but the relationship between the two.

As my choice of pronouns indicates, even though I know that Dil is a man, I continue to read her gender as feminine. If gender as a categorical signifier is determined by culture, and if biological sexual anatomy is determined by genetic makeup, the relationship between the two is overdetermined by symbolic forces that virtually undermine any absolute distinction between nature and culture. In his theory of the mirror stage, Lacan describes "the effect in man of an organic insufficiency in his natural reality – insofar as any meaning can be given to the word 'nature.'"[71] Nature, for Lacan, as opposed to what he calls the Real, articulates or represents the limitations of the human organism, the gap or contradiction between its biological needs and the linguistic nature of its demands. There is no way to unravel completely the entanglement of needs and demands in the logic of desire: as Lacan writes,

Desire begins to take shape in the margin in which demand becomes separated from need: this margin being that which is opened up by demand, the appeal of which can be unconditional only in regard to the Other, under the form of a possible defect, which need may introduce into it, of having no universal satisfaction.

At the risk of oversimplifying, desire is the dialectical relationship between need and demand. Human need brings to the surface the alterity of its own ground by virtue of its dependency on the symbolic function. It is not that the organism is inherently defective but that the dependency of the organism on the symbolic function for the satisfaction of its needs opens it to the play of desire as the excess of signification inherent in the instability of the signifier/signified relationship. Meaning in the absolute sense is no more attainable than "universal satisfaction." For Lacan, the propagation of the human species requires the movement of desire as an excess of signification; but this effect of desire, which turns out to be what we call its natural function, is irreducible to natural law as the ground of normal sexuality:

What psychoanalysis shows us about desire ... is not only that it is subjected ... to the accidents of the subject's history ... but also that all this requires the cooperation of structural elements, which, in order to

[71] Lacan, *"Ecrits": A Selection*, p. 4

143

intervene, can do very well without these accidents, whose effects, so unharmonious, so unexpected, so difficult to reduce, certainly seem to leave to experience a remainder that drove Freud to admit that sexuality must be the mark of some unnatural split (*fêlure*).[72]

In other words, without desire, the species would never achieve the self-propagation for which it has been biologically programmed; yet desire itself exceeds and cannot be governed by the program which determines it. Because desire is overdetermined by the actual and unpredictable events of a subject's history (which is to say, finally, by history itself), it exceeds any program of nature, even though without what we call nature there would be no desire. The upshot of this logic is that sexuality in itself cannot be reduced to nature, and certainly not to reproduction, although it is not the plaything of culture either. It is the undecidable border between nature and culture, one that calls into question any attempt to rationalize this difference by subordinating one term to the other or by extending the law of this binarism to other relationships. In short, there is no such thing as normal sexuality that would be purely natural or purely cultural and that would enable one to determine the proper ground of abnormal sexuality. Dil's sexuality, like Jody's, is "as different as it's possible to be" (*NJR* 224) because it cannot be reduced to a gender-identity or defined within the dyad homosexual/heterosexual. Dil can be classified as a homosexual; but this label, while not meaningless, does not capture the truth of her sexuality. The truth would be the excess or remainder of signification that marks each subject with a radical difference that cannot be entered into the account of an absolute identity. This difference results from the dialectic of desire through which the structural determinations of biology interact with the accidents of history. From this perspective, every sexuality is radically different or incommensurable: "man's desire is the *désir de l'Autre* (the desire of the Other) in which the *de* provides what grammarians call the 'subjective determination', namely that it is *qua* Other that he desires."[73] In this remark, the Other is neither nature nor culture but what exceeds that binarism as its ground, or the ground of desire.

When Dil says, "Can't help what I am" (*NJR* 257), she appeals to the Other in Fergus, the totally other that constitutes his desire as

[72] Lacan, *"Ecrits": A Selection*, pp. 310–11.
[73] *Ibid.*, p. 312.

an answer to the demand for love. After Fergus discovers that Dil is a man, he returns to his apartment where he has one last dream about Jody, who this time is grinning ironically as he throws the cricket ball up and down. Fergus may feel betrayed by his own desire, but he will not be able to give it up. On the contrary, he returns to the Metro the next evening looking for Dil because, in a sense different from what he thought before, *she is what he desires*. After her performance of "The Crying Game" earlier in the film, Dil asks Fergus what he wants. When he has no answer, she concludes that he must be "old-fashioned." This phrase resonates with Jude's description of him as "a walking cliché" when he gets angry about her threat to hurt Dil (*NJR* 216, 240). The meaning of these labels emerges when Dil tries to push Fergus into articulating his true desire:

DIL: So what do you want with me, Jimmy?
FERGUS: Want to look after you.
DIL: What does that mean?
FERGUS: Something I heard someone say once.
She draws back and looks at him.
DIL: You mean that?
FERGUS: Yeah.   (*NJR* 227)

As these lines suggest, Fergus is *a walking cliché who always means what he heard someone else say*. If Dil is the other (small o) as the object of his desire, Jody is the big Other, or the intersubjective ground from which Fergus desires. It is Jody who said what Fergus says; and it is through his identification with Jody, with Jody's desire as the desire of the Other, that Fergus desires Dil. For when Dil uncovers her body, she discloses not the structure of the lie but the structure of truth that explodes the imaginary form that Fergus's desire has taken. Fergus is then confronted with his desire as the desire of the Other, as the desire for the absolute difference that cannot be reduced to the binary opposition and that virtually explodes the imaginary divisions of nationality, gender, race, and sexual orientation.

When Dil removes her robe, she does not reveal the phallus as the constitutive signifier of sexual difference within the patriarchal economy. As I suggested earlier, Jude is the woman with the phallus since she must enforce the laws of sexual and national identity. Dil eventually claims the phallus when she kills Jude; but when she undresses for Fergus, she reveals a sexual organ that has no symbolic value but is simply *real*. It is real because it is unexpected. For Jude, the phallus is a weapon with which she intends to kill the other who threatens the unity of the one sex, the one nation, and the one race. That the one sex she would defend is masculine is not the issue because it is the economy that matters, the patriarchal/heterosexual economy, the nationalist/imperialist economy, and the racial economy. When Fergus confronts the truth about Dil's sexuality, he is forced to confront a division for which there are no opposing sides, a difference against which there is no identity to be defined; it is what Lacan would call the Other that has no Other.

The irony is that a scene, which must appear to a significant portion of the audience as a reversal of the plot, should, in retrospect, appear to be the logical and even inevitable repetition of the reversal that concludes the film's first half. When Jody dies and Fergus screams, a process of mourning begins that is charted in the film's second half as Fergus seeks to understand the meaning of this event and the irreversible difference it has introduced into his life. Jody's death confronts Fergus with the truth that suffering and love are almost the same thing. On one level, it could be said that Fergus falls in love with Jody and then transfers that love to Dil. On another level, it is not love that Fergus seeks but the meaning of desire – in fact, the meaning of Jody's desire or the desire of the Other. Just before Fergus discovers the truth about Dil's biological sex, he asks why she is not in mourning for Jody, and she implies that in her own way she is. In fact, it is the process of mourning that brings Fergus and Dil together and actually creates the hope that almost overcomes Fergus's revolutionary melancholy. At an allegorical level, it is possible to read Fergus's transformation through Freud's distinction between mourning and melancholia. Both of these processes involve grief and the process of working through the loss of a loved object; but while mourning only lasts as long as it takes to withdraw the psychic investments a subject has placed in a person or a thing, melancholia becomes a generalized state of mind and view of the world that seems to lose sight of the lost object that was its cause.

As a postcolonial Irish revolutionary, Fergus has identified with the lost object of national desire, namely, the *Symbolical Living Republic*. As Freud explains, in melancholia the lost object of desire takes over part of the ego in order to become "a special mental faculty" that can criticize the ego as if it were an agency outside of it. When Fergus tells Jody that he is not good for much, he is identifying himself with the failed object of his revolutionary desire. In other words, Fergus's relation to the symbolic republic expresses not only his ambivalence toward the state as it actually exists in Ireland and Britain but his ambivalence toward his own identity as a national subject. With the capture of Jody, Fergus enters into a new kind of relationship, one that virtually restructures his identity. The bond between the two men articulates not only an imaginary identification (the "narcissistic identification" that Freud saw as the basis of melancholia) but also an intersubjective recognition.[74] When Jody dies, Fergus is confronted with a loss that is real, not symbolic or imaginary; and he begins a process of genuine mourning which means, as Freud argued, reality-testing to establish that the object no longer exists. I would argue that from the moment of Jody's death Fergus is torn between melancholy as the death wish, which drives him toward revolutionary suicide, and mourning as a confrontation of the Real, or the inexorable form of historical events.

Fergus tries to come to terms with the meaning of Jody's life and death as a way of coming to terms with the meaning of his desire. He tries to desire what Jody desired. To this extent, he nearly subordinates the structure of mourning to the structure of melancholy through narcissistic identification. Then Dil undresses and in an instant destroys that possibility. She confronts Fergus with the Real in two senses. First, he discovers that the meaning of desire cannot be reduced to a symbolic representation or an imaginary identification. Second, he discovers that the answer to his own desire is not the other, for the other is never the true object of desire. The true object of desire is the Real, and the Real cannot be represented or defined or identified with. It is the Thing that is nothing in itself – the limit of our representations, our definitions, and our identifications. Beyond the phallus, Dil's sexuality confronts Fergus with his own *real* sex. John Rajchman explains that, in Lacan's reading of Freud, the definition of sex cannot be reduced to the mutuality of "genital love." Sex is always perverse and refuses the ideal relationship between two autonomous subjects who would unite "in the reciprocity of given equal

[74] S. Freud, *General Psychological Theory: Papers on Metapsychology* (New York: Collier, 1963), p. 170.

147

positions, or in the mutuality in which we would compensate for what is lacking in one another." Sex is the incommensurable in each subject and cannot be classified by categories of identity. On the contrary, "sex singularizes us in our libidinal destinies, and so divides us from ourselves and one another." This is the meaning of Lacan's often misunderstood remark, *there is no sexual relation*.[75]

Rajchman's analysis suggests that normal sex is an idealization of sexuality in a culture dominated by the binarisms: man/woman, heterosexual/homosexual, white/black, British/Irish, and so forth. The sexual Real explodes these binarisms by replacing the logic of $1 + 0 = 1$ with $1 + 1 + 1 + 1 + 1$ *ad infinitum*. True sexuality is perverse not because it deviates from the norm within the space of social convention but because it operates outside of that space altogether. It should be clear by now that this deconstruction of normative sexuality has resonances across the field of social activity and is not limited in its impact to sexuality in itself. As Sedgwick stresses, if the new institutional discourses which propagated the social division of human sexuality according to the homosexual/heterosexual definition expanded rapidly at the turn of the century, this cultural event also functioned as a symptom of a larger social crisis that comprehends such diverse forces as the women's movement and the conflicts centered around nationalism and imperialism. It follows from this that changes in sexual discourse cannot be confined exclusively to the domain of sexuality but have a transformative effect on every aspect of human culture and the social relations of knowledge.[76] In other words, Dil's sexuality calls into question not only Fergus's sexuality but his national and racial identities, which are also founded on idealized constructions of the self.

If there is no sexual relation, that is to say, a binary relation that adds up to one, then there is only the dispersed configuration of incommensurable sexualities. No category of abstract identity escapes the disruptive law of desire that singularizes each being and refuses any undivided associations. Alliances are possible, but they can never be based on the knowledge of an identity that transcends difference. Such an identity would sacrifice knowledge to the imaginary closure of meaning and thus reproduce the

---

[75] J. Rajchman, *Truth and Eros: Foucault, Lacan, and the Question of Ethics* (New York: Routledge, 1991), pp. 43–44.

[76] Sedgwick, *Epistemology of the Closet*, pp. 2–3.

epistemological occlusions of both patriarchy and imperialism. Sexuality constitutes itself as a difference that adds to cultural knowledge without adding up to a system of culture.[77]

Sexual nations

The knowledge that adds to but does not add up is the knowledge of what I will call the sexual nations. With this term, I combine the concept of the incommensurable sexual difference determined by the dialectic of desire with the concept of the political alliance based on symbolic exchange. There may not be any sexual relation, as Lacan would argue; but there are alliances between sexual nations. In *The Crying Game*, the possibility of such an alliance unfolds during the scene in which Dil visits Fergus at work. Fergus is in the process of fitting a window into a wall when he notices Dil walking across the cricket green. According to directions in the original screenplay, *"On the pitch we see the cricketers, distorted through the moving glass of the window. Across the pitch Dil walks, with a lunch basket in her hand, dressed in a very short skirt with high heels. As she approaches the site a chorus of whistles breaks out"* (NJR 232). In the film itself, the camera faces Fergus who holds the window in front of him and looks to the side to see Dil crossing the green. She enters Fergus's visual field from an unexpected angle as she walks across the space that signifies Jody's cultural difference. Just as Jody's relation to cricket subversively posits a cultural difference that adds to, without adding up to, the culture of empire, so Dil's relation to gender articulates her sexual difference as adding to, without adding up to, the normative or rule-governed sexuality determined by the homosexual/heterosexual dyad. Fergus is so disconcerted by the sight of Dil in this context that he drops the frame and breaks the window. In effect, his historical perspective has been shattered. At that moment, the contractor, Deveroux, responds with more stereotypes of race and class, calling Fergus "Pat" as he berates him for breaking the glass. He calls Dil a tart; and when Fergus defends her, he sarcastically calls her a lady. Fergus responds ambivalently that she is neither one nor the other.

[77] On this view of cultural difference, see Homi Bhabha, "DissemiNation: Time, Narrative and the Margins of the Modern Nation," in *The Location of Culture* (London: Routledge, 1994), pp. 162–64.

Cinema, theory, and political responsibility

By standing in *"the gap where the window should be"* (*NJR* 233), Dil
has symbolically taken over Jody's position in Fergus's history. At
the same time, by defending her in front of Deveroux, Fergus
expresses a social connection with her that subverts the identity
thinking common to both imperialist and nationalist ideology.
Fergus has learned to see Dil as "something else" without a
homophobic reaction; implicitly, he now understands that Jody
was also something else and that their bond was never a form of
sexual identification but a reciprocal exchange of incommensurable differences. Such an exchange is not based on mutual
equality, which presupposes a common measure, or reciprocal
compensation for the other's difference understood as lack. It is an
exchange or social tie unmediated by the logic of value. When Dil
starts crying, Fergus plays the crying game for the second time not
only because he is sympathetic but because he has confronted the
intersubjective ground of his own identity, the nonidentity of
identity, or what Derrida would call the totally other. He implicitly
recognizes identity as a position within a game-structure. When
Deveroux interrupts this moment by calling Fergus "Paddy" and
Dil a "bloody tart" one more time, Fergus responds with violent
language: "Did you ever pick your teeth up with broken fingers?"
(*NJR* 235). With this threat, Fergus announces the formation of a
coalition which is based on a metonymical rather than a metaphorical social tie. As Gayatri Spivak has suggested, such a
coalition distinguishes itself from identity politics by constructing
a relation of kinship without identification, though by *kinship* she
probably means something like Stuart Hall's concept of *articulation* as it might be applied to subject-positions as opposed to texts –
in this case, a connection or linkage between subjects "which is not
necessary, determined, absolute and essential for all time."[78] The
crying game expresses not the mutual, reciprocal identification of
love but the impossibility of identification as the condition of
social kinship and exchange.

With the term "sexual nation," I am arguing that beyond the
nationalist ideology there is a relation to nation as the incommensurable. In terms of their histories, Fergus cannot cease to be Irish

[78] Hall, "Postmodernism and Articulation," p. 53. For more on the Spivak reference, see my essay, "History's Echo: Joyce, Nationalism, and Decolonization,"
in *Voices from Elsewhere: Essays on Cross-Cultural Studies*, ed. David Wills and
Patrick Mensah (forthcoming).

anymore than Dil can escape being identified as a homosexual. These identities, however, are not determined exclusively by biology or culture; on the contrary, they are the overdetermined effects of a dialectical interaction between chance and necessity, accident and structure, history and biology. Every human subject is a nation unto itself insofar as its identity is incommensurable and therefore not exchangeable through the economic formulas of identity thinking. This does not mean that people cannot change but rather that change cannot be programmed, predicted, or manipulated with absolute certainty as to the result. Every human subject is a sexual nation that can enter into negotiations and constitute alliances with the other. Yet the sexual nation is neither self-identical nor fully autonomous. For the identity of the nation would require the rule of equivalence, or what Marx called exchange value, by which the multitude of irreducible and ungovernable differences are constituted as autonomous wholes, each one reflecting the greater whole of which it is a part. The term "sexual nation" represents the determinate negation of social identity. In a sense, there could never be any nationalist struggle without the eruption of the sexual nations that construct alliances with each other not through the discovery of a common identity but through the refusal of an oppressive identity and the symbolic exchange of suffering. The nationalist ideology which arises out of the struggle against imperialist domination or hegemonic culture inevitably represses the movement of human desire that animated it in the first place. But if it is in the nature of desire to be repressed, it is also true that historically, whether we speak of colonial or postcolonial repression, desire always gets a new start from the very law that represses it.

The sexual nation, therefore, is the unstable law of desire, the law that must preexist the movement of desire and the creation of culture. As Frantz Fanon wrote, "The nation is not only the condition of culture, its fruitfulness, its continuous renewal, and its deepening. It is also a necessity. It is the fight for national existence which sets culture moving and opens to it the doors of creation."[79] In this thought of the nation as origin of culture, however, Fanon distinguished between nationalism and national consciousness, between an ideology of national identity and the

[79] F. Fanon, *The Wretched of the Earth*, trans. Constance Farrington (New York: Grove Weidenfeld, 1991), p. 244.

self-subversive dialectic of collective human desire. Nationalism focuses on the past; but national consciousness is the necessary condition of the future, not as utopia but as permanent cultural revolution. Nationalism as an ideology depends on the definition of the nation as an *imagined community*, to use Benedict Anderson's term,[80] that occludes social differences in the interest of social identities. The sexual nation is the site of the incommensurable from which culture and national consciousness originate. Nationalism constitutes legal subjects that are mirror reflections of one another, while national consciousness arises from acts of symbolic exchange between points of incommensurable difference.

Each difference is a nation, and each nation is sexual because it is constituted by the difference between the satisfaction of human need and the demand for absolute love. That difference is desire. As Lacan states it,

In place of the unconditional aspect of demand, desire substitutes the "absolute" condition: in effect this condition releases that part of the proof of love which is resistant to the satisfaction of a need. Thus desire is neither the appetite for satisfaction, nor the demand for love, but the difference resulting from the subtraction of the first from the second, the very phenomenon of their splitting.[81]

As Lacan suggests, it is the splitting of need from demand, this division of/as hope, that creates desire as the absolute condition. Without this division, hope would quickly become despair since the immediate satisfaction of physical need requires the disappointment of unconditional demand. Desire divides hope and thus saves it from authoritarian utopias and the illusion of progress; it makes hope particular and concrete in the *time of the now*. By accepting Dil's sexuality and admitting that he cares, Fergus surrenders his national/sexual identity as Irish/man to a desire whose law cannot be mastered or rationalized or reduced to an essence. In other words, he confronts his own singular sexuality beyond the categories that have defined and measured it so that it can fit into the social imaginary like a window into a wall. Since the frame and the glass have been shattered, there will be a change of frame and a change of view. It is desire that shatters the glass and

---

[80] B. Anderson, *Imagined Communities: Reflections on the Origin and Spread of Nationalism*, rev. edn. (London: Verso, 1991), pp. 6–7.

[81] J. Lacan, *Feminine Sexuality: Jacques Lacan and the "école freudienne,"* ed. J. Mitchell and J. Rose, trans. J. Rose (New York: Norton, 1985), p. 81.

becomes the absolute condition for the survival of hope. The mechanism by which this survival assumes a material form is what Freud called *sublimation*. According to Lacan, "if one looks at the most esoteric formulation of the concept in Freud, in the context of his representing it as realized preeminently in the activity of the artist, it literally means that man has the possibility of making his desires tradable or salable in the form of products." Sublimation makes possible the satisfaction of need without the repression of desire and shows that "desire is nothing more than the metonymy of the discourse of demand." Escaping the metaphorical closure of repressed desire requires the metonymic shift of desire away from identity. As this shift, sublimation "is change as such": "the properly metonymic relation between one signifier and another that we call desire is not a new object or a previous object, but the change of object in itself" (*E* 293).

For Lacan, desire is either repressed or sublimated. If it is repressed, then its effect as the absolute condition, and therefore limit, of demand undergoes denegation through the metaphorical closure of the symptom; and thus the impossible demand is compelled to find its only possible satisfaction in the absolute authority of the master or the state or death itself. If desire is sublimated, it is unleashed on the symbolic as the absolute condition of culture, a source of its continuous renewal; and only the most rigid traditionalism can subject this metonymic process to rule by metaphor. It is the difference between the fascist identification with the leader as symbol of the nation, on the one hand, and the postcolonial appropriation of a game like cricket as the expression of national consciousness, on the other. As Rajchman stresses, unlike repression that produces symptoms or compulsions, sublimation "acquires a 'public' approval, or is introduced into a socially acceptable place." Curiously, Rajchman then misquotes Lacan: "Sublimation ... is always individual."[82] Lacan's French says quite the opposite: "toute sublimation n'est pas possible chez l'individu" or "complete sublimation is not possible for the individual" (*E* 91).[83] Still, Rajchman's error is a telling one since it underscores the relation of sublimation to the singularity of desire. For Rajchman, the public that sublimation

---

[82] Rajchman, *Truth and Eros*, p. 72–73.

[83] J. Lacan, *L'éthique de la psychanalyse 1959–1960*, book 7 of *Le séminaire*, ed. J.-A. Miller (Paris: Seuil, 1986), p. 110.

requires is not based on a common denominator or collective identification. Rather, sublimation constitutes itself as the public space "in which our singular perverse bodies may make contact with one another through the creation of beautiful objects that stand for them, without thereby abolishing what makes them singular." Such a space does not create a public based on the pursuit of common goods or on identification with common ideals. It involves a different bond.[84]

In *The Crying Game*, the public of sublimation is the community of the Metro, which could never be mistaken for a utopia but nevertheless captures in microcosm the multicultural, multisexual *nation* that is postcolonial Britain. This would not be the official nation but the sublimated nation. The "beautiful objects" that stand for "our singular perverse bodies" in this space are those bodies themselves made into beautiful objects. This is the meaning of Dil's performance and the performance of the others who act out the unmasterable law of desire on the stage. The bond that defines this community is the symbolic exchange of the sublimated body; but although this body expresses the singularity of desire, it does not follow that sublimation is always individual. On the contrary, it is only through the exchange of the unexchangeable that the body can be sublimated in order to give ground to new values. Sublimation is intersubjective; it disrupts the body's autonomy as an object of desire (the *objet a*) by subjecting it to metonymic displacement, a change of object. In the scene where everyone in the bar joins in singing "The White Cliffs of Dover," there appears a form of bonding that contrasts dramatically with the use of intimidation and violence by the characters in the IRA. The song itself, though it nostalgically recalls the British empire before the eruption of postcolonial difference, has been forced to undergo a change of object in this polymorphously perverse community. As Dil and Fergus dance, there is a tracking shot of the clientele standing against the bar, with Col in the background singing along with them in a deep bass voice. The camera comes to rest on the silent figure of Dave, who looks lonely and isolated. By trying to force Dil to live out his sexual fantasies, Dave has betrayed the community. Yet he is not totally excluded; and the composition of the shot, like the song itself, seems almost to invite

[84] Rajchman, *Truth and Eros*, p. 73.

him back into the community if he can undergo a change of object.

The sexual nation is neither one nor many but the identity of nonidentity and the incommensurable difference whose complete sublimation is not possible for the individual. As such an entity, Fergus is confronted with a seemingly irresolvable contradiction between the ideology of nationalism and the law of desire, which carries within it the implicit contradiction between gender and sex. For can it really be said that Neil Jordan escapes the tragic ending that he associates with the works of O'Connor and Behan from which, in some way, his story derives? Or is it that happiness, since it can only be achieved through the division of hope, has its own tragic dimension? It seems to me that the last question posed by *The Crying Game*, the question that it fails to answer and the one that destroys its illusion and thus reveals its historical truth, is the question of misogyny as the destiny of sexual difference. I use the term "destiny" in this context to signify not transcendent fate but historical determination. This determination can be reversed but not without social transformation through collective political action. If sexuality is inextricably bound to the historical constructions of national, racial, and gender differences, it is the hatred of women that continues to support these binary economies even after the system of patriarchal–imperialist representations has entered into a state of crisis. *The Crying Game* poses this question: can we escape this destiny or are we doomed to repeat it? By failing to answer this question definitively, it almost subverts the hope it tries to construct.

Desire and hope

The signifier of destiny is the national identity that Fergus loses at the farmhouse when he fails to kill Jody, the signifier that follows him across the sea and undergoes its own version of sublimation or change of object. This phallic signifier passes to Jude who, as the symbol of postcolonial Ireland, fuses the sublime and the beautiful. In effect, the symbolic republic as the object of revolutionary desire changes into its other, death as the end of history. Fergus thinks he can lose himself and his national identity, that he can get out of something; but every time he seeks to unravel the strings that tie him to the national destiny, he finds that he has only made the knot tighter in ways that he never expected. He leaves Jude and the IRA behind only to find them again where he least expects them and in a *tougher* form. After Jude hands the phallus back to Fergus in the shape of an assassin's gun, he concocts a plan to save Dil; but, as destiny would have it, Dil takes the phallus away from him. Fergus tries to change Dil into the man she really is and hide her from Jude and Peter, but in the end he has to tell her the truth about the death of her soldier. Dil finally takes his gun and ties him to her bed, which represents the historical destiny of his own sexual ambivalence. When he fails to keep his appointment with Jude and Peter, Peter does the hit and sacrifices his own life in Fergus's place. Jude then goes to Dil's flat to kill both Fergus and Dil but fails to realize that the phallus is no longer hers. It now belongs to Dil.

Dil is the one who *real*izes Fergus's destiny by killing Jude. For it turns out that the national identity Fergus tries to escape harbors the object of his love as well as the object of his hate. It is this unity of love and hate in the national identity as woman, as the object of desire, that Fergus both runs away from and continues to seek; for the more he distances himself from this symbolic woman, the more *real* she becomes. Consequently, the more he hates her, the more he loves her. Lacan insisted that "there is no love without hate"; and the way man withdraws from this economy is to confuse the woman with "what it is she comes from," whether it is God or some ideal like the symbolic republic.[85] In the original French of *Encore*, Lacan writes what Jacqueline Rose translates as "what it is she comes from" in this way: "ce dont elle jouit."[86] In other words, it is not a question of the origin of woman but of an experience, a sexual experience beyond the phallus and the human economy of love/hate. Fergus is torn between Dil and Jude, between a different kind of love that virtually explodes his heterosexual identity and the absolute expression of love/hate, which commands him to sacrifice his life in order to resolve the contradiction between desire as the absolute condition and the drive as the absolute demand. I would speculate that in the unconscious Fergus knows everything that he should have known about Jody and Dil. He desires something he thinks they have, a passion beyond the phallus, beyond the gender division, beyond the misogyny at the heart of

[85] Lacan, *Feminine Sexuality*, p. 160.
[86] J. Lacan, *Encore*, book 20 of *Le séminaire*, ed. J.-A. Miller (Paris: Seuil, 1975), p. 82.

conventional love and the love of nation itself. Ironically, as long as Fergus believed in the transcendent law of the symbolic republic and the principle of self-sacrifice it imposed on him, as long as he could keep the faith, in accordance with Jude's command, he was able to master his own sexual ambivalence. When that faith was unconsciously called into question by Jody, Fergus discovered a desire that bypasses the laws of gender and of national identity. In pursuing Dil, he imagines that he wants another object of love; but what he really wants is the change of object, or a relation to the Thing. He relates to Dil not as the object of love/hate but as the subject of his "care," a symbolic exchange that does not presuppose binary opposition.

Nevertheless, he cannot escape his own history. Though he wants to save Dil, he has no intention of missing his appointment with death, who is the real *one* he loves and hates. And he would have succeeded if Dil had not taken the phallus away from him and confronted with it the signifier of his love/hate, Jude. Dil wants to kill Fergus; but her ambivalence prevents her from doing it. When Jude arrives, however, that ambivalence is divided between the heterosexual couple. Dil can love Fergus by hating Jude, who now embodies the law of gender that Dil associates with Jody's death. Jude, of course, is not an innocent victim; she has come to kill what does not conform to the law of her own identity, not only those who have lost the faith like Fergus but the racial and sexual other like Dil. After she is shot, she screams at Fergus: "Get that thing off me, Fergus – ... I said get it off me, Fergus." There is no mistaking the equation of racial difference and death in the swan-song of Jude's ideological existence. Meanwhile Dil has become the instrument of misogyny as she denounces "those tits and that ass" which Jude used to capture and finally kill her soldier (*NJR* 264–65). After she kills Jude, Dil turns the gun on Fergus; but she cannot kill him, because, as she says, Jody will not let her.

With the gun in hand, Dil is completely under the rule of the phallic signifier. Fergus has transferred to her the thing he tried to escape; and she puts the gun in her mouth to complete the process by becoming a thing. He takes it away in time, however, and does what he has never done before. He assumes responsibility for his own destiny. Before Jude arrived at the apartment, Dil had insisted that Fergus make a pledge. She made him tell her that he loves her and then asked him, "What would you do for me?" Fergus admitted that he would do anything for her. As Dil started crying, she untied his bonds and finally asked, "And you'll never leave me?" (*NJR* 263). Fergus tells her what she wants to hear; and she likes hearing it even though she believes that he lies. But Fergus is not altogether lying though he may not know the truth. He loves Dil in some way that he can never say or represent or even recognize, a way beyond the economy of love/hate that determined his relation to Jude. Fergus breaks his promise never to leave Dil because only by leaving her and going to prison can he be with her and love her. So Dil speaks truthfully when she comments later, "No greater love, as the man says" (*NJR* 267). Dil refers to John 15: 13: "Greater love hath no man than this, that a man lay down his life for his friends." The irony is that the word "friend" in the context of *The Crying Game* must necessarily carry a connotation of homoerotic love; but it also articulates a different, incommensurable love beyond love/hate. When Lacan argues that the sexual relation does not exist, he means that it "does not know that it is only the desire to be One";[87] but there is the possibility of a relationship that is not founded on the desire to be one but starts from the suspension of desire in the recognition of irreducible difference. In *The Crying Game*, Fergus refuses to be Dil's lover; and one could argue that the relation between them is not a sexual one in the way that Lacan understands that term. It is a relation that is based not on the desire to be one but on the knowledge that two sexualities can never add up. Žižek may be partially right, therefore, in arguing that this is "an 'impossible' love which will never be consummated": "Herein resides the film's paradox and, at the same time, its irresistible charm: far from denouncing heterosexual love as a product of male repression, it renders the precise circumstances in which this love can today retain its absolute, unconditional character."[88] In effect, heterosexual love has become the absolute norm of perversity, the norm of the non-universalization of sexual identity, the impossible love that makes desire into the prison-house of the body instead of the other way around. It is the absolute condition of an unconditional demand. But ironically, heterosexual love can maintain its

---

[87] Lacan, *Encore*, p. 12.
[88] S. Žižek, *The Metastases of Enjoyment: Six Essays on Woman and Causality* (London: Verso, 1994), p. 105.

normative force only by deconstructing itself and thus displacing the binary system that constitutes its identity in the first place. Heterosexual love redeems itself by puncturing the illusion of its self-identity as the norm of a relation that does not exist. It is no longer the love between man and woman but the love of the Other, of the Thing.

In the introduction to the screenplay, Jordan says of the final scene in the prison: "But for the lovers, it was the irony of what divided them that allowed them to smile" (*NJR* xiii). They are divided not only by the glass screen, which in a sense symbolizes the seeming transparency of gender difference, but by the Real itself, a sexual difference that resists representation. Fergus remains, in some sense, a heterosexual, while Dil indicates absolutely no interest in undergoing a surgical change of sex. Fergus refuses to be called "honey" and "my love," while Dil refuses to stop "loving" him. Yet they are able to smile because they know that the divisions between them are the absolute condition of their love. Their differences are the intersubjective ground from which the possibility of social relationship through mimetic adaptation proceeds in the first place. It is through such a mutual adaptation or symbolic exchange that hope arises as a form of historical consciousness.

The tragedy of *The Crying Game* is that it creates *a kind of happiness* only by failing to resolve the historical contradictions that determine the conflicts it dramatizes. These contradictions between freedom and law, sex and gender, desire and demand, are condensed into the figure of misogyny. When the film ends, misogyny still dominates the relations between men and women. The father's law still condemns the mother to death, and the sons are virtually paralyzed before his authority. The historical truth of *The Crying Game* lies in its failure to overcome this contradiction and thus transcend its own historical context. This is not to say that the film remains politically neutral toward the relations of power that have a vested interest in maintaining the binarisms of contemporary culture. Fergus's solution can be considered more than a personal one to the extent that it imagines new forms of alliance between different sexes and nations, or between the different parties who experience victimization in the postcolonial world. Yet *The Crying Game* finally negates itself and the happiness it promises: the price of love is the death of the other and submission to the unquestionable authority of the state. The mother can threaten and cajole, but the father keeps the keys to the prison-house. This self-negation subverts any totalizing interpretation of the sort that would resolve all contradictions and eliminate the heterogeneity of the work of art as a historical symptom. Such a symptom expresses the existence of desire as the absolute condition of history. It also expresses the division of hope between the impossibility of utopia and the necessity of change. In other words, as long as there is desire, there is hope.

4

❖❖❖

Deconstruction and responsibility: the question of freedom in the place of the undecidable

❖❖❖

What does criticism want?

What does it have to have to constitute a beginning? Does it have to want or be wanting as the condition of saying anything? Does the process begin with some form of absence?

Or at least with a difference?

I have tried to raise the question of the political in art in a context in which such a question is hardly novel. Yet I have raised the question of the political only to shortcircuit the question itself. If art cannot be politically correct, can it be political in any meaningful sense? To give an example, in her more negative reading of *The Crying Game*, bell hooks suggests that the film is "conservative–reactionary" by comparison with a more conventional Hollywood melodrama, *The Bodyguard*. The former suggests that transvestites and homosexuals in general hate women to the extent of battering and killing them, that heterosexual white men will surrender their homophobia and enter homosexual relationships with black men in order "to get that 'down-home' service only a 'black female' can give," and that the world should just forget about the messages of recent race and gender theorists and become the exclusive domain of white heterosexual couples.[1] Hooks implies that art can and should be politically correct, that content must take precedence over form in the determination of value. Yet I would argue that she actually engages with *The Crying Game* in a provocative and useful way to drive home to those who

---

[1] b. hooks, "Seduction and Betrayal," *Visions* (Fall 1993), 51.

would dismiss a film like *The Bodyguard* out of hand as non-art that there is always something more at stake in any kind of work than can be derived from the values of a traditional concept of the aesthetic. I read her essay after completing the first draft of my essay on *The Crying Game*; but I would like to think that her position and that of others, which more often came to me by word of mouth, began to haunt my work through every subsequent revision. In some sense, what I have written responds to them, but I do not think it refutes them. There is a place for debate and refutation; but while such an act can emerge from the need to defend the stakes of a particular field or to demand the right to a voice, it does not get to the heart of interpretation as a desiring process. Derrida uses the word *specters* to refer to those forces, those voices of the other, that haunt any writing, both inside and outside.[2] These specters are the possible differences of desire that could, and in some sense always do, structure its meaning. There is no escaping the function of desire in the production of meaning; and the challenge of criticism is to engage desire in this process without ceding it to the formal closure of a *final* meaning. Every interpretation is haunted by the interpretations it excludes. Responsibility in this process is not only a question of content but of style. One needs to leave some space, some margin of uncertainty, for the specters that form the margin of the text, that are both inside and outside.

My purpose in this chapter is to expand the arguments about reading as an act with political and ethical content to a larger institutional context in which I can make clear the limitations and responsibilities of such an act. I realize that reading and interpretation are not necessarily the most important forms of political activity, but the accumulation of these acts in an institution like the university is an important dimension of contemporary culture, not only in the West but throughout the world. I approach this question through the work of Derrida because Derrida has foregrounded the concept of responsibility in the ethics of reading and discussion in a way that is crucial to understanding the social and political responsibilities of academic work. My strategy is a somewhat defensive reading of Derrida because, ironically, the political and ethical side of his work has been observed best by his

[2] J. Derrida, *Specters of Marx: The State of the Debt, the Work of Mourning, and the New International*, trans. P. Kamuf (New York: Routledge, 1994).

critics and overt opponents. My goal is to connect the Adornian concept of autonomy as a historical category (I should even say, historically variable category) and the Derridean concept of undecidability as the historical limit of any discursive theorizing that calls forth the necessity of ethics in critical discussion. I move from an ethics of reading and discussion in Derrida to the contemporary institutional context of the university, where one can see this ethics in action. In other words, I show that the criticisms of Derrida which derive from and, to some extent, culminate in the work of Habermas – criticisms that claim to expose a certain political irresponsibility in Derrida's work – can be turned inside out and made to support an argument for the political significance of Derrida's work. I would not describe this significance as a political philosophy because it does not attempt to be a systematic theory of political power, the state, and the economy. Rather, it theorizes what would constitute the form of responsibility in any political philosophy.[3] It also addresses some of the crucial debates about the nature of freedom and the ethics of intellectual work that have emerged in social institutions like the university.

Derrida and his critics

The politics of art and interpretation has recently been the subject of studies that challenge the methodology of deconstruction, and in particular the work of Derrida. Patrick Colm Hogan, for example, argues for the political inefficacy of deconstruction – and by implication of most of the trends in Euro-American literary theory over the last two decades – as a form of irrationalism that can be dismissed almost as easily as Dr. Johnson once dismissed Berkeley's idealism by kicking a stone. Hogan overtly claims to speak with the authority of reason; and one underlying presupposition of his study, *The Politics of Interpretation*, is that deconstruction ignores, avoids, or somehow undermines that authority and the concept of truth derived from it.

By contrast, I want to argue that deconstruction is a rational, perhaps hyperrational, critical practice governed by a strict use of logic. Nevertheless, it is the aim of deconstruction to push logic

---

[3] See D. Cornell, *The Philosophy of the Limit* (New York: Routledge, 1992), p. 170. All of this work is relevant to the present discussion.

and the principle of reason to the point at which one discovers the limit of such totalizing concepts and systems. This limit is the undecidable. It operates more or less like the metamathematical concept of undecidability. It refers to a proposition that emerges at some point in the elaboration of a system of thought and produces a crisis in that system by suggesting that its premises are incomplete. One can determine an undecidable in thought only through a rigorous practice of logic just as one can determine the undecidable in metamathematics only by reconstructing the entire series of premises from which a true proposition of number theory is supposed to derive. According to Gödel's theorem, sooner or later in number theory one generates a proposition that is true and yet contradicts the theoretical premises of the system. If one writes a new premise to account for this undecidable proposition, one will generate yet another undecidable, and this process continues to infinity. In other words, in terms of its theoretical systematicity, metamathematics never reaches closure or completion. Jonathan Culler observes that the demonstration of Gödel's theorem has not led mathematicians to give up their field out of some sort of despair over the inadequacies of mathematical reason.[4] It does not suggest that mathematics is irrational or phantasmatic. In the same way, Derrida's work is not vilified as rational analysis because it leads to concepts that appear to contradict or undermine the systematic premises from which they derive.

Hogan repeats what has become almost a cliché in some of the more disingenuous arguments against deconstruction. He argues that Derrida has privileged writing over speech, a point that I would flatly contest and that Derrida has rebutted on numerous occasions. Hogan treats this reading as if it were uncontroversial and self-evident and then leaps to this categorical judgment: "To valorize writing is to reinforce a prejudice which tends to or has in the past tended to exclude Blacks, as well as Southerners, Irish, lower class English, and others, from intellectual dialogue."[5] In response, I would argue that Derrida has never valorized writing over speech but has systematically and logically demonstrated that those characteristics attributed to writing in a specific philo-

---

[4] J. Culler, *On Deconstruction: Theory and Criticism after Structuralism* (Ithaca: Cornell University Press, 1982), p. 133.

[5] P. C. Hogan, *The Politics of Interpretation: Ideology, Professionalism, and the Study of Literature* (New York: Oxford University Press, 1990), p. 78.

sophical tradition which privileges speech over writing with
respect to the proximity of truth are also the characteristics
attributed to speech at another moment in the same discourse.[6] For
example, in *Of Grammatology*, his reading of Rousseau reaches
conclusions about the logic of the supplement as the thought of a
writing *before the letter*. Derrida argues that Rousseau cannot
imagine a writing "that takes place *before* and *within* speech." For
this reason, he participates in the production of what Derrida calls
the metaphysics of presence which presupposes "the simple
exteriority of death to life, evil to good, mask to face, writing to
speech." The supplement breaks away from these terms by
refusing the metaphysical separation that they posit. It does not
privilege the signified over the signifier, presence over representation, speech over writing.[7] When Derrida speaks of a writing
before the letter, or before the distinction between writing and
speech, he carefully distinguishes it from writing in its restricted
sense. Such *general writing* is not posited as a metaphysical truth
but as a critical response to a specific argument within the history
of philosophy. Its truth, in other words, is relational and historical.
The argument Derrida challenges (that speech is closer to truth
than writing) leads to the concept of a general writing when the
premises of the argument are driven to their logical end without
excluding any logical possibility. This deconstruction of the
relation between writing and speech does not necessarily lead to a
reinforcement of the historical exclusion of those social and ethnic
groups with less access to the technology of writing and probably
leads to the opposite by challenging the hierarchy that privileges
one over the other. Writing, even when it is valorized, is never
exclusively an instrument for the domination of cultures and
peoples. James Joyce, Zora Neale Hurston, Chinua Achebe, and
Ishmael Reed all use writing to validate the authority of repressed
oral traditions. By the same token, imperialist culture has never
hesitated to use the appeal to the orality of native cultures in order
to delegitimate the writing of minority or postcolonial authors.
(On this subject, read the first chapter of Joyce's *Ulysses* in which
the Englishman Haines, a student of Irish language and literature,

---

[6] J. Derrida, *Margins of Philosophy*, trans. A. Bass (Chicago: University of Chicago
Press, 1982), pp. 7–10.
[7] J. Derrida, *Of Grammatology*, trans. G. C. Spivak (Baltimore: The Johns Hopkins
University Press, 1976), p. 315.

makes both the aging working-class Irishwoman and the potential young author feel ashamed for not knowing Gaelic. Or, better yet, read Yambo Ouologuem's brutally sarcastic portrait of the anthropologist and collector Frobenius, author of *African Genesis*, in the character Shrobenius in *Le devoir de violence*.)

More can be said about Hogan's critique of deconstruction, but I want to get at the larger implications of his position; and, as a first step in that direction, I need to explain why a genuine politics of interpretation requires the concept of the undecidable. Hogan warns us away from the path of deconstruction as a form of irrationality that cannot lead to liberation or freedom;[8] but his procedure ignores not only the logical necessity of the undecidable but the historical symptoms it generates. Can there possibly exist any concept of freedom that does not lead directly to the experience of the undecidable? I will try to explain what I mean. Hogan is correct when he associates liberation with rationality because freedom has become the name of a post-Enlightenment discourse whose first premises are the principle of reason and the autonomy of reason implied by that principle. The principle of reason ("Nothing is without reason, no effect is without cause" – Leibniz) may have no other reason than reason itself, as Derrida has pointed out;[9] but it still defines and delimits the world in such a way that freedom becomes a necessary possibility. Under the rule of reason, human actions and thoughts no longer have to be referred to God or to some other transcendent authority; they are judged according to the rules of logic and some notion of internal consistency. Reason itself may be what Kenneth Burke calls a God-term; but if we accept the principle of reason we posit a world in which everything has a reason and call into question any system of rules governing social relationships that appeals to some absolute authority beyond human thought and society itself.

In *The Philosophical Discourse of Modernity*, Habermas describes the conditions of post-Enlightenment discourse: "modernity can and will no longer borrow the criteria by which it takes its orientation from the models supplied by another epoch; *it has to create normativity out of itself*. Modernity sees itself cast back upon itself without any possibility of escape."[10] This concept of modern-

---

[8] Hogan, *Politics*, p. 81.
[9] J. Derrida, "The Principle of Reason: The University in the Eyes of Its Pupils," *Diacritics* 13.3 (1983), 7.   [10] Habermas, *Discourse of Modernity*, p. 7.

ity refers to the history of thought since Descartes, who, if he had to accept God's benevolence as a matter of faith, nonetheless subjected everything else to the principle of reason. John McGowan, whose critique of Derrida in *Postmodernism and Its Critics* more directly concerns the question of freedom that we are interested in here, clarifies Habermas's concept when he describes modernity as a condition in which society legitimates itself by reference to its own "self-generated principles," without appeal to any transcendent metaphysical authority or truth. McGowan also focuses on the key term that defines the discourses of modernity at every phase of their history: *autonomy.* This term names the process by which society forges its own practices and recognizes its ground without appealing to any external determination or influence. Still, McGowan qualifies this viewpoint in suggesting that autonomy may not be a predictable guide. For one thing, the concept of autonomy derives from humanism which claims that human beings make themselves and the world around them. Since most postmodernists are antihumanists, they have usually denied the possibility of autonomy as an actual social condition while insisting on its "pernicious consequences." From another perspective, the value of autonomy as a concept depends on where it is located in the social order. If autonomy resides in some Hegelian notion of "Reason as a totality," then the actions of individual subjects will be determined from the outside by that totality and, to that extent, will not be autonomous. By contrast, liberalism advocates the autonomy of the individual insofar as he or she has the freedom to choose his or her own ends and the means of achieving them. Between these extremes lies the Kantian division of the world into the autonomous realms of pure reason, practical reason, and judgment, which can be correlated with Habermas's argument about the differentiated social systems of modernity (the economic, the legal/administrative, and the aesthetic) which break away from the social totality or the *lifeworld* as the horizon of social interaction in order "to develop autonomously according to their own traditions, logics, and procedures, with little interference from other systems or from the practices of the lifeworld."[11]

McGowan's observations serve to complicate the argument I want to make. The post-Enlightenment concept of freedom neces-

---

[11] J. McGowan, *Postmodernism and Its Critics* (Ithaca: Cornell University Press, 1991), pp. 3–5.

sarily produces the concept of autonomy as its concrete expression. It is the autonomy of *reason as a totality* that makes freedom in this world possible. Individuals could not act freely if they could not appeal to some form of autonomous reason against the claims of unquestioned tradition or dogmatic faith. There may be a God who created reason, but after that, reason is autonomous and everything that follows from reason requires no further justification, no other outside authority. If, at the other extreme, liberalism insists on the autonomy of the individual who is free to act according to his or her own interests, that ideology also presupposes the autonomy of *reason as a totalized form* within the individual. The basis of the individual's claim to autonomy is the appeal to such reason; and at the same time, the seat of reason lies in the individual. The reason individuals can choose their own ends and the means of achieving such ends is that they all have the same access to universal reason. This does not mean, of course, that any choice made by an individual is always equal to the choice made by any other individual. Reason has generated rules and procedures for determining when a choice derives from rational grounds and when it appeals to some other ground, including irrational faith or unmitigated power. Consequently, although McGowan does not make this perfectly clear in the passage I have referred to, the autonomy of reason as a totality and the autonomy of the individual are two sides of the same coin. There can be no principle of reason without the assertion of reason's autonomy; and the autonomy of reason necessarily produces and guarantees the autonomy of the individual as a subject who can appeal to reason.

Now, according to McGowan, postmodernism has produced a critique of the principle of reason insofar as it makes the rather strange claim that autonomy is both impossible and pernicious. McGowan implies that postmodernism contradicts itself and the principle of reason when it produces an ethical judgment of something it claims cannot exist. Since he considers Derrida a postmodern theorist, he presumably attributes this kind of thinking to Derrida. I will have more to say about his overall critique of Derrida in a moment, but let me say in this context that I can find no moment in Derrida when he dismisses a concept like autonomy as simply pernicious. On the contrary, it seems to me that McGowan misconstrues what Derrida might call the undecidability of a term or proposition with a denial of its existence. Derrida has never denied something like the autonomy of the subject or of reason, or, for that matter, the autonomy of the aesthetic (for example, in the case of literature), economics, or the law (in line with the Habermasian reappropriation of Weber and Kant). McGowan wants to substitute the term *semiautonomy* for autonomy as a more realistic description of how the sphere of normed social activity works; but this gesture misses the point of Derridean critique altogether. There is either a claim to autonomy or there is not: these are all-or-nothing propositions. It seems to me that words like "semiautonomy" or "relative autonomy" (after Althusser) are useful insofar as they clarify the limits of the concept of autonomy but misleading when they imply that there is a pure autonomy to which we can oppose, or from which we can derive, "relative" or "semi" versions. The point of a deconstructive critique of autonomy is not to prove that autonomy does not exist (although the question of its existence may be problematic and even unanswerable). The point is rather that the concept itself is impure or incomplete at its origin or center. Relative autonomy is simply autonomy. Semiautonomy is simply autonomy.

Having said this, I may seem to be going back to Adorno's theory of the autonomy of art and, in particular, to the concept of the individual work of art as a *windowless monad*. Unquestionably, Adorno offers the most rigorous analysis that I am familiar with of the autonomous work of art, an analysis which does not lead him to the conclusion that there is no autonomy or that the solution to the problem lies in words like "semiautonomy" or "relative autonomy" but that autonomy is determined both internally and externally by the history of form, social context, the economy, and so forth. For Adorno, the autonomous work of art is the absolute commodity or the defetishizing fetish because autonomy is the form of its social determination – or, rather, overdetermination, since we are not talking about a simple cause-and-effect relationship. Does this make Adorno a deconstructionist? I would rather say what Derrida says when he explains to Gerald Graff why deconstruction is not inherently conservative or revolutionary: deconstruction is "'inherently' nothing at all" because from the start it calls into question the oppositions between essence and accident, proper and improper, extrinsic and inherent, on the basis of which such a claim about deconstruction's defining qualities would have to be made.[12] Adorno is not a deconstructionist, but then deconstruction is *inherently nothing at all*. Still, Adorno's analysis of the autonomous work of art certainly implies the deconstruction of the concept of autonomy, a point to which I will return later.

I am suggesting that autonomy is not so much the condition as the realization of the post-Enlightenment concept of freedom. McGowan argues that postmodernist critiques contradict themselves by, on the one hand, ruling out autonomy as impossible and pernicious, and, on the other, adopting "strategies of resistance" that appear to contradict their own implicit social theories. He says that all of the different versions of postmodernism postulate a concept of *negative freedom* that resembles the modernist concept of autonomy. His alternative is *positive freedom* that presupposes a more strict view of authority as the ground for legitimating intellectual work and social arrangements. The overemphasis of negative freedom, in his view, leads to a situation in which the postmodern theorist refuses to make any distinction between legitimate and illegitimate social action. I find this argument very compelling, for McGowan takes into account the antifoundationalism that has dominated most postmodern discourses and points out that foundational truths are not required for the maintenance of the current capitalist social system. Furthermore, he makes a strong case for the failure of the postmodernist critique of totality to challenge the capitalist system because the latter's tendency to alienate the individual and compartmentalize the social experiences derived from economic and cultural differences can easily incorporate the celebration of difference as a fetish in its own right. By comparison with Hogan's, McGowan's critique of postmodern theory seems more rigorous. Hogan concludes his book with his own speculative description of the anarchist university, the details of which seem incoherent and finally trivial. McGowan, however, has touched a nerve. He counters the "anarchistic heterogeneity" of postmodernism with the argument that the capitalist principle of universal exchangeability can only be restrained in such a way as to give ground to a true pluralism of interests by the construction of political and ethical norms that become the ground of social consensus. Freedom itself requires

[12] J. Derrida, *Limited Inc*, trans. S. Weber and J. Mehlman (Evanston: Northwestern University Press, 1988), p. 141.

membership in a society that is based on specific and universally accepted terms which "are not foundational but are produced by society itself." Social identity, in other words, is based on positive freedom, which must be absolutely differentiated from negative freedom. The latter valorizes exclusion, otherness, and distance; and this valorization has characterized postmodern theories from the start and foregrounded their "strange affinity with traditional liberalism." According to McGowan, only the most irresponsible sort of political neutrality could reject the claim that "a humanly created norm of democracy" is the key to Western political culture and makes possible legitimate human actions that can ensure and expand the realm of freedom.[13]

McGowan's critique advances deconstructive cultural theory in the right direction. Still, I think we have to analyze his criticisms with some care. When people start waving the banners of freedom and democracy, there is always the risk that we will get in line to make our commitments before we have given these terms any real thought. I would still insist that deconstruction is not anarchy but a form of caution before the moment of decision, before the act of taking responsibility. It is an *ethical* imperative. Frequently, in the criticisms of deconstruction that seem to emerge from everywhere these days, there is the unstated presupposition that deconstructive thought disables one from political engagement. I have seen no compelling evidence that would support such an empirical claim. For example, most of the political positions that Hogan aligns himself with in *The Politics of Interpretation* are identical to my own. I do appreciate the possible significance of his making his positions public. However, I do not think we gain much from a bragging contest between university professors about who has the strongest credentials in the realm of political activism. There is no evidence that the critics of deconstruction or of poststructuralist theory or of postmodernism in general, however one understands that term, have been more politically effective than those they criticize.

In any case, Derrida himself has frequently associated his name and more than his name with specific political causes; but if he has usually avoided the celebration of his own political engagement in the manner of Hogan, it may be in part that he has another ethical

---

[13] McGowan, *Postmodernism*, pp. 2, 15, 28.

imperative, another political duty as a critical philosopher. Before there can be any political engagement or decision, there must be the assumption of a responsibility that I would call the moment of a deconstructive politics. Such a politics does not naively insist on the negative freedom of individuals over and against the positive freedom derived from laws that determine membership in society as a whole. Deconstructive politics calls into question the bipolar structure of positive and negative freedom that McGowan takes for granted and on which he bases his critique of Derrida. This interrogation does not mean that one category slides over into the other. On the contrary, although Derrida does not use this particular terminology, he maintains in his writing a rigorous distinction between what would be called positive freedom, on the one hand, and negative freedom, on the other. He even insists on the duty of assuming and defending what he identifies as the historically *European* norm of democracy, as I will show in a moment.

McGowan discusses a reading of Levinas in which Derrida formulates an "encounter with the absolutely-other." This other is neither a representation, nor a boundary, nor a self-identical concept. The ego and the other are not dominated by their relationship to one another as self-contained totalities. This is true because the concept that we give to the other, which must be taken from the material of language, "cannot encompass the other, cannot include the other."[14] In reading this argument, McGowan surmises that, despite Derrida's ambivalence about the import of Levinas's work, he tends to endorse Levinas's view of *the other* as something which exceeds language as the medium of conceptualization and "thus can be said to exist outside of thought." McGowan identifies this kind of thinking as negative mysticism.[15] If the other is beyond language and thought, then the freedom of the other, or negative freedom, must be grounded in an appeal to the mystical rather than to the collectively generated norms and rules of society.

McGowan is almost right but not in the way he thinks. Derrida *reads or interprets* the meaning of the Other in the work of Levinas. In the same context referred to above, Derrida goes on to describe

[14] J. Derrida, *Writing and Difference*, trans. A. Bass (Chicago: University of Chicago Press, 1978), p. 95.
[15] McGowan, *Postmodernism*, pp. 99, 101.

the face-to-face encounter between the ego and the other as taking place "within a glance *and* a speech which both maintain distance and interrupt all totalities." This encounter is a form of "being-together as separation" which "precedes or exceeds society, collectivity, community. Levinas calls it *religion*. It opens ethics." It is not religion as an institution or mysticism as an experience that Derrida identifies, but "the religiosity of the religious." He articulates, after Levinas, the logical place of the mystical. While, as Derrida suggests, the "original direction of language" lies in its relationship to the other as the object of its address, language itself cannot enter into, or be modified by, the condition of objectivity, including its own status as an object, without violence. In that sense, language carries the absolutely-other within itself as the impossibility of its own self-identity as a concept: "Language ... cannot make its own possibility a totality and *include* within itself its own origin or its own end."[16] In all of this, Derrida is saying nothing more than that language as a system can never totalize or complete its code. There is an other, the absolutely-other, which is not something metaphysically present outside of language, but the trace within language of its own incompleteness. Language is never fully self-adequate; there is always something that exceeds its concepts, some undecidable remainder that is *neither* inside *nor* outside the system or *both* inside *and* outside. If it were absolutely outside the system, it would not contaminate the system with the irreducible mark of incompleteness. If it were legitimately inside, it would be accounted for by the code of the system and again would not threaten it with incompleteness. This mark of the other signifies through its inability to signify (and this paradoxical logic becomes inescapable if one attempts to theorize or account for the totality of language). It signifies undecidability not as the indeterminacy of meaning but as the impossibility of closing the system of language in such a way that it will account for every possible meaning-effect. Ironically, this incompleteness of language as a system makes possible or conditions not only the historical development of language (including linguistics as the articulation of language as a system) but of history itself and everything that exists within history as recorded or re*membered* experience.

It is almost amusing that while the popular press faults Derrida

---

[16] Derrida, *Writing*, pp. 95–96.

for supposedly saying that everything is language, academic critics like McGowan turn around and fault him for saying that there is something that exists beyond language or outside of thought. If Derrida believes that the absolutely-other is outside of thought, then why does he insist that *there is nothing outside the text*? As he explains, such a remark

> does not mean that all referents are extended, denied, or enclosed in a book, as people have claimed, or have been naive enough to believe and to have accused me of believing. But it does mean that every referent, all reality has the structure of a differential trace, and that one cannot refer to this "real" except in an interpretive experience. The latter neither yields meaning nor assumes it except in a movement of differential referring.[17]

There is nothing outside the text not because everything is a written text in the narrow sense. Rather, Derrida suggests that there is no place from which one escapes the necessity of some form of interpretation, and this requirement constitutes experience as a *general writing*. He insists not only that there is nothing outside of thought or writing in the general sense but that thought is never adequate to itself. It can never articulate its own border with finality. Language is never transparent. The ego in its relation to the other as its outside can never be fully accounted for by such a relationship, for the ego is already contaminated by the other it seeks to master and define. Neither the ego nor the other can be made into totalities, that is to say, into self-adequate concepts. And yet one arrives at the knowledge of the incompleteness of this relationship only through the most rigorous differentiation of the ego and the other. One arrives at the experience of the undecidable in the relation of subject to object through the most rigorous logical effort to distinguish subject from object.

This does not mean that one arrives at the Hegelian absolute through the back door of such terms as *différance*. Such a term is no more a concept with a decidable meaning and value than the absolutely-other is a code word for the substance of God. *Différance* is an arbitrary signifier. As such, and in the context in which it is used, it foregrounds *both* the logical necessity of the thought of the origin of language *and* the impossibility of the decision that would produce that thought within language in such a way as to

[17] Derrida, *Limited Inc*, p. 148.

bring the question itself to closure or resolution. Derrida has never denied that the thought of *différance*, which is indistinguishable from writing *différance* (substituting an *a* for the *e* in *différence*), resembles the thought of negative theology, "occasionally even to the point of being indistinguishable from negative theology." *Différance* is the mark of the other not as something outside of language that can decide its limit but as the undecidable within language. Negative theologies, by contrast, "are always concerned with disengaging a superessentiality beyond the finite categories of essence and existence, that is, of presence, and always hastening to recall that God is refused the predicate of existence, only in order to acknowledge his superior, inconceivable, and ineffable mode of being."[18]

With this last remark, however, someone will surely say that deconstruction has been caught in the act of expressing its passion for metaphysics. How can one distinguish God's *superessentiality* and his superexistence from the nonexistence and nonessentiality of *différance*? If God as a concept refers to something beyond essence and existence, something that refuses these predicates, can we not simply say that this *something* is nothing, or, in other words, that God is *différance*? Of course, there is a superficial truth in this claim, and Derrida implies that the concepts of God and *différance* are, at some point in their elaboration, indistinguishable. I would add that at such a point the difference between deconstruction and negative theology becomes undecidable. But it is one thing to say that there is a God (or, to be more specific in one's example, that there is a God who would guarantee every American citizen the right to bear arms) and another to say that the difference between negative theology and deconstruction is undecidable. As Derrida stresses in another discussion of this question, deconstruction can always be reappropriated by onto-theology and to some extent that is inevitable because onto-theological logic and grammar haunt the philosophical language that makes deconstruction possible. Nevertheless, because this possibility is circumscribed by the undecidability of the distinction it presupposes, it must necessarily fail as a philosophical concept that wants to transcend deconstructive logic. Derrida concludes that the

---

[18] Derrida, *Margins*, p. 6.

relation between negative theology and deconstruction simply remains open.[19] Though critics like McGowan imagine that they have avoided any contamination by theology altogether, they usually avoid a rigorous formulation of the question. The result, as I will show later, is that they let in theology or onto-theological values through the back door.

McGowan wants to suggest that while Derrida can only conceive of freedom in the negative, he nevertheless relies on positive law by referring to existing norms in order to justify his "visionary politics." McGowan is particularly concerned with Derrida's appeal to nonviolence, "even while he resists more specific norms of legitimacy as forged by particular societies."[20] I have already cited Derrida's appeal to the norm of democracy, but let me quote here, at some length, the passage from which I took that idea, which I will then comment on in some detail:

Hence the *duty* to respond to the call of European memory, to recall what has been promised under the name Europe, to re-identify Europe – this *duty* is without common measure with all that is generally understood by the name duty, though it could be shown that all other duties perhaps presuppose it in silence.

This *duty* also dictates opening Europe, from the heading that is divided because it is also a shoreline: opening it onto that which is not, never was, and never will be Europe.

The *same duty* also dictates welcoming foreigners in order not only to integrate them but to recognize and accept their alterity: two concepts of hospitality that today divide our European and national consciousness.

The *same duty* dictates *criticizing* ("in-both-theory-and-in-practice," and relentlessly) a totalitarian dogmatism that, under the pretense of putting an end to capital, destroyed democracy and the European heritage. But it also dictates criticizing a religion of capital that institutes its dogmatism under new guises, which we must also learn to identify – for this is the future itself, and there will be none otherwise.

The *same duty* dictates cultivating the virtue of such *critique, of the critical idea, the critical tradition*, but also submitting it, beyond critique and questioning, to a deconstructive genealogy that thinks and exceeds it without yet compromising it.

The *same duty* dictates assuming the European, and uniquely European, heritage of an idea of democracy, while also recognizing that this idea, like

[19] J. Derrida, "How to Avoid Speaking: Denials," trans. K. Frieden, in *Languages of the Unsayable: The Play of Negativity in Literature and Literary Theory*, ed. S. Budick and W. Iser (New York: Columbia University Press, 1989), p. 9.

[20] McGowan, *Postmodernism*, p. 112.

that of international law, is never simply given, that its status is not even that of a regulative idea in the Kantian sense, but rather something that remains to be thought and *to come [à venir]*: not something that is certain to happen tomorrow, not the democracy (national or international, state or trans-state) of the *future*, but a democracy that must have the structure of a promise – *and thus the memory of that which carries the future, the to-come, here and now.*

The *same duty* dictates respecting differences, idioms, minorities, singularities, but also the universality of formal law, the desire for translation, agreement and univocity, the law of the majority, opposition to racism, nationalism, and xenophobia.

The *same duty* demands tolerating and respecting all that is not placed under the authority of reason. It may have to do with faith, with different forms of faith. It may also have to do with certain thoughts, whether questioning or not, thoughts that, while attempting to think reason and the history of reason, necessarily exceed its order, without becoming, simply because of this, irrational, and much less irrationalist. For these thoughts may in fact also try to remain faithful to the idea of the Enlightenment, the *Aufklärung*, the *Illuminismo*, while yet acknowledging its limits, in order to work on the Enlightenment of this time, this time that is ours – *today*.[21]

I want to look at this passage in light of McGowan's criticisms. As a preliminary gesture, however, I should mention that it was probably not possible for McGowan to have read this material before his book went to publication. "The Other Heading: Memories, Responses, and Responsibilities" was originally published in the October 1990 issue of *Liber, Revue européenne des livres*. In France, the essay appeared in book form in 1991, the same year in which McGowan's book came out. Yet I cannot imagine that McGowan or any other serious reader of Derrida would be surprised by what he says in the passage quoted.

I want to emphasize the first paragraph of that passage because it reminds us that for Derrida the first duty is always, in a sense, to the call of the past, to a tradition, to values and norms that make it possible for us to begin to talk, to write, and to think in the present tense. Yet this duty, this call to recognize the past, entails other responsibilities, precisely because it privileges a certain heading or direction in human history. The first and most general responsibility – and the one that McGowan has the most difficult time reconciling with his understanding of positive law – is the

---

[21] J. Derrida, *The Other Heading: Reflections on Today's Europe*, trans. P.-A. Brault and M.-B. Naas (Bloomington: Indiana University Press, 1992), pp. 76–79.

responsibility to the other heading, other directions, other (if you will) human desires. For McGowan, this gesture would represent, once again, the Derridean emphasis on the freedom of the other, negative freedom, negative autonomy, which calls into question the authority of the norms, values, and ideas that determine positive freedom (for example, the norms of Western democracy that historically have been a ground for constructing human communities based on liberty, though it would be a mistake, in my view, to read Derrida's references to European duty and memory as an attempt to identify democracy exclusively with the West rather than as an appeal to Western responsibility for its history, including responsibility for the historical effects of imperialism). Nevertheless, McGowan presupposes that the second gesture simply negates or undermines the first gesture – that any appeal or reference to the call of the past as the recognition of a European direction which must not be surrendered is undermined by the imperative to recognize the other as another heading or direction. McGowan sees in this relationship an irreconcilable contradiction. Before I go on to say what I think this contradiction really is, we need to look more closely at what follows in Derrida's statement.

In many ways, the next few paragraphs resonate with what one might want to call liberalism. Derrida suggests that we should welcome foreigners by accepting their differences, and there is no question that he is encouraging a reversal of recent European (and American) tendencies toward, on the one hand, keeping people out through more strict immigration laws, and, on the other, forcing those who are in to conform to some version of cultural nationalism or become the victims of cultural and physical violence. Would McGowan want to argue that this sort of "liberalism" undermines the necessity of developing Western norms of democracy? Perhaps not. Let me go on.

In the next paragraph, Derrida talks about the duty of relentless criticism. In effect, it is necessary to criticize both the "totalitarian dogmatism" that we commonly associate with China and the former communist societies of Eastern Europe *and* the "religion of capital" that took on new life in the eighties and now promises a *new world order* through military interventions. As the gap between the wealthy and the poor continues to increase both inside and outside the Western nation-state, capitalist institutions have become more self-conscious and sophisticated about planning and implementing strategies of ideological control and containment. Surely McGowan would not disagree with the call for relentless criticism. It is the condition of the construction of positive freedom through law.

But it is necessary to go further, says Derrida. Criticism must be self-critical. It must recognize its own limits, where it has had to make decisions and, consequently, where it must assume responsibility for its own violence. This call for a "deconstructive genealogy" raises the question of the undecidable in the history of thought that McGowan seems to refuse. I will come back to it when I take up the question of violence.

Finally, Derrida makes his own appeal to the idea of democracy as a European heritage, which must be in some sense unique. I take the word *unique* in this context to refer not to the exclusivity of the idea's European genealogy but to the specificity of that connection. With reference to a public lecture that Derrida gave, McGowan expresses his interest in, but also his distrust of, Derrida's appeal to a democracy that is somehow still to come; he claims that Derrida only gestures toward a future without certainty.[22] I would not argue with the assertion that Derrida has not said enough (would Derrida himself argue with this? Has he not repeated over and over again that more needs to be said? Must he say it all?), but I still think it is important to understand what he has said. The concept of democracy should never be taken for granted as simply given. It is a dynamic concept that must mean something very different today, for example, from what it meant in the nineteenth century when it coexisted with the institution of slavery in the United States and the disenfranchisement of women throughout the Western world. Democracy is not a Kantian regulative idea because it is an attempt at the pragmatic realization of the meaning of the regulative idea of freedom. When Derrida speaks of democracy as something that has not yet been thought or ever fully realized, he explicitly distinguishes this concept from the notion of a democracy of the future. He is not talking about the future of democracy but about the structure of the concept of democracy as a promise. As such, it is not a dream that can only be realized completely in the future but a relationship of the future, as a direction of thought, to the present through the mediation of

---

[22] McGowan, *Postmodernism*, p. 115.

historical memory. Democracy is and has always been a promise. It is the memory of the promise to realize freedom through the construction of practical social institutions and positive laws. It has yet to be thought because this concept of democracy as the realization of freedom can have no end, no closure, in itself. While the concept of democracy and the systems to which it gives rise could possibly be eradicated from the face of the earth, the concept itself contains within its own structure as a concept the yet-to-be-thought. The institutions that appeal to democracy for legitimation and justification must presuppose the necessity of this yet-to-be-thought as the condition of their survival. In principle, democracy is the form of government and social organization that seeks to articulate and materially realize collective human desire; but collective human desire cannot be answered once and for all by one set of laws and one institutional order. Democracy, *insofar as it lives up to its promise*, institutionalizes hope. As Derrida writes in *Specters of Marx*, "the effectivity or actuality of the democratic promise ... will always keep within it ... this absolutely undetermined messianic hope at its heart, this eschatological relation to the to-come of an event *and* of a singularity, of an alterity that cannot be anticipated."[23] In other words, desire is dynamic; and democracy as system, if it is truly guided by the concept of democracy, answers to this movement of desire through its guarantee of the specific freedoms (of the press, of speech, of assembly, and so forth) that make relentless criticism and social debate possible. On the other hand, democracy fails to live up to its promise when it limits or abuses those freedoms in the interest of an economic system that refuses to hear the demand for economic justice as a form of hope. McGowan has simplified Derrida's understanding of democracy; and certainly, while more needs to be said, that fact in itself does not vilify the importance of what has been said.

The next paragraph repeats the need to respect difference, alterity, and so forth; but it also links this respect for singularity to the universality of law. As I tried to argue earlier about the interdependent relation between the autonomy of reason and the autonomy of the individual who can appeal to reason, there can be no universal that is not rooted in the particular, in the example that

[23] Derrida, *Specters*, p. 65.

claims to be exemplary by inscribing "the universal in the proper body of a singularity, of an idiom or a culture, whether this singularity be individual, social, national, state, federal, confederal, or not."[24] This passage from *The Other Heading* can be further illuminated by reference to my earlier reading of Monique Wittig in which I argue that the universal is not a value, a law, or a norm in any metaphysical sense but rather "a simulacrum, a copy of a copy, without any absolute origin."[25] In other words, the universal is nothing in itself – like deconstruction, like *différance*. That does not mean that the universal is not absolutely essential to the possibility of any social interaction or consensus-formation. The universality of law lies in its capacity for translating and retranslating collective human desire. Universality is the trace-structure of language that makes translation possible but never complete. The appeal to the universality of law means the appeal to what has been written (including oral forms of transmission which are also a kind of writing), the trace of human consensus and desire, as the condition of rewriting and retranslation. How could McGowan disagree with Derrida on these issues when he himself refers to the insecurity of the social consensus in terms of its "historical and social specificity"? Such insecurity, he suggests, can give us pause or occasion for rejoicing, depending on the content of our own desires for radical change.[26]

The last paragraph of the long passage I have quoted will probably be the most difficult one for McGowan (and Hogan) to swallow. Reason does not explain everything, including itself. Yet the imperative to tolerate faith in the world today is a challenging one and requires a willingness to negotiate and seek compromises in contexts where this kind of negotiation seems self-contradictory and impossible. (Witness Salman Rushdie's attempt to seek reconciliation with the Islamic fundamentalists who have sentenced him to death.) Nevertheless, deconstruction carries within itself, in my opinion, the imperative to negotiate, always negotiate, even when negotiation seems impossible. And the same rule applies to the philosophical analysis of the discourse of reason. Deconstruction has the impossible imperative of saying the unsayable; and while this act may seem to privilege or celebrate

---

[24] Derrida, *Other Heading*, p. 72.
[25] McGee, *Telling the Other*, p. 187. See also p. 190.
[26] McGowan, *Postmodernism*, p. 264.

the mystical (as it does to Hogan and McGowan), it may be the only true way to demystify the mystical: it illuminates the darkness of language by foregrounding its trace-structure. Unlike the early Wittgenstein, deconstruction cannot pass over in silence what cannot be said clearly but must say the unsayable, repeat its trace-structure, in order to destroy any metaphysical illusion that there is anything like the mystical outside of language and culture.

As for the norm of nonviolence to which, according to McGowan, deconstruction appeals, I agree that a norm of some sort must exist for deconstruction but I would think of it as a responsibility for violence rather than a rule of nonviolence. In his interview with Gerald Graff, Derrida notes that there is a violence in academic discussions, sometimes with political implications, that must be recognized. Furthermore, he concludes that though such violence may be unavoidable in critical thought, it can be analyzed; and such an analysis, which takes into account the conditions of violence in discourse, may be the only way of resisting violence. It may even be a nonviolent way of transforming "the legal-ethical-political rules: *in* the university and *outside* the university."[27] Derrida's so-called appeal to nonviolence does not suggest *an absolute norm of nonviolence*, though it does point toward the undecidability of the question at issue. Freedom, as I have asserted, is undecidable. By this phrase, I mean that the discourse of freedom always sediments as the by-product of whatever definition or theory or law it formulates (the ground of positive freedom) the necessary possibility of its self-negation, of producing the opposite of freedom. This possibility demands some response, some concept of negative freedom. There is no way of separating these two gestures or of avoiding the decision they require one to make. Laws have to be written or there would be no freedom, no concept of freedom, no discourse of freedom, including no discourse of negative freedom; but every law necessarily creates the possibility of violence, every freedom guaranteed by law carries within itself the possibility of the negation of freedom. It is this undecidability within the structure of the concept of freedom that creates the demand for responsibility. This responsibility is not addressed exclusively to something that lies beyond the law. This responsibility must be to law itself. It

---

[27] Derrida, *Limited Inc*, p. 112.

is a responsibility for the violence inherent to law that can only be addressed through law understood as a process of negotiation and compromise.

Actually, in the essay on "The Politics of Friendship" that McGowan takes particular issue with, Derrida suggests that there is a violence *before* the law, preceding the formulation of laws; and this violence is itself a sort of law. "Before even having taken responsibility for any given affirmation," he says, "we are already caught up in a kind of asymmetrical and heteronomical curvature of the social space, more precisely, in the relation to the Other prior to any organized *socius*, to any determined 'government,' to any 'law.'"[28] In Derrida's work, whenever there is a relation to the other, there is always some implicit violence, some division or marking of difference, that has the logical effect of creating a heteronomical inflection of social space through exclusion. Before laws can be determined and written down, there must already exist some compulsion to negotiate and compromise, to come to terms with the other through the formulation of positive laws, to respond to the call for justice.[29] As I said before, McGowan believes that freedom is possible *only* in a society that has laid down the terms of its membership. Still, before the rules of membership can be formulated and identities constructed, there must exist a relation to the other and some sort of general law. As Derrida continues, "This heteronomical and asymmetrical curvature of a sort of originary sociality is a law, perhaps the very essence of law." Now McGowan or Hogan would probably insist at this point that Derrida is falling back into metaphysics, but I would respond that he is insisting on a rigorous logic that leads inevitably to the place of metaphysics, that is to say, to the place where metaphysics would assert its authority. Nevertheless, he does not legitimate that authority except in the form of a violence that he calls strange. McGowan refers explicitly to the part of Derrida's essay that follows the statement about the essence of law. Derrida argues that a "strange violence has since forever insinuated itself into the origin of the most innocent experiences of

---

[28] J. Derrida, "The Politics of Friendship," *The Journal of Philosophy* 85.11 (1988), 633–34.

[29] Elsewhere Derrida refers to this paradoxical condition as the limit of deconstruction itself. See *Specters*, p. 59; see also J. Derrida, "Force of Law: 'The Mystical Foundation of Authority,'" *Cardoza Law Review* 11.5–6 (1990), 919–1045.

friendship or justice." To that violence, we begin to respond insofar as we are caught by a responsibility that must precede freedom and yet is unthinkable without the concept of freedom. Derrida says that this responsibility surprises us; and one can only assume that the desire for freedom itself comes as a sort of surprise, something in excess of historical determination, which cannot be explained in terms of cause-and-effect. As soon as we begin to signify something, which presupposes the intersubjective ground of relationship between self and other, we encounter a responsibility which "assigns us our freedom without leaving it with us." It poses the question of freedom as the open promise that governs any ethical relationship between self and other. This responsibility to freedom comes from the Other as the intersubjective ground itself, the general signifiability of things, "before any hope of reappropriation permits us to assume this responsibility in the space of what could be called *autonomy*."[30]

McGowan identifies the freedom spoken of here as positive. Against that view, I would say that Derrida speaks of a freedom that precedes and remains after the decision between positive and negative freedom. The decision that makes these two dimensions of freedom possible is the form that responsibility takes. There is no way of making this decision without taking responsibility; there is no way in which this decision can be programmed in advance so that its outcome would be predictable and fully accounted for by the code from which it derives. Herein lies the strange violence Derrida speaks of. McGowan notes that the Other in this passage is capitalized, which identifies it as the big Other of Lacanian discourse or "the order of signification that 'assigns' responsibility, freedom, and personhood to the subject." This reading ignores Derrida's difficult relation to Lacan while it oversimplifies Lacan's concept of the subject. Lacan does not say that the subject is assigned responsibility, freedom, and personhood by the order of signification *as if the subject preexisted that order as a real thing* but that the subject is the logical condition of the general possibility of signification while it can have no existence outside of that process. The subject, for Lacan, is free only insofar as it signifies nothing, as it is ontologically empty. Derrida's work presupposes that before we can even talk about the subject or

---

[30] Derrida, "Politics of Friendship," p. 634.

responsibility or freedom we have already encountered a strange violence that constitutes a responsibility and assigns freedom as the undecidable. This responsibility precedes the subject and any autonomy it can lay claim to; and yet it is impossible to assume this responsibility without some reference by way of anticipation to autonomy and heteronomy, to the subject and its other. This is why the violence of the origin is so strange.

McGowan interprets Derrida's use of the phrase "strange violence" as a protest "against the very terms of political and social life that he presents as 'ineluctable.'" This violence "marks the subjection of the subject to the conditions imposed by the Other."[31] Derrida's admittedly paradoxical formulations do not protest against anything but rather foreground both the impossibility and the necessity of thinking the origin of the discourse of freedom, autonomy, law, and reason itself. The strange violence Derrida speaks of is this impossible necessity. In pursuing a politics based on the norms of freedom, autonomy, law, and reason, it is necessary to take this violence into account because the thought of the origin continues to influence and determine every political act. Every friendship, every social bond, and every commitment to justice in any particular case presupposes some thought of the origin as the very basis of any normativity and of every seemingly stable signification. This originary normativity necessarily arises in response to the call of the other, from what Lacan would call *the desire of the Other* that is both a desire from the Other and for the Other. It precedes the formation of autonomy and succeeds autonomy not as the heteronomy that would be its opposite and negation but as an asymmetrical, heteronomical inflection of the social space. This social space is not heteronomous in itself but the asymmetrical and impossible ground of the relation between autonomy and heteronomy, or the ground of the intersubject that must necessarily precede and succeed any formation of subject and object.

In the passage I have referred to above, Derrida continues his argument by describing the experience of responsibility as one in which the Other somehow "appears without appearing." That is to say, it has no substance in itself that can appear but yet appears as a relation to the alterity or thingness of things, including the subject as

---

[31] McGowan, *Postmodernism*, p. 114.

a thing. It comes before autonomy and yet exceeds it – succeeds, survives, and surpasses it (just as, in Marxist theory, use-value can be said to precede but also exceed the exchange-value of the commodity). If law usually presupposes an opposition between autonomy and heteronomy, it may be necessary "to deform this oppositional logic and prepare, from very far away, its political translation."[32] The Other appears without appearing because it is nothing in itself. This does not mean that the Other is not the ground of law, of normativity and universality, and even of what passes as the mystical. The Other cannot be reduced to that which is different from a subject, a self, an ego, or any other marked position within a discourse or symbolic system. The Other is the trace-structure that precedes the formation of a position. It is the mark that is re-marked by any position and yet remains outside that position as the possibility of its being marked or written again.

Here we should try to consider in more detail the translation into politics Derrida speaks of. How does one translate the undecidability of freedom into a practical politics? Whether one speaks of the norm of nonviolence or the norm of responsibility for violence, one still insists that the thought of the origin continues to haunt every norm. This thought must be addressed and accounted for. Derrida's argument implies that the thought of the origin is violence itself. It seems to follow that the originary responsibility is the responsibility for the thought of the origin. But is it not possible to think politically without any appeal to origins or to any metaphysical foundation? McGowan would say that it is both possible and necessary. Thomas McCarthy, on the other hand, would go so far as to say that the Derridean critique of some foundational concepts is politically vicious because it undercuts the authority of reason, truth, and justice "as presently 'coded,' without offering alternatives." Far from promising a better world, deconstruction both predicts and constitutes "the 'danger' of some 'monstrous mutation.'"[33] The use of the word "coded" suggests that McCarthy knows as well as Derrida does that the concepts of reason, truth, and justice are human constructions that can only be justified by their history and not by some appeal to metaphysical transcendence. But, to give McCarthy his due, are

[32] Derrida, "Politics of Friendship," p. 634.
[33] T. McCarthy, *Ideals and Illusions: On Reconstruction and Deconstruction in Contemporary Critical Theory* (Cambridge, Massachusetts: MIT, 1991), p. 112.

we not bound as responsible political beings to respect the codes that do exist in the absence of metaphysical authority? Why must we repeat again and again the same deconstruction of the origin if it fails to lead us to any form of practical action? McCarthy argues that whenever Derrida has tried to identify deconstruction as a useful tool for social and political practice, he encounters the same objection that it has never made any "positive ethicopolitical proposals."[34] For example, even if McGowan has oversimplified Derrida's concept of freedom, he could be on the mark in claiming that deconstruction is too negative, that its relentless criticism destroys any possibility of a positive political practice aiming at the construction of law as the condition of freedom.

In the present context, I will not try to criticize everything McCarthy says about Derrida; but I will pose a few questions. If deconstruction is so utterly ineffective and without any positive ethical or political proposals, why is it so dangerous? What sort of threat does it pose? Is it possible to pose a threat without such proposals? In McCarthy's statement about the "monstrous muta-tion," he actually quotes Derrida's own words in an interview with Richard Kearney. There Derrida describes *Glas* as an attempt to produce a new form of writing through catachresis, "a violent writing which stakes out the faults (*failles*) and deviations of language." Such a text wants to achieve a particular form of language, "which while continuing to work through tradition emerges at a given moment as a *monster*, a monstrous mutation without tradition or normative precedent."[35] If we compare these remarks about *Glas* with McCarthy's criticism of deconstruction as a sort of monster, it should become clear that McCarthy's commit-ment to normativity *can only be rooted in a metaphysical concept of tradition.* When Derrida says that *Glas* has no tradition or preced-ent, he does not mean that it ignores tradition or fails to account for it or can never be incorporated into it. It is a monstrosity *at the moment of its emergence* because of its relation to tradition. In *Glas*, Derrida produces a *violent* writing that takes responsibility for that relation – in this case, for the intersection of philosophical and literary traditions – and calls into question the stability that every

[34] McCarthey, *Ideals and Illusions*, p. 107.
[35] J. Derrida, "Deconstruction and the Other," in *Dialogues with Contemporary Continental Thinkers: The Phenomenological Heritage*, ed. R. Kearney (Manchester: Manchester University Press, 1984), p. 123.

tradition in some way claims for itself. His work appears beyond the normativity of tradition because it has articulated its own norm and thus insists that normativity itself does not have any kind of metaphysical guarantee but constantly undergoes revision through technical innovation in different social contexts. His understanding of normativity bears a striking resemblance to Adorno's understanding of the normativity of art in *Aesthetic Theory*.

Of course, Derrida chooses the words "monster" and "monstrous mutation" because he can more or less predict the sort of response he gets from McCarthy, and that response is either metaphysical in its ultimate implication or ridiculous. McCarthy quotes the word "danger" from this passage in *Of Grammatology*: "The future can only be anticipated in the form of an absolute danger. It is that which breaks absolutely with constituted normality and can only be proclaimed, *presented*, as a sort of monstrosity."[36] The future is a dangerous monstrosity *only* from the perspective of the present, only in the form of something anticipated. This somewhat Nietzschean perspective is finally a historical one. Things change; and there is no way of accounting for that change absolutely without an appeal to metaphysics, to some form of transcendent value. McCarthy implies that any threat to normativity constitutes a danger rather than a promise, and there is no perspectivism in this viewpoint. He presupposes that there is some safety in the norm, some limited ability to predict the future and govern it. Now it is important to keep in mind that Derrida himself never calls for the mindless abolition of norms or traditions but insists that these be inculcated in ways that are responsible to the undecidable from which they derive. In this sense, he insists that we take responsibility for the violence of the origin of any value or norm. Does this mean that he undercuts our present understanding of reason, truth, and justice without proposing alternatives? The only alternative, he implies, is to continue to argue for these concepts, to appeal to their authority, while at the same time submitting them to relentless criticism and scrutiny. It is to recognize norms as tentative agreements within a process of ongoing negotiations.

Those who see this alternative as a threat to the certainty and

---

[36] Derrida, *Of Grammatology*, p. 5.

stability of the norms that guarantee the safety of our future should take a good look at the historical record. As Jeffrey Nealon sums up, McCarthy's claim that deconstruction is an inadequate defense against "ethico-politico backsliding" ignores the actual experience of history. Marxist theory did not predict or prevent the Stalinist and other crimes committed in its name. Habermasian communicative rationality has not had much influence on our recent global crises (say, in Bosnia or the Middle East). To Nealon, this suggests that no ethical or political system can predict the future. Deconstruction nevertheless wants to protect the future's promise – *in the present* – by devising norms and laws that teach respect for other contexts, that take into account the necessity of social transformations in the future, and that refuse every form of repression. According to Nealon, "the only thing that deconstruction excludes is totalization."[37] I would qualify this last statement. In fact deconstruction does not exclude totalization but subjects every system that aims at totalization to a deconstructive analysis and finds in every case that the system has produced at least one term or proposition that is true even though it contradicts the premises from which it logically derives. The act of deconstruction has to be repeated again and again because there is no universal law of the undecidable. Each undecidable is particular to its contextual framework. Deconstruction does not exclude totalization but finds, repeatedly, that every totalized system is incomplete not in the sense that there are parts missing but in the sense that it is impossible to draw the boundaries of the system once and for all. The undecidable is not the antithesis of totalization but its effect, perhaps even its condition.

McGowan's argument for positive freedom based on norms and consensus can never escape the appeal to metaphysical authority and foundation as long as it bypasses the experience of the undecidable. For example, he argues that in the United States virtually everyone takes seriously "the charge that an action is fundamentally undemocratic." Everyone identifies their cause as "compatible with democracy." In such a context, ethics has more to do with meaning than with values *per se*. In the area of official discourse, no one ever challenges the norm of democracy; only its meaning and "the interpretation of particular actions as compat-

---

[37] J. T. Nealon, *Double Reading: Postmodernism after Deconstruction* (Ithaca: Cornell University Press, 1993), p. 172.

ible with it or not" can be subject to serious criticism.[38] But one wonders if it is really possible to separate debates over the meaning of democracy from the stability of the norm itself. Is not the norm always at stake in every challenge to some current interpretation of its meaning? In my experiences as a teacher, I have found that my students have radically different views of democracy, and I am not always sure about where the norm lies within these interpretations unless the norm is simply the word "democracy." Furthermore, I have had students who did not favor the term "democracy" over terms like "republic," "free enterprise," and so forth, as the key to American ideology. Some think that democracy means majority rule and resent the arguments that have been made for the protection of minority rights. Others think that democracy is a utopian fantasy and that the real issue is power. The point is that democracy, if it is not identical with its specific meanings in specific contexts, has the structure of a promise. Every attempt to define democracy assumes that a promise has been made that can only be kept by recognizing the true meaning of democracy in a specific way. If one assumes that democracy is a stable norm (that is, a norm that is never at stake in debates over its meaning), then one has appealed to an idea of democracy that is metaphysically transcendent. This would be a sort of Platonic idea of democracy. Such an absolute norm could be called mysticism.

The arguments I have examined thus far all derive to one extent or the other from Habermas's argument in the "Excursus on Leveling the Genre Distinction between Philosophy and Literature," the second chapter on Derrida in *The Philosophical Discourse of Modernity* (though McGowan's argument against Derrida is, in my view, more rigorous than Habermas's). Basically, Habermas faults Derrida with "standing the primacy of logic over rhetoric, canonized since Aristotle, on its head." He describes deconstruction in this way: "Derrida does not proceed analytically, in the sense of identifying hidden presuppositions or implications," the technique approved of by Habermas because it conforms to the philosophical tradition as he understands it. "Instead," he continues, "Derrida proceeds by a critique of style, in that he finds something like indirect communications, by which the text itself

---

[38] McGowan, *Postmodernism*, p. 232.

denies its manifest content, in the rhetorical surplus of meaning inherent in the literary strata of texts that present themselves as nonliterary."[39] Those familiar with Derrida's texts must surely find these statements utterly bizarre. Derrida does not identify "hidden presuppositions or implications"? What else does he do, and what has Habermas read that would create this confusion?

Ironically, Derrida has admitted that because he primarily identifies hidden or at least unrecognized presuppositions and implications, he does what successive generations of philosophers have always done, and in that sense he is conservative and traditional. But Habermas is not satisfied with having demonstrated his ignorance of Derrida's texts. He goes on to make the remarkably incoherent statement that Derrida produces only a "critique of style" through which he arrives at some sort of "indirect communication" in the texts he reads, a communication that contradicts or denies "manifest content." Indirect communications are distinguished from hidden presuppositions or implications, apparently, by virtue of the fact that the former are derived from a "rhetorical surplus of meaning" while the latter are merely hidden or unstated but logically necessary to the argument being made in a text. Rhetorical communications are literary and therefore have no serious relation to the argument that is made in a nonliterary text. In effect, Habermas begs the very question that Derrida poses (particularly in the debate with Searle, which seems to be the extent of Habermas's knowledge of Derrida's work in the "Excursus").

In response to Habermas, Derrida has pointed out that in making the argument against him Habermas has not paraphrased carefully or quoted a single word from his texts.[40] Nevertheless, unlike Habermas, Derrida unquestionably does make it a methodological point *not* to resolve all the ambiguities and contradictions that emerge in reading a philosophical text simply by excluding as not serious all those meanings that derive from the rhetorical dimension of language. At the same time, he does not understand rhetoric as forming a stable opposition to logic so that it would be possible to read any text, including a literary text, as simply rhetorical and not producing any logical or propositional meaning. Does this mean that there is no difference between rhetoric

[39] Habermas, *Discourse of Modernity*, pp. 187–89.
[40] Derrida, *Limited Inc*, pp. 156–58.

and logic, between literature and philosophy? Derrida's argument is more subtle than that. One need only go back to the essay on genre where he argues not against the law of genre as somehow inappropriate or misleading but for an understanding of "the law of the law of genre." It is only by producing the law of genre, which says that "Genres are not to be mixed," that one is forced to recognize the law of the law of genre as "a principle of contamination, a law of impurity, a parasitical economy."[41] It is only by defining the limits of genre as rigorously as possible that the transgression of those limits becomes a necessary possibility. Before there is a law of genre, transgression makes no sense. Once there is a law of genre, it is impossible not to have to confront at some level the law of the law of genre as the necessary possibility of contamination. This rule also applies to the genre distinction between philosophy and literature.

These observations recall Rodolphe Gasché's discussion of Derrida's position on literature: "If it were possible to draw one major proposition from Derrida's statements on literature, it would certainly not be that everything is literature, but on the contrary that 'there is no – or hardly any, ever so little – literature.'" Gasché's point is that Derrida recognizes all too well the truth of Habermas's claim about the primacy of logic over rhetoric in the history of Western philosophy. Historically, as Gasché stresses, the concepts and values of philosophy have always dominated literature and forced it to act as the mouthpiece of philosophy. Of course, Gasché prefaces these remarks by noting that there are exceptions to the rule, certain literary works that resist appropriation by philosophy.[42] Much of Derrida's writing focuses on such examples: Genet, Blanchot, Joyce, and so forth. His readings of philosophy always challenge the experience of the limits of philosophy, the moment when philosophy must confront the law of its own law, that is, of its genre. Never does Derrida simply argue that philosophy is literature or that literature is philosophy. In fact, his readings of literature and philosophy, even

[41] J. Derrida, "The Law of Genre/*La loi du genre*," trans. A. Ronnell, *Glyph* 7 (1980), 206.

[42] R. Gasché, *The Tain in the Mirror: Derrida and the Philosophy of Reflection* (Cambridge, Massachusetts: Harvard University Press, 1986), p. 256. See J. Derrida, *Dissemination*, trans. Barbara Johnson (Chicago: University of Chicago Press, 1981), p. 223.

when they are most transgressive, presuppose a certain rigorous autonomy. Still, Habermas is absolutely right to say that Derrida's readings of literature and philosophy call into question the primacy of logic over rhetoric, of philosophy over literature. Calling into question a canonical rule or norm does not automatically posit an antithetical norm, however. Nowhere does Derrida simply substitute rhetoric or rhetoricism for logic or logocentrism. As he says in a note on Habermas, deconstruction, as he practices it, is not a form of rhetoricism, which would just be another version of logocentrism. Indeed, to the extent that Derrida has taken an interest in the rhetorical organization or literary form of philosophical discourse, his purpose has not been to reduce, level, or assimilate. Rather, his aim is "to refine the differences."[43]

In the last analysis, Derrida and Adorno share some common ground in the attempt to distinguish and understand the relation between philosophy and art. For Adorno, as I noted in chapter 2 of this study, aesthetics is not something that philosophy can completely expel from itself. On the contrary, the mimetic experience that art foregrounds can never be completely effaced by the concepts of philosophy: "To represent the mimesis it supplanted, the concept has no other way than to adopt something mimetic in its own conduct, without abandoning itself" (*ND* 14). While philosophy must get rid of its aestheticism in order to preserve its autonomy, it can only perform this task by incorporating some aspect of the mimetic impulse into itself. At the same time, art or literature can never fully extract itself from the conceptual because it is only the illusion of totalized meaning in the midst of reified meanings and values that enables art to posit the desire for authentic meaning as its proper content (*AT* 222). This negative desire becomes the basis and guarantee of art's negative autonomy. Still, neither the autonomy of art nor the autonomy of philosophical discourse is ever pure or beyond contamination by its other. The genre distinction between philosophy and literature requires the possibility of contamination as the condition of its law, as the law of its law. Contamination by the other is the ground of rigorous autonomy in either cultural field. This poses yet another question: is not this concept of contamination an indirect way of reconciling contraries through some form of identity-

---

[43] Derrida, *Limited Inc*, p. 156.

thinking? Peter Dews argues that the difference between Adorno and Derrida finally lies in the latter's attempt to overcome oppositions with concepts (or pseudo-concepts), such as *différance*, that insist on the contamination of identity by the other which identity excludes. Adorno's position is different: for example, while he calls for the abolition of the hierarchy between subject and object, he does not imagine that this gesture abolishes the subject – object relation or any other binary opposition. In *Negative Dialectics*, as Dews notes, Adorno argues for an inequality between subject and object in the process of mediation. The subject does not enter the object in the same way that the object enters the subject. Though an object requires a subject, it is always something different from the subject, while the latter is also an object, even to itself.[44]

Dews uses the word "overcoming" to describe the effect of deconstructive concepts, and this word carries the connotation of a Hegelian sublation or *Aufhebung*. Derrida, by contrast, describes the effect of deconstructive terms as the opposite of the Hegelian synthesis: they limit, interrupt, and destroy the sublation wherever it appears. Later, he clarifies this destruction of the *relève* or *Aufhebung* through the example of the deconstruction of the concept of history. Derrida challenges the traditional concept of history as the history of univocal meanings derived from the ontological *presencing* of events. He overturns that concept of history by positing another history that would foreground contradictions and conflicts of interpretation and that would not presuppose the possibility of a context saturated with meaning. However, in overturning an idealist concept of history by articulating a materialist concept, it is necessary to recognize the relational interdependence between these terms, which Derrida calls *marking the interval*. Otherwise, one can reproduce in materialism the same conceptualization that underlies idealism. One may not be able to escape that conceptualization, but one can at least take it into account as a part of the general problem of historical representation itself. A materialist view of history escapes the pitfalls of idealism not by transcending them but by accounting for the tendency toward idealism in the materialist/idealist distinction itself. Derrida also suggests that such work on the concept of

---

[44] Dews, *Logics of Disintegration*, p. 40.

history is never purely theoretical, conceptual, or discursive, since historically the terms "theoretical," "conceptual," and "discursive" derive from the very conceptual framework that the deconstruction of idealist history calls into question, that is, a discourse "entirely regulated by essence, meaning, truth, consciousness, ideality, etc."[45]

In a sense, Dews's critique of the potential danger in the deconstructive gesture is not only correct but already anticipated by Derrida himself. For Dews, the deconstructive overturning of the hierarchical relationship between the terms of a metaphysical opposition is "merely a stage on the way to its overcoming."[46] The term Derrida generally uses, however, is not "overcoming" but "displacement." "Overcoming" carries the connotation of neutralization; but, according to Derrida, the end of deconstruction is never the neutralization of conceptual oppositions but rather the disclosure of the contradictory relations between the terms and the marking of the interval that makes contradiction necessary. Rather than neutralizing contradictions, deconstruction tries to displace the system that produces them, which moves the analysis from the conceptual to the historical as the open field of interpretive possibilities, the promise of a future open to unlimited transformation. To sum up, Derrida's double science or double writing involves "an *overturning* of the classical opposition *and* a general *displacement* of the system."[47] According to Dews, any new concept that deconstruction proposes necessarily neutralizes the original opposition; but this view completely ignores the nature of deconstructive writing which presupposes that the boundary between logic and rhetoric, though not indeterminate, is undecidable.

Derrida does not call for the abolition of the distinction between rhetoric and logic anymore than he calls for the abolition of the distinction between subject and object. On these points, his work is completely consistent with Adorno's. He does insist that the only way to guarantee an absolute autonomy of these spheres or of the concepts that govern them is by appealing to metaphysical authority. By absolute autonomy, I mean an autonomy that is pure

[45] J. Derrida, *Positions*, trans. A. Bass (Chicago: University of Chicago Press, 1981), pp. 40–41, 56–59.
[46] Dews, *Logics of Disintegration*, p. 40.
[47] Derrida, *Margins*, p. 329.

and without any trace of the other. Derrida never argues against the autonomy of logic and reason or against aesthetic autonomy, for without taking their autonomy for granted it would be impossible to deconstruct these categories. However, deconstruction repeatedly demonstrates that autonomous reason always contains within itself some trace of the other in the form of its own lack: reason itself has no reason. The autonomous work of art never transcends its own immanent sociality as the absolute commodity. Adorno's writing on the relation between subject and object is not inconsistent with Derrida's position, for Derrida never claims simply that the object is a subject. On the contrary, he would agree, I think, that "an object can only be conceived by a subject" and yet remains "something other" than a subject. The subject itself is contaminated by this "something other," which is to say that the subject is also an object (*ND* 183). However, it is necessary to go further and say that the subject is an object for another subject. There is an alterity, an intersubjectivity, that is the necessary precondition for the formation of any subjectivity whatsoever. Lacan called it an *inmixing of otherness*.[48] While objects need not be subjects, there can be no objects without subjects; and the subject itself, while historically autonomous, is never pure. It always carries the trace of the other within itself as the condition of its possibility.

Still, Dews insists that Adorno, unlike Derrida, never appeals to any thought of the origin. In *Against Epistemology*, Adorno argues that "The theoretical limit against idealism does not lie in the content of the determination of ontological substrates or primal words [which suggests perhaps something like the Derridean concept of *différance*], but first of all in consciousness of *the irreducibility of what is* to a pole of *uncancellable difference*, whatever its nature might be. This consciousness must be unfolded in concrete experience" (my emphases).[49] Supposedly, Derrida *never* allows for a similar appeal to experience or to what Adorno calls "the logically consistent consciousness of non-identity [*das kon-*

[48] J. Lacan, "Of Structure as an Inmixing of an Otherness Prerequisite to Any Subject Whatever," in *The Structuralist Controversy: The Languages of Criticism and the Sciences of Man*, ed. R. Macksey and E. Donato (Baltimore: The Johns Hopkins University Press, 1972), pp. 186–95.
[49] T. W. Adorno, *Against Epistemology: A Metacritique*, trans. Willis Domingo (Oxford: Oxford University Press, 1982), p. 183.

sequente Bewüsstsein des Nichtidentität]" (Dews's translation). According to Dews, Derrida jettisons the concepts of experience *and* consciousness, while Adorno claims that something is given in experience *but never immediately*. Still, Derrida's concept of *différance* is not irreconcilable with Adorno's insistence on the irreducibility of being to an uncancelable difference. Derrida's term or anticoncept is one way of writing this law of the irreducibility of experience to some ultimate ground of difference that cannot be canceled because it is absolute and nonrelational. This difference is a form of identity – the identity of nonidentity. For Derrida, experience is *différance* because once one has granted that nothing is given immediately, then experience itself becomes a complicated movement or interplay. Adorno's position, as described by Dews, involves a similar conceptualization: experience is the interplay of presence and absence, of the immediate and the mediated, and of the identical and the nonidentical, since without immediacy mediation itself would become immediate and overwhelm the particular.[50] Derrida would not disagree that experience is an interplay of this sort, which does not mean that the oppositions in question have been overcome or synthesized. It is the interplay itself that challenges a metaphysical way of understanding these terms. Adorno never has any illusions about the sort of *delusion* that must underlie any simple notion of direct experience. In *Negative Dialectics*, he refers to the delusion of the transcendental subject as "the Archimedean fixed point from which the world can be lifted out of its hinges." This delusion cannot be overcome by subjective analysis because contained within it is "the truth that society comes before the individual consciousness and before all its experience" (*ND* 181). In other words, experience is always socially mediated; and Adorno's warning about the delusion of transcendental subjectivity correlates with Derrida's warning that metaphysical thought is not limited to the writings of philosophers but plays a role in the everyday perception of the world.

As evidence of Derrida's refusal of experience, Dews refers to the well-known remarks about perception in the discussion at the end of the version of "Structure, Sign, and Play in the Discourse of the Humanities" published in *The Structuralist Controversy*. Der-

---

[50] Dews, *Logics of Disintegration*, pp. 41–42. See *ND* 15.

rida describes perception as a concept that postulates a pure intuition of what is given directly by the thing itself, transparent to itself and in its meaning, beyond language and interpretation. Derrida says that he does not believe in such a concept of perception as the absolutely unmediated datum. From an ideological perspective, this concept participates in the privileging of origins and centers; and any philosophical move that undermines metaphysics also undermines the concept of pure perception.[51] In *Negative Dialectics*, Adorno also argues that the thing itself is never "positively and immediately at hand." Yet Adorno goes on to note that such a thing in itself is not a product of thought but the articulation of nonidentity through identity (*ND* 189). Derrida's use of the word "concept" may suggest that he understands perception or experience as simply mental. However, this reading would misconstrue the logic of *différance* which calls into question not only the simple immediacy of experience but the transparency of thought to itself. *Différance* is a structural movement or interplay that cannot be conceived through the opposition between presence and absence. It postulates *and* presupposes a relational system of traces in which, while no term or difference is uncancelable, every difference remains incommensurable, that is, irreducible to an absolute law of identity.[52] *Différance* is not a rejection of consciousness or of historical experience although it certainly complicates any reductive understanding of those terms. It designates the process or movement by which language as a code or any symbolic system of referral "is constituted 'historically' as a weave of differences." At the same time, Derrida insists that the concepts *constitution, production, creation, movement,* and *history* must be understood in ways that subvert their metaphysical implications even as their capture by the language of metaphysics is taken into account.[53] As Derrida indicates, one does not simply step aside from or transcend the appeal to metaphysics. It is embedded in the history of our languages, in the words we have to use in order to raise any questions about our historical emplacement and political

[51] J. Derrida, "Structure, Sign, and Play in the Discourse of the Humanities," in *The Structuralist Controversy: The Languages of Criticism and the Sciences of Man,* ed. R. Macksey and E. Donato (Baltimore: The Johns Hopkins University Press, 1972), p. 272.
[52] Derrida, *Positions,* p. 27.
[53] Derrida, *Margins,* p. 12.

formation. Perhaps there is a *beyond* somewhere, but for the moment there is no way of conceptualizing a place beyond metaphysics and the old systems of value without employing words and concepts that carry within themselves traces of these same values and metaphysical presuppositions.

Deconstructive politics and the university

Finally, we are left with the question we have wanted to pose: is a deconstructive politics possible? And our discussion suggests that the answer is yes and no. It is possible, but it should not be thought of as a political system or program. A deconstructive politics is nothing in itself; it is certainly not a program with rules that anyone could follow. It is not a political science and probably not even a political philosophy in the classical sense. It is a moment within politics in general, a moment that makes it possible for us to come to a decision and to act responsibly. The deconstructive moment is not merely an opening or an ending but the constant reopening of the question of the political within the political. Without this moment, the political ceases to be political, or rather ceases to be a practice based on responsible decisions, and becomes another form of dogmatism. To the extent that a political movement always emerges within the framework of a conflict of interpretations, it must aim at a specific stabilization of context in order to communicate successfully to the other who represents a different or opposing viewpoint. Yet this stabilization of context can destroy the political if it does not allow for or take into account the reopening of the question of context that necessarily requires a redefinition and reconceptualization of the political. As I see it, there is no escaping this dialectic, and I would not hesitate to call it a *negative dialectic*. It does not promote negative freedom to the exclusion of positive freedom, as McGowan argues, but guarantees the survival of positive freedom on the basis of laws. The law must never be seen as a closed book, however, but as writing, as a trace that is always subject to revision, renegotiation, and compromise. Freedom, as I argued earlier, is undecidable, which means that finally the question of freedom can never be laid to rest. This question must be posed again and again; it must be reconceived, renegotiated, and always recontextualized.

I have been thinking at a very general level, but it may be useful to consider more particular issues. As far as I am concerned, all of the texts I have discussed in this essay are productive criticisms of deconstruction because, whatever their intention (and even if in some places they are animated by intellectual resentment), they have forced deconstruction to confront its own political and institutional situation. Derrida himself notes that the enemies of deconstruction often have a more vital grasp of what is at stake in it than do those who call themselves deconstructionists. Still, in the note to the Graff interview I referred to earlier, Derrida responds very negatively to the type of criticisms that have been inspired by the work of Habermas. He refers to philosophers, theorists, and ideologists in the United States and Europe who see themselves as the defenders of communication and consensus, who insist on the univocity and transparency of terms, and who argue for classical logic as the ethical basis of proof and debate. Curiously, from Derrida's viewpoint, these defenders of logical clarity and self-evident truth are often guilty of not reading or listening carefully to those whom they criticize, sometimes to the point of not respecting the elementary rules of philological interpretation. In this kind of critique, which often borders on "chatter" rather than analysis, Derrida sees a form of intellectual dogmatism that recoils from deconstructive arguments as if out of fear. When the advocates of communication are exposed "to the slightest difficulty, the slightest complication, the slightest transformation of the rules," they "denounce the absence of rules and confusion."[54] The real question for Derrida concerns the emotional nature of this reaction which suggests the fear of something.

I will propose a theory about the fear that deconstruction arouses in critics and historians and play the devil's advocate for a moment. This fear is, ironically, the fear of context. I mean the fear of an ungovernable context that would undermine the possibility of any stable communication or informed consensus, the fear of a context that is never, in Derrida's own formulation, saturated. *At bottom*, this fear may be the fear of history itself, though most of those who express it believe themselves to be the defenders of the historical perspective in criticism and thought. Nevertheless, one has to concede that this fear has some legitimate motivations. For

---

[54] Derrida, *Limited Inc*, pp. 140, 157–58.

example, we hear about surveys indicating that many young people today either do not know about the Holocaust or doubt that it ever took place. Is this a subject the members of a "free" society can afford to forget or even have a debate about? Can we risk saying that the truth about the Holocaust is undecidable? If we cannot stabilize the historical context to the extent of recognizing the Holocaust as a simple fact, beyond argument, how can we convey to our children the historical responsibility that this particular knowledge must convey?

Or, to choose a less painful example, one should consider that today in the university there appears to be a struggle taking place between liberal (and sometimes radical) pluralism, on the one hand, and conservative traditionalism, on the other. Both sides of this debate have expressed a fear of deconstruction as a methodology that undermines any stable ground for positing values; both accuse deconstruction of inadvertently supporting the other side by leaving that ground open.[55] Conservatives fault deconstruction with undermining the Western tradition and the values it inculcates by insisting on an instability of meaning that makes it impossible to construct universal norms. Without these norms, there is no way of asserting and arguing for a hierarchy of social values that could become the basis for a New World Order, for the benign or not-so-benign dominance of the West at a dangerous historical juncture in which national, racial, and religious conflicts threaten to tear the fabric of modern civilization to pieces.[56] Some liberals and radicals, on the other hand, distrust the fact that deconstruction appears to be nothing in itself, that it constructs an intellectual position which makes it almost impossible to choose sides. They fear the experience of the undecidable as a refusal to support and defend basic democratic and social democratic

---

[55] For an overview of this debate, see G. Graff, *Beyond the Culture Wars: How Teaching the Conflicts Can Revitalize American Education* (New York: Norton, 1992).

[56] See W. J. Bennett, "To Reclaim a Legacy," 1984 Report on Humanities in Education, *Chronicle of Higher Education* (November 28, 1984):1, 14–21; A. Bloom, *The Closing of the American Mind: How Higher Education Has Failed Democracy and Impoverished the Souls of Today's Students* (New York: Simon and Schuster, 1987); E. D. Hirsch, Jr., *Cultural Literacy: What Every American Needs to Know* (Boston: Houghton Mifflin, 1987); and D. D'Souza, *Illiberal Education: The Politics of Race and Sex on Campus* (New York: Free Press, 1991).

principles that seek to guarantee freedom and some degree of social and economic equality to all people.[57]

So, in the last analysis, the left is not that different from the right on this issue: they want the recognition of norms that are pragmatically stable even if they are not universal. To cite a particular instance, in the university deconstructive analyses have sometimes called into question certain common-sense assumptions about the nature of the canon and the function of writing in the curriculum. While these critiques annoy conservatives who want to see the canon and standard English as the expression of self-evidently pragmatic or transcendent values, they annoy pluralists perhaps even more by questioning the political efficacy of recent efforts at revising the canon and producing critical pedagogies in order to make education more responsive to a diverse, multicultural society. Writing specialists in particular, regardless of political identity, face a legitimate dilemma in trying to imagine teaching practices that do not reinforce the authority of standard English. Canon-revisionists, by contrast, have always argued that the canon is intrinsically vicious in consciously or unconsciously promoting the agenda of the social class and gender which have historically monopolized the power of the state and its cultural institutions. Yet the ordinary response to the hegemony of the canon has been to revise syllabuses so that they include the category of *the noncanonical*. Unfortunately, as John Guillory points out, changing the syllabus does not change or challenge the principle of canon-formation, since every attempt to make a new syllabus virtually re*institutes* the process. Guillory's critique questions the efficacy of any principled curriculum reform that tries to reverse the political effects of the traditional canon by constructing yet another canon.[58]

It is not my intention to respond to these problems by producing a plan for the reform of the university. Such a critical gesture presupposes that one can arrive at some ideal model of the university within the purely conceptual realm and then put it to a

[57] For an example of this viewpoint, see M. Zavarzadeh and D. Morton, *Theory, (Post)Modernity, Opposition: An "Other" Introduction to Literary and Cultural Theory* (Washington, DC: Maissoneuve Press, 1991), especially chapter 6, "Deconstructive Critique, Ideology Critique, and Radical Critique-Al Theory."

[58] J. Guillory, *Cultural Capital: The Problem of Literary Canon Formation* (Chicago: University of Chicago Press, 1993), p. 31. The entire first chapter of this book is relevant to the present context.

vote, so to speak, without entering into a complex dialogue with the members of the university community and without confronting any number of complicated and, in some sense, unanswerable questions. Such proposals usually result in absurdities that have little or nothing to do with what is practically possible in the university as it exists at the present time or in cosmetic trivialities that would make the university a more comfortable place for some but would not fundamentally challenge its current organization. Now, having made this qualification, I do think it possible to propose some guidelines and a direction for our discussion of the university and of the social production of knowledge in general. With this in mind, I will address the questions proposed because they articulate local issues that have implications for the university as a whole.

I cannot do justice to the subject of the Holocaust in this context, though I believe it is an issue that has to be considered here because there is no other event in the consciousness of the West that competes with it as a challenge to the metaphysical presuppositions of European culture (though there is nothing innocent about the failure of Western education to foreground the histories of slavery and imperialism to the same degree). As Adorno explains, after Auschwitz, "Our metaphysical faculty is paralyzed because actual events have shattered the basis on which speculative metaphysical thought could be reconciled with experience" (*ND* 363). These words suggest that the Holocaust not only has the effect of destabilizing our direct experience of the world; it challenges the continuity of experience as mediated by values and thus calls into question any idealized or metaphysical concept of tradition. How can we trust our experiences or even our ordinary grasp of the facts when we know that it is possible for ordinary human beings – including those who have been inculcated with the values of Western humanism – to tolerate, live with, and participate in the most shocking forms of evil as if they were normal events, or when we know that human beings can witness such evil without seeming to recognize it, which must cast some doubt upon the notion that evil is naturally abhorrent to human nature? And these recognitions call into question our use of the term "evil" itself: can we speak of it in the same way, within the classical opposition between good and evil, after Auschwitz? In other words, the Holocaust is the event in European history (along with slavery and imperialism with which it has intimate historical links) that produces the most profound destabilization of the historical context.

For these reasons, it should not come as a surprise that there are individuals – in some cases, scholars – who are bent on *normalizing* or *domesticating* the Holocaust. I do not doubt for a moment that most of these individuals, especially those who have tried to popularize the notion that the Holocaust never took place, are motivated by vicious ideologies. At the same time, it would be brutally ironic if those who want to defend the memory of the dead inadvertently contributed to the normalization process by insisting that the Holocaust does not change the way we view or understand Western history. The deconstructive method does not deny the facts of the Holocaust; but, as Hayden White argues, there is no escaping the moment of interpretation in the constitution of historical facts.[59] The context that we refer to as European culture can no longer be viewed or interpreted in exactly the same way after the Holocaust as it was before. Therefore, any examination of the evidence of the Holocaust can no longer take for granted the contextual framework within which that evidence is to be evaluated. Certain humanistic values that are supposed to govern and justify our moral outrage at the evidence of the Holocaust must also be analyzed coldly for the possibility that they may have shaped the context in which the Holocaust took place.

A deconstructive analysis would never suggest that the evidence of the Holocaust is in itself undecidable. It does suggest that no individual can interpret the evidence of the Holocaust in terms of its ethical, political, and historical significance without making a decision after having passed through the experience of the undecidable. That experience does not emerge from the evidence as a set of isolated facts but from the relation of the evidence to the ethical, political, and historical contexts of which it is a part. The Holocaust as an event constitutes such a profound crisis in the history of Western values and cultural practices that it cannot be uncritically interpreted and evaluated within that framework without violently producing the effect of normalization. The evidence itself, however, works against that

[59] H. White, *The Content of the Form: Narrative Discourse and Historical Representation* (Baltimore: The Johns Hopkins University Press, 1987), pp. 58–82.

effect and, by insisting on the undecidability of contextual boundaries, makes the Holocaust a living issue that cannot be forgotten through the normal processes of historical classification and representation. Though it may be painful, the issue of the Holocaust will remain with us. It is not really the evidence that is in question, though there are unscrupulous ideologues who will try to argue that it is. It is the ethical-political framework of Western culture that has been destabilized by this event. A deconstructive analysis only discloses this instability. The decision that is made after that disclosure is the moment of responsibility. Deconstructive pedagogy should aim at this responsibility of decision, not at the justification of irresponsibility before the abyss of uncertainty.

But what of those who say that it can go either way, that deconstruction justifies the act of indecision as much as it forces one to make a decision? For example, Deborah Lipstadt has argued, using the case of Paul de Man as support, that deconstruction encourages attempts to falsify history and has created an "atmosphere of permissiveness" that indirectly supports efforts to deny the Holocaust.[60] Though one should point out the blatant tendentiousness and inaccuracy of Lipstadt's characterizations of critical theories, one should also admit that deconstructive pedagogy involves risk. It is always possible that someone will make a decision that is inconsistent with our deepest feelings and values. But is this risk not, finally, the risk of thought itself? In the face of an event like the Holocaust, how can we begin to think through the grounds of our feelings and values without risking them, without putting them at stake? Nevertheless, it seems to me that the one thing deconstruction does not allow is an absolute indecision. Now I realize that the celebration of the *mise-en-abyme* by the Yale school of deconstruction has created exactly the opposite impression in the United States. This is not the appropriate context in which to investigate that school of thought, but it seems to me that we have completely misunderstood the concept of undecidability if we see it as a justification for neutrality or indifference. On the contrary, the experience of the undecidable forces us to realize that a decision must be made without metaphysical guarantees or programmatic

[60] D. Lipstadt, *Denying the Holocaust: The Growing Assault on Truth and Memory* (New York: Plume, 1994), pp. 18, 29.

authority. In the face of the undecidable, every act is a decision, even if it is the decision not to act. As there is no other court of appeal, the decision itself articulates the form of responsibility. Or, as Derrida writes in his essay on de Man, one cannot assume responsibility without the experience of the undecidable that involves recognizing the irreducibility of the other.[61] The other in this context is the realm of nonidentity, or historical experience itself, that cannot be reduced to a calculus of univocal values. Nothing guarantees that anyone will take responsibility, but there is no chance for responsibility unless the destabilization of context that the Holocaust as a historical event brings about is fully confronted and worked through. Consequently, responsibility requires that we teach the Holocaust, present its evidence, and carefully explore the relationship between this factual evidence and the contextual framework. In this area, deconstructive pedagogy is not inconsistent with a strict historical methodology.

But what about de Man, whose name both Lipstadt and Derrida invoke? Did he take responsibility? In my view, he did not. But it seems to me that the question for us today is not about de Man's responsibility but about ours. How do we take responsibility for de Man? How do we take responsibility for those many other ordinary Europeans who collaborated with the Nazis by failing to oppose them or who directly participated in the *final solution*? First, we have to establish and defend the facts; but then it is not enough to assign guilt to the other. We have to confront the other in ourselves, to confront our own implication in the historical situation that the evidence of the Holocaust presents us with. This means confronting not only the way the Holocaust has transformed our understanding of Western culture and tradition but the way it forces us to reread the history of Western violence against others, including violence against women and the violence of imperialism, slavery, and so forth. Under no circumstances should such a historical revision become a debate about which group is the most oppressed. The Holocaust and the violent events that make up the history of European colonialism are not strictly commensurable, but knowledge of one transforms our understanding of the other. And of course violence against others is not exclusive to the West.

[61] J. Derrida, "Like the Sound of the Sea Deep within a Shell: Paul de Man's War," *Critical Inquiry* 14 (1988), 639.

Having said that, it is appropriate that I now address the issues concerning curriculum and pedagogy that have sometimes become volatile in the context of the *culture wars*. According to Gauri Viswanathan, in her brilliant work on English studies in nineteenth-century British India, curriculum should not be seen as a collection of texts but as an activity that involves the acquisition and exercise of power. From this perspective, those who describe the content of curriculum as the expression of universal values or as the ground for emerging identities in a pluralistic, secular society fail to confront the hegemonic functions of curriculum.[62] Though they would probably not identify themselves as deconstructionists, scholars like Viswanathan and Guillory produce the effect in their work of deconstructing stable, everyday concepts of canonicity and curriculum by rearticulating the historical context in such a way as to destabilize the vision of cultural continuity and political innocence that characterizes most conservative views of curriculum. Their work contributes to what I would call a radical deconstruction, or indeed a responsible deconstruction, which is the kind that Derrida, in my view, has always practiced. The word "responsible" in this context should be understood as signifying not only the accountability of an individual or group for the decision made but also the right of response granted to those who did not make it. A responsible decision as the aim or end of deconstruction is a decision that remains open to the voice and the desire of the other. This kind of decision presupposes that the minimal stability of context which it establishes can and will be displaced by the historical movement of social desire.

Even this form of deconstruction threatens certain proponents of pluralism who feel that it subverts minority or oppositional traditions in the same way that it threatens so-called dominant traditions. This fear, as I see it, derives from a misunderstanding of the relation between the two aspects of the deconstructive gesture: overturning and displacement. Initially, any deconstructive analysis of the curriculum would have to recognize the necessity of a reversal, of challenging the dominance of the traditional canon by introducing into the curriculum those writers and movements that have historically been marginalized by the institutional construction of the canon itself in the form of a curriculum.

[62] G. Viswanathan, *Masks of Conquest: Literary Study and British Rule in India* (New York: Columbia University Press, 1989), p. 167.

Programs in Women's and Gender Studies, African-American Studies, Gay and Lesbian Studies, and Cultural Studies try to produce exactly this sort of reversal when they invert the relationship between the center and the margin of the traditional canon. But if things are left this way, the effort at curriculum reform through the greater representation of minorities only succeeds in creating pockets of opposition within a field that remains dominated by the traditional canon. As Guillory implies, this kind of curriculum reform by itself ultimately reinforces the legitimacy of the traditional canon by suggesting that canon-formation is a natural process that transcends the politico-pedagogical context.

A deconstructive curriculum reform must go beyond constructing new programs with new canons or adding new works to the traditional canon. It must displace the system of canon-formation through the act of radical contextualization. Guillory describes this process when he explains why text traditions, whether they are dominant or subordinate, are never sufficient in and of themselves to shape and transmit a culture. The culture of the school is only a part of the complex acculturation process, which operates through multiple insitutional sites. As the instrument of cultural hegemony, the school projects an image of itself as a neutral and disinterested environment for cultural reproduction by occluding the contextual framework (for example, the culture of the commodity) in which cultural production and consumption take place. It forces students to read texts out of context and produces the illusion of a cultural self-identity (pitting *our* culture against *their* culture) which proclaims itself the outcome of a natural transmission process through direct contact with the works. Guillory then addresses the possibility of another pedagogy that challenges the traditional functions of the school, that, while recognizing the "intertextual dialogue" of tradition, insists on the recognition of the discontinuity and heterogeneity of culture. This different pedagogy, by emphasizing historical contextualization, "would ... inhibit the assimilation of cultural works to the agenda of constituting a national culture, or the Western culture which is its ideological support." At the same time, it would challenge a naive countercultural pedagogy that believes it "can make the works of the multicultural curriculum stand in a 'subversive' relation to Western culture." For Guillory, while cultural production has many different sites, it does not for that reason produce a

multiplicity of cultures, as though every cultural work were only the organic expression of a discrete and autonomous culture. The fact that we now expect the curriculum to reflect as a principle of its organization the very distinctness of cultures, Western or non-Western, canonical or noncanonical, points to a certain insistent error of culturalist politics, its elision of the difference the school itself makes in the supposed transmission of culture.[63]

Guillory's observations suggest two conclusions to me. First, though canon-formation may be one of the effects of the pedagogical process, it need not be the ultimate goal of teaching. Whenever a teacher writes down a list of works in the form of a syllabus, he or she projects a canon in the form of what Guillory calls the *pedagogic imaginary*.[64] This imaginary is not natural but arises out of the history of the institution with its claims to cultural authority. Though there is nothing *intrinsically* vicious about this pedagogic imaginary, it can be vicious when it becomes an end in itself, when the institution identifies its purpose with the reproduction of this pedagogic imaginary as the form of cultural unity and continuity and tries to suppress any pedagogical action that would call that unity into question. In such a case, the institution takes the imaginary for the real. The antidote to this institutional tendency is radical contextualization, and by that I mean a process of contextualization that focuses not only on the historical background of individual works or texts but on the history of canon-formation itself and of the institutional framework within which it takes place. Furthermore, although Guillory does not make this point, such contextualization must be interminable: it can never allow the context to become rigid and completely stable and, for that reason, resistant to any further questions and interpretive strategies. If the context is allowed to stabilize to this extent, it becomes a mere shadow of the canon and projects an image of cultural continuity that lacks any real historical content. Radical contextualization prohibits such stability by insisting that the boundary between text and context, work and historical background, is undecidable. While the distinction between text and context is absolutely necessary, it can never be determined with finality

---

[63] Guillory, *Cultural Capital*, pp. 43–44.   [64] *Ibid.*, pp. 28–38.

since the text always remains at some level of analysis a part of the context and the context is always included within the text it frames. There is no site in the text–context relationship that transcends the possibility of interpretation. There is no event in history that transcends history, that is, the possibility of its reinterpretation. Consequently, radical contextualization necessarily leads to the recognition of cultural discontinuity and heterogeneity.

Second, such radical contextualization calls into question any simplified understanding of the relation between dominant and subordinate cultural formations. I do not mean that a deconstructive pedagogy would make these formations disappear with a wave of its magic wand. It merely complicates the relation between formations by disclosing their interdependence within the institutional framework. Guillory makes the rather canny observation that only a very naive concept of multicultural curriculum can imagine that the works it proposes for inclusion in the curriculum will have the effect of subverting the hegemonic formations of Western culture. This does not mean that such a curriculum will have no transformative impact on Western culture, since the curricular representation of minority literatures at least suggests that Western culture can no longer afford to ignore its others. The subversive force of such representation is severely limited, however. In order to maintain it, we would have to suppress the hybridity of both the postcolonial and the metropolitan artifact, both of which articulate within themselves the contradiction between dominant and subordinate cultures. Still, though the cultural unities posited by a multicultural curriculum often serve to legitimate the unity of the dominant national culture and ultimately of Western culture itself, they should not become the reason for abandoning diversity in curriculum design. They should, rather, point to the need for radical contextualization that would subject the curriculum to a double reading. We need to subvert the dominant tradition of Western culture not only by reversing its relation to other cultures and giving those cultures more representation within the canon, but also by displacing the system of canon-formation itself, by disclosing the historical contexts and institutional desires that underlie the formation of a multicultural curriculum. Among other things, such contextualization calls into question the assumption of cultural unity and, consequently, the attribution of pure and noncontradictory autonomy not only to the cultural formation but to the cultural artifact. As Guillory suggests, the university is anything but neutral and disinterested in mediating the forms of cultural reproduction. It plays an active, political role, in coordination with other institutional sites, in shaping that process.

Now I want to take a closer look at what happens in departments of English as the institutional context of writing and literary pedagogy. I choose to focus on English departments because this is the area from which my own experience of work derives. In *Work Time: English Departments and the Circulation of Cultural Value*, Evan Watkins argues that English departments have the social function in capitalist societies of producing evaluations that circulate throughout the system as forms of commodity value. Whether professors teach radical deconstructive theory, the traditions of European white males, or the African Diaspora, the legacy that their students carry away from them and onto the job market where students become commodities in their own right is a list of grades. They are able to exchange their grades, degrees, and institutional affiliations for jobs and social prestige. Watkins uses the Marxist distinction between concrete and abstract labor to explain this process. For Marx, these terms articulate two different ways of understanding the process of work in the capitalist system which centers on the factory: "'Concrete labor' names the actual effort of work, the physical/intellectual process whereby a particular material is transformed by work into something else. 'Abstract labor' in contrast points to the social organization of work, the relations among people at the work location."[65] If one compares the university as a field of cultural production to the factory as a field of material production, one can infer that abstract labor expresses itself in the grades and evaluations by which teachers transform students into commodities, while concrete labor is the substance of what teachers and students actually do in the classroom.

Yet there is a significant difference between the university and the factory. The history of capitalism is largely the history of the gradual subordination of concrete labor, or what workers actually do, to abstract labor, or the social organization of work for the

[65] E. Watkins, *Work Time: English Departments and the Circulation of Cultural Value* (Stanford: Stanford University Press, 1989), p. 16.

production of surplus value or profit. In the factory, as opposed to the earlier craft guild, the worker has little or no autonomy; through processes like Taylorization and the Fordist assembly line, his or her concrete labor has been made to conform to the requirements of abstract labor. As Stanley Aronowitz and William DiFazio demonstrate, for the majority of workers, even computerization in the workplace has only increased their subordination and their general irrelevance to the production process.[66] In the college classroom, on the other hand, the teacher has an unusually high degree of autonomy in the form of intellectual freedom. Within some limits, teachers choose their own subject matter, pedagogical styles, and methods of evaluating. Admittedly, there are standards, usually written down, that every teacher is expected to maintain; but these are normally vague and general enough to allow enormous scope for interpretation by the individual teacher. Teachers, in other words, are able to produce surplus value simply by handing out grades and evaluations that their students can then trade for monetary rewards and social distinctions.

While, as Watkins stresses, English teachers usually think of themselves as full participants in the circulation of cultural values, they are really doing something else. Of course, they may have an impact on the production of cultural values through acts of research and critical interpretation, but they can hardly compete with the field of advertising and the media when it comes to circulation. Rush Limbaugh, who may not be very original as a critical thinker, nonetheless has resources at his command, both financial and technological, that give him a capacity for intervention in the social circulation of ideas and beliefs far beyond what teachers can do in the classroom. He reaches more people in a day than any teacher can reach in a lifetime. Although teachers play some role in the circulation of values, their primary function lies in the way they facilitate the circulation of people.[67] Sooner or later, from elementary school to the university, virtually everyone in the United States passes through the English classroom; and if college teachers only reach a portion of them directly, they reach all of them indirectly because they teach the other teachers. Through a

[66] S. Aronowitz and W. DiFazio, *The Jobless Future: Sci-Tech and the Dogma of Work* (Minneapolis: University of Minnesota Press, 1994), p. 33.
[67] Watkins, *Work Time*, pp. 271–72.

process of training and sorting, teachers shape their human subjects into a vast labor reserve of individuals who have been identified by a list of grades as having specific capacities or skills.[68] The debate continues as to whether teachers actually teach these skills or merely validate them, as to whether, for example, they teach their students how to write standard English or identify those students who do write standard English.

At a hearing of the US Senate on "Competitiveness and the Quality of the American Work Force" in 1987, Owen B. Butler, a former chairman of the board of Proctor and Gamble, described the criteria for employability in the corporate world. Prospective employees, he said, need two things: first, "true literacy, the ability to speak and to hear, to read and write the English language fluently and with true comprehension and true ability to articulate ideas"; and second, "work habits, attitudes, and behavior patterns."[69] Most college professors, in my view, would support the value of true literacy, although many would be suspicious of the need to indoctrinate students with a work ethic that operates as a normative system beyond critical thought. But how is true literacy achieved? If many businessmen and college professors agree on the value of true literacy, they do not always agree on the means of achieving such a goal. As Watkins stresses, literacy as a set of learned skills is not the highest priority of English departments. On the contrary, such departments emphasize the study of English and American literature, literary criticism, and, more recently, cultural theory, even though the practices inculcated by these studies have almost no utility outside of academic departments themselves.[70] Recent proposals for a conservative curriculum do not offer any serious solution to this problem, since learning how to appreciate the classics of Western literature surely inculcates the values and skills of business no better than learning how to deconstruct popular culture. Yet the views of William Bennett, Allan Bloom, and E. D. Hirsch seem to have some support in the business community, though it cannot be based on commitment to purely functional education. Perhaps the idea is that respect for

[68] Watkins, *Work Time*, pp. 127–33.
[69] Quoted in M. Blitz and C. M. Hurlbert, "Cults of Culture," in *Cultural Studies in the Classroom*, ed. J. A. Berlin and M. J. Vivion (Portsmouth: Boynton/Cook, Heinemann, 1992), p. 9.
[70] Watkins, *Work Time*, p. 89.

the classics and the "right" ideas means respect for authority, which inculcates the attitudes and behaviors businessmen want in their employees. Still, in the current climate of layoffs and the probable reality of what Aronowitz and DiFazio have called the "jobless future," trying to streamline higher education to serve the needs of business exclusively is not only inconsistent with democracy but a Quixotic gesture of futility. Is rising unemployment caused by the failure of higher education to prepare students for the jobs that exist or is it the structural result of the new production and information technologies? As George F. Will likes to say, reducing labor costs through increased productivity is one of the goals of capitalism. The NAFTA and GATT treaties may create the need for a more educated work force in the United States, but there is no guarantee they will create more instead of fewer high-paying jobs in the long run.

Democratic education has been called the practice of freedom.[71] If these words are to mean anything, however, they should require that college teachers make some effort to determine the needs and interests of students and the general community rather than simply assuming these are the same as the needs and interests of business. Watkins interprets this responsibility as the call "to support multiple practices of resistance."[72] Throughout his study, he identifies such resistance with a Gramscian war of position, that is, an intellectual war over ideas and values. I would prefer to qualify his terms somewhat in order to avoid the Manichean logic they imply. I think it is naive to imagine the university as the site of any great opposition or effective resistance to the dominant values of capitalist culture. Rather than enabling opposition or resistance, the university enables the articulation of radical differences that would threaten the dominant culture with a war of movement, that is, a real war, if these differences were not accounted for and assimilated by a war of position. Nonetheless, this assimilation as the practice of freedom is not an illusion but a real practice. As long as the democratic university can support the discourse of freedom

[71] See P. Freire, *The Politics of Education: Culture, Power, and Liberation* (South Hadley: Bergin, 1985); S. Aronowitz and H. A. Giroux, *Education Still under Siege*, 2nd edn (Westport, Connecticut: Bergin and Garvey, 1993), especially chapter 6, "Curriculum Theory, Power, and Cultural Politics"; and b. hooks, *Teaching to Transgress: Education as the Practice of Freedom* (New York: Routledge, 1994).
[72] Watkins, *Work Time*, p. 28.

as the response of the other to the dominant forces in Euro-American culture, then democratic society, even within a capitalist economic system, can be said to have remained faithful to its promise. The history of socialist and capitalist states in this century does not support the Manichean division of the world into the absolutely good and the absolutely evil. As Ernesto Laclau and Chantal Mouffe argue, the war of position leads not only to a "demilitarization of war"; it also makes visible the "radical ambiguity" of the social by privileging discourse and the signifier over "any transcendent signified" that would constrain and block the articulation of social desire.[73] As the institutionalized site of the undecidable or *radical ambiguity* (a point to which I will return), the university is the place where every transcendent signified – whether it calls itself *universal tradition, free enterprise,* or *communism* – can be called into question.

Nevertheless, the concept *war of position* projects a Manichean view of things by employing the metaphor of war to describe the process of social and cultural change. The metaphor creates the illusion of two opposing sides that can be reduced to an absolutely positive and an absolutely negative position within the field of culture. Yet it makes little sense to identify capitalism as absolutely negative in a culture where it continues to command the consent of the people and where it continues to permit and even to respond to the struggle for social and cultural change through peaceful and sometimes violent means. The Gramscian concept of hegemony refers to the totality of culture, even though this culture, as Raymond Williams stresses, involves "the lived dominance and subordination of particular classes."[74] The war of position is not a war against that culture but a process of transformation from within. Of course, if the hegemony should break down, if the dominant forces in this society should be required to resort to coercion and repression as the *primary* means of legitimating their authority, then a war of movement would be the result. Then the university would no longer be a viable site for any practice of freedom.

[73] E. Laclau and C. Mouffe, *Hegemony and Socialist Strategy: Toward a Radical Democratic Politics,* trans. W. Moore and P. Cammack (London: Verso, 1985), p. 137.
[74] R. Williams, *Marxism and Literature* (Oxford: Oxford University Press, 1977), p. 110.

Though university professors should not be the agents of business, they also do not make credible revolutionaries despite the posturing and rhetoric of some critical theorists. Their job is to support and nurture the practice of freedom in a democratic society. Unfortunately, they make this task difficult when they insist on being linguistic policemen and literary custodians. Watkins criticizes what he calls the "ideologies of the new" that have virtually taken over the field of critical discourse in English studies. While such a tendency is the logical consequence of modernist ideologies and New Critical practices, and has homologous relations to a culture that privileges technological innovation for its own sake, it has led to the overproduction and dissemination of new theories in the last twenty years. One does not have to be against theory, and that is neither my position nor Watkins's, to see that innovative and/or oppositional critical practices, which are viewed by conservatives as forms of terror and by radicals as forms of resistance, require conditions of work that are not universally available. The problem with ideologies of the new is their dangerous assumption that "our political responsibility lies in passing on our work skills and knowledges to others to practice as we do."[75] In other words, teachers of writing and literature subordinate their concrete labor to the ends of abstract labor when they insist that their job in the classroom is to enforce the rules of standard English and to transfer to students their own work skills, including the work skills that they associate with so-called oppositional criticism.

Of course, I realize that English teachers should give their students a realistic view of the function of standard English in their society; they should instruct students on the rules of grammar and the norms of standard usage, insofar as they can. However, teachers will convey to students an ideological view of language, and not true literacy, if they start out from the assumption that standard English is simply correct English without any relation to power or class. As long as teachers refuse to recognize the political nature of so-called *standard* English, they will fail to see that their students are not the subjects of a lack, that is, of an inability to use language properly. They do not come to the teacher empty; they come with practices of their own, with an understand-

[75] Watkins, *Work Time*, p. 28.

ing of, and a relation to, language derived from their own social and cultural contexts, from their own histories.

Similarly, teachers frequently kill their students' curiosity about literature, films, and other forms of cultural expression when they insist that students master the work skills of the teachers. For example, *Goals and Objectives for the English Curriculum*, a document produced in 1990 by the Department of English at Louisiana State University, my own workplace, lists the objectives for introductory literature courses. Not surprisingly, it says that students should exit these courses with the ability to paraphrase literary texts, to read them closely, to identify themes, structures, and patterns, to recognize genres and traditions, and to understand cultural contexts.[76] In other words, introductory literature courses should teach students how to be critics. The problem, of course, is not with the individual skill, which probably should be taught, but with our expectation that these skills in the aggregate will add up to the written performance of a literary criticism, to a performance that teachers judge according to a model based on their own work practices. By failing to recognize these practices as something specific to their work location, college teachers judge their students by a model that, with some exceptions, students cannot possibly live up to. While few of them will ever become literary critics, many of them have already developed practices for reading and writing about literary and other kinds of texts that could be explored and developed in the classroom if teachers would take the time to recognize them as legitimate forms of critical and linguistic expression. Teachers should, of course, expose their students to the models of criticism that they practice, including the models of contemporary theory; but if they make these practices into the norm by which they judge and evaluate student work, they destroy the legitimacy of student practices and of the cultural contexts from which they derive.[77]

Curriculum, therefore, should not be isolated from the question of pedagogical practice. A curriculum that works is one that

[76] Committee for the Revision of the Undergraduate Curriculum, *Goals and Objectives for the English Curriculum* (Department of English, Louisiana State University, 1990), p. 4.

[77] For different but related viewpoints, see Aronowitz and Giroux, *Education*, p. 153; and J. Merod, *The Political Responsibility of the Critic* (Ithaca: Cornell University Press, 1987), p. 11.

facilitates effective pedagogy by fostering a dialogical, interactive exchange between teachers and students. The political responsibility of the teacher lies in recognizing and exploiting the gap between concrete and abstract labor in the English department as a workplace. This gap exists because, despite the repeated appeals to standards throughout the history of democratic education and the demands that we go back to the basics, language as a social practice is dynamic and cannot be reduced to one universal norm. In the early nineteenth century, as Gerald Graff reminds us in *Professing Literature*, the students who attended American colleges were not expected to prove themselves as writers but rather to master the art of speaking. They studied oratory, not English.[78] For the most part, they were upper-class white men; and the language they spoke was probably some version of what we now call standard English. As the institutions of democratic education developed from the end of the nineteenth century to the present, the new voices that entered higher education represented differences of race, gender, and class. These voices might have threatened the authority of standard English if they had not been contained by the introduction into the curriculum of the composition course as the institutional site of the low or disempowered. As Susan Miller notes, in this new curriculum the history of literature was told "as a history of authorship and of the authorized voice, whose origins, successes, and privileges are not bound to the material circumstances of either readers or writers." Composition, on the other hand, became "a national course in silence."[79] I would qualify Miller's remark and say that disempowered students never went silent without a protest. Despite the dominance of standard English, it did not go unchallenged or unchanged over the years as the university was opening its doors to new generations of students from diverse cultural and class backgrounds. Today, literature itself, at least in its postmodern and postcolonial forms, is no longer the safe haven of any linguistic norm; and if students do not find teachers who will affirm their linguistic differences, they do find authors who will – authors like Ishmael Reed, Thomas Pynchon, Toni Morrison, Kathy Acker, and Chinua

---

[78] G. Graff, *Professing Literature: An Institutional History* (Chicago: University of Chicago Press, 1987), pp. 19–51.

[79] S. Miller, *Textual Carnivals: The Politics of Composition* (Carbondale and Edwardsville: Southern Illinois University Press, 1991), pp. 27, 55.

Achebe. By allowing students to explore and experiment with their own language practices, teachers create the context in which students can understand these practices in relation to *standard* English as a complex hybrid in its own right. In this way, teachers not only give students the freedom to choose how they are going to write; they also begin to teach them about the responsibility that such a choice entails.

So rather than designing curriculums that channel our concrete labor into practices that readily lend themselves to the goals of abstract labor, namely grading and evaluation, we should do the opposite. The courses we design should facilitate the kind of dialogical interactions between teachers and students that make it extremely difficult to evaluate the individual performance. Only when teachers have experienced the undecidability of student writing, its irreducibility to an absolute norm, do they make a truly responsible decision about the overall quality of a student's performance. We should encourage students to try different writing styles, including popular styles, in an effort to find a voice in writing with which they are able to communicate effectively. We should introduce them to the kinds of literature that interest us, but we should also make an effort to discover the kinds of writing and cultural expression that interest them and relate both – that is, traditional literature and more popular literature – to culture as a total way of life. The classrooms in which we work should not be the panoptical sites of discipline and surveillance in which we teach students how to recognize and live with their own inadequacies and failures. The classroom should be a place of discovery and excitement, of symbolic exchange and self-actualization. Although part of our job is to instruct our students by giving directions and conveying information to them, there is always a gap between instruction as passive learning and education as the practice of freedom. As Gramsci elaborates, "There is no unity between school and life, and so there is no automatic unity between instruction and education. In the school, the nexus between instruction and education can only be realized by the living work of the teacher."[80] Only the teacher can create a bridge of communication between the cultural differences of the student body and the cultural authority of the institution the teacher represents.

[80] Gramsci, *Reader*, pp. 312–13.

What I have said about pedagogy and its institutional context certainly calls into question the concept of autonomy in its ideological form. Nevertheless, though the university can never be totally neutral or disinterested, teachers in the university should defend and maintain its autonomy. Like a work of art, the university internalizes its social context without necessarily becoming the instrument of the dominant powers of that context. The university is not exclusively the site of affirmative culture in the Marcusian sense because it carries within itself the contradictions and antagonisms of the society from which it symptomatically derives. What distinguishes the university from the rest of society as the ground of its negative autonomy is the relatively safe haven it gives to the experience of the undecidable. Insofar as the university has a relation to the future of culture, it must permit and even encourage the sort of research and critical thought that brings about the crisis of reason that I have called, after Derrida, the undecidable. Furthermore, it fosters this experience not as a value in itself but as a necessary dimension of the educational process. However detached the researchers in a university may become from their teaching duties, the only justification for having universities in which freedom of thought is not only allowed but desired is that the production of knowledge and its transference from one generation to the next require it. Without the experience of the undecidable, the university would only produce technicians who can apply the knowledge achieved by earlier generations without any sense of its limitations and social implications. They would lose the capacity for innovation, which often derives from chance and imagination. It goes without saying that universities *do* produce technicians, but if that were their exclusive function they would not require the degree of autonomy and freedom they claim as their right.

Today any concept of the autonomous work of art must also be framed by this context. Insofar as the term "autonomy" signifies a claim to absolute purity through a separation from and transcendence of the social context – which would be the claim to autonomy that we associate with the ideology of "art for art's sake" and, to some extent, with modernism – it can and must be deconstructed. But I do not think the question of autonomy finds an answer in terms like "relative autonomy" or "semiautonomy." Cultural processes since the Enlightenment, and throughout the colonial and now postcolonial periods, have undergone a certain historical autonomization. Today *minority* cultures and the cultures of the formerly colonized struggle for autonomy against cultural imperialism, and it would be a gross oversimplification to say they are deluded. These cultures understand autonomy not in a metaphysical sense but in a relational – and, therefore, historical – sense. According to Peter Bürger, aesthetic autonomy as a historical category refers to the separation of art as "a special sphere of human activity" from life as a social practice. While the process that produces this separation is real, it nevertheless operates through concepts that block the recognition of art's social determination. As a category of bourgeois society in the West, the autonomy of art both discloses and hides its real historical origins.[81]

Still, the situation of postcolonial and feminist writers would suggest that reducing the autonomy of art to a bourgeois category may be an oversimplification in itself. Without using the word "autonomy," for example, Monique Wittig has argued for the usefulness of such a concept of art through the metaphor of the Trojan Horse. She suggests that any new aesthetic form is a war machine because it aims at the destruction of the old forms and conventions that have made it possible. While a literary work can have a political effect, it does not represent history, politics, or ideology directly because the political and the aesthetic produce "parallel systems of signs which function differently in the social corpus and use language in a different way."[82] The Trojan Horse metaphor carries the implication that for Wittig, as for Adorno, "the social meaning of the work of art is expressed through technique rather than through specific themes and motifs."[83] Or, perhaps more accurately, art is autonomous to the extent that its meaning is a function of the dialectical relation between aesthetic form and social content. Of course, there is always the risk that autonomy will become a metaphysical category as it does not only in aestheticism but in *nativist* theories of culture. Those risks are the reasons why deconstructive pedagogy and criticism remain useful in the present global context.

A work of art – and by that I mean anything, a television sitcom,

---

[81] Bürger, *Theory*, pp. 35–36.
[82] M. Wittig, *The Straight Mind and Other Essays* (Boston: Beacon Press, 1992), p. 69.
[83] Hohendahl, *Reappraisals*, p. 66.

a movie, a rock video, a literary classic – produces its aesthetic effect when it carries us to the moment of decision by way of the undecidable. As I said at the end of chapter 2, art itself never chooses. But it forces us to make a choice at a moment of terrifying freedom. I call this freedom terrifying because one can never know absolutely if it is truly free. It is the freedom of responsibility, the freedom that requires you to make a decision without knowing where it will take you or what kind of historical effect it will produce. I do not mean that the decision is carefree but that it requires the assumption of a responsibility that has no point of termination.

Today the Western university as an institution of cultural reproduction is not the site exclusively of social determination *or* of freedom. There is freedom in the university; and, despite the efforts of private individuals, corporations, and state governments to subordinate the university to their interests, it nevertheless remains an autonomous institution to the extent that it nurtures freedom by creating a space for the experience of the undecidable. Even those research programs in science that are most blatantly governed by outside interests still manage to produce students who make decisions against those interests. Sometimes the outside interests discover that their interests are different from what they originally thought. Historically, the university has never been autonomous if by that term one means that it transcends the social antagonisms and contradictions that exist outside of it. Nevertheless, I will insist that the concept of *autonomy*, like the concept of *freedom*, is never pure and reducible to a univocal definition because it is never a state of being-in-itself but a dialectical relationship. When I say that teachers must defend and maintain the autonomy of the university, I do not mean that they must defend a state of affairs that already exists in some idealized form. In such a form, there is no autonomy. Nevertheless, they must defend the concept of autonomy and the practical relationships it fosters on a day-to-day basis within the university. Otherwise, they surrender to a program, even if it calls itself *accountability*, that would destroy not only the future of thought but the thought of the future. This thought, as I see it, is the responsibility of those of us who live *in the present*; and the university is one of the institutions of social reproduction in which this responsibility must remain possible.

Such a possibility expresses the desire that I continue to find in art even when art appears to be completely irresponsible. Perhaps the irresponsibility of art is not so much a refusal of responsibility as a quest for it. Art seeks the threshold from which responsibility arises. Still, this threshold is never the termination of the quest, for it is the nature of this responsibility that it must remain open to the response of the other, to the other's desire, and to the possibility that what has been called responsibility harbors something irresponsible. The threshold is never surpassed once and for all because the desire that directs us to the threshold always comes from the other, the other that is both inside and outside of us. "Desire" is only a word. A word with a history and therefore with more than one meaning. It refers to something real but not something given to us without mediation. This mediation is the experience of interpretation – and finally the history of interpretation. Desire addresses the other of representation, the other that marks the internal boundary of representation, its incompleteness. It is the direction of speech and writing. It is what requires a subject to say something, anything.

But no matter what anyone says or writes, it is never without the possibility of a response.

Adams, Gerry. *The Politics of Irish Freedom*. Wolfeboro, New Hampshire: Brandon, 1987.

Adorno, Theodor W. *Negative Dialektik*. Frankfurt am Main: Suhrkamp, 1970.

    Kritik: Kleine Schriften zur Gesellschaft. Frankfurt am Main: Suhrkamp, 1971.

    Negative Dialectics. Trans. E. B. Ashton. New York: Continuum, 1973.

    Minima Moralia: Reflections from Damaged Life. Trans. E. F. N. Jephcott. London: Verso, 1978.

    Ästhetische Theorie. Ed. Gretel Adorno and Rolf Tiedemann. Frankfurt am Main: Suhrkamp, 1980.

    Prisms. Trans. Samuel and Shierry Weber. Cambridge, Massachusetts: MIT, 1981.

    "Transparencies on Film." *New German Critique* 24–25 (Fall–Winter 1981–82): 199–205.

    Against Epistemology: A Metacritique. Trans. Willis Domingo. Oxford: Oxford University Press, 1982.

    Aesthetic Theory. Ed. Gretel Adorno and Rolf Tiedemann. Trans. C. Lenhardt. London: Routledge and Kegan Paul, 1984.

    Notes to Literature. Ed. Rolf Tiedemann. Trans. Shierry Weber Nicholsen. New York: Columbia University Press, 1991.

Anderson, Benedict. *Imagined Communities: Reflections on the Origin and Spread of Nationalism*. Revised edition. London: Verso, 1991.

Aronowitz, Stanley, and William DiFazio. *The Jobless Future: Sci-Tech and the Dogma of Work*. Minneapolis: University of Minnesota Press, 1994.

Aronowitz, Stanley, and Henry A. Giroux. *Education Still under Siege*. Second edition. Westport, Connecticut: Bergin and Garvey, 1993.

Ashcroft, Bill, Gareth Griffiths, and Helen Tiffin. *The Empire Writes Back: Theory and Practice in Post-Colonial Literatures*. London: Routledge, 1989.

Baudry, Jean-Louis. "Ideological Effects of the Basic Cinematographic Apparatus." Trans. Alan Williams. *Apparatus: Cinematic Apparatus, Selected Writings*. Ed. Theresa Hak Kyung Cha. New York: Tanam Press, 1980, pp. 25–37.

Beckett, Samuel. "Dante … Bruno. Vico … Joyce." *Our Exagmination*

Round his Factification for Incamination of Work in Progress, by Samuel Beckett et al. London: Faber and Faber, 1972. Originally published in 1929.

Benjamin, Walter. *Illuminations*. Trans. Harry Zohn. New York: Schocken, 1969.

    The Origin of German Tragic Drama. Trans. John Osborne. London: NLB, 1977.

Bennett, William J. "To Reclaim a Legacy." 1984 Report on Humanities in Education, *Chronicle of Higher Education* (November 28, 1984):1, 14–21.

Bhabha, Homi. *The Location of Culture*. London: Routledge, 1994.

Blitz, Michael, and C. Mark Hurlbert. "Cults of Culture." *Cultural Studies in the Classroom*. Ed. James A. Berlin and Michael J. Vivion. Portsmouth: Boynton/Cook, Heinemann, 1992, pp. 5–23.

Bloch, Ernst, et al. *Aesthetics and Politics*. Afterword by Fredric Jameson. London: NLB, 1977.

Bloom, Allan. *The Closing of the American Mind: How Higher Education Has Failed Democracy and Impoverished the Souls of Today's Students*. New York: Simon and Schuster, 1987.

Brenkman, John. *Culture and Domination*. Ithaca: Cornell University Press, 1987.

Buck-Morss, Susan. *The Origin of Negative Dialectics: Theodor W. Adorno, Walter Benjamin, and the Frankfurt Institute*. New York: Free Press, 1977.

Bürger, Peter. *Theory of the Avant-Garde*. Trans. Michael Shaw. Minneapolis: University of Minnesota Press, 1984.

Cahn, Michael. "Subversive Mimesis: Theodor W. Adorno and the Modern Impasse of Critique." *Mimesis in Contemporary Theory*. Vol. I. Ed. M. Spariosu. Philadelphia: J. Benjamins, 1984, pp. 27–64.

Committee for the Revision of the Undergraduate Curriculum. *Goals and Objectives for the English Curriculum*. Department of English, Louisiana State University, 1990.

Coogan, Tim Pat. *The IRA: A History*. Niwot, Colorado: Roberts Rinehart, 1994.

Cornell, Drucilla. *The Philosophy of the Limit*. New York: Routledge, 1992.

Culler, Jonathan. *On Deconstruction: Theory and Criticism after Structuralism*. Ithaca: Cornell University Press, 1982.

Curtis, L. P., Jr. *Anglo-Saxons and Celts: A Study of Anti-Irish Prejudice in Victorian England*. Bridgeport, Connecticut: University of Bridgeport Press, 1968.

de Lauretis, Teresa. "Oedipus Interruptus." *Wide Angle* 7 (1985): 34–40.

de Man, Paul. *The Resistance to Theory*. Minneapolis: University of Minnesota Press, 1986.

Derrida, Jacques. "Structure, Sign, and Play in the Discourse of the Humanities." *The Structuralist Controversy: The Languages of Criticism and the Sciences of Man.* Ed. Richard Macksey and Eugenio Donato. Baltimore: The Johns Hopkins University Press, 1972, pp. 247–65.

Of Grammatology. Trans. Gayatri Chakravorty Spivak. Baltimore: The Johns Hopkins University Press, 1976.

Writing and Difference. Trans. Alan Bass. Chicago: University of Chicago Press, 1978.

"Living On: Borderlines." *Deconstruction and Criticism.* Ed. Harold Bloom. New York: Seabury, 1979, pp. 75–175.

"The Law of Genre/*La loi du genre.*" Trans. Avita Ronnell. *Glyph* 7 (1980): 202–32.

Dissemination. Trans. Barbara Johnson. Chicago: University of Chicago Press, 1981.

Positions. Trans. Alan Bass. Chicago: University of Chicago Press, 1981.

Margins of Philosophy. Trans. Alan Bass. Chicago: University of Chicago Press, 1982.

"The Principle of Reason: The University in the Eyes of Its Pupils." *Diacritics* 13.3 (1983): 3–20.

"Deconstruction and the Other." *Dialogues with Contemporary Continental Thinkers: The Phenomenological Heritage,* by Richard Kearney. Manchester: Manchester University Press, 1984, pp. 107–26.

"Like the Sound of the Sea Deep within a Shell: Paul de Man's War." *Critical Inquiry* 14 (1988): 590–652.

Limited Inc. Trans. Samuel Weber and Jeffrey Mehlman. Evanston: Northwestern University Press, 1988.

"The Politics of Friendship." *The Journal of Philosophy* 85.11 (1988): 632–44.

'How to Avoid Speaking: Denials." Trans. Ken Frieden. *Languages of the Unsayable: The Play of Negativity in Literature and Literary Theory.* Ed. Sanford Budick and Wolfgang Iser. New York: Columbia University Press, 1989, pp. 3–70.

"Force of Law: 'The Mystical Foundation of Authority.'" *Cardoza Law Review* 11.5–6 (1990): 919–1045.

The Other Heading: Reflections on Today's Europe. Trans. Pascale-Anne Brault and Michael B. Naas. Bloomington: Indiana University Press, 1992.

Specters of Marx: The State of the Debt, the Work of Mourning, and the New International. Trans. Peggy Kamuf. New York: Routledge, 1994.

Dews, Peter. *Logics of Disintegration: Post-Structuralist Thought and the Claims of Critical Theory.* London: Verso, 1987.

Doane, Mary Ann. "Film and the Masquerade: Theorizing the Female Spectator." *Issues in Feminist Film Criticism.* Ed. Patricia Erens. Bloomington: Indiana University Press, 1990, pp. 41–57.

D'Souza, Dinesh. *Illiberal Education: The Politics of Race and Sex on Campus.* New York: Free Press, 1991.

Dworkin, Dennis L. "Cultural Studies and the Crisis in British Radical Thought." *Views Beyond the Border Country: Raymond Williams and*

Cultural Politics. Ed. Dennis L. Dworkin and Leslie G. Roman. New York: Routledge, 1993, pp. 38–54.

Eagleton, Terry. *The Ideology of the Aesthetic*. Oxford: Basil Blackwell, 1990.

Eliot, T. S. "Tradition and the Individual Talent." *Selected Essays*. New York: Harcourt, Brace, 1950, pp. 3–11.

Fanon, Frantz. *The Wretched of the Earth*. New York: Grove Weidenfeld, 1991.

The Field Day Anthology of Irish Writing. Ed. Seamus Deane. Derry: Field Day Publications, 1991.

Freire, Paolo. *The Politics of Education: Culture, Power, and Liberation*. South Hadley: Bergin, 1985.

Freud, Sigmund. *General Psychological Theory: Papers on Metapsychology*. New York: Collier, 1963.

Gadamer, Hans-Georg. *Truth and Method*. Trans. Garrett Barden and John Cumming. New York: Crossroad, 1986.

Gallop, Jane. *The Daughter's Seduction: Feminism and Psychoanalysis*. Ithaca: Cornell University Press, 1982.

Gasché, Rodolphe. *The Tain in the Mirror: Derrida and the Philosophy of Reflection*. Cambridge, Massachusetts: Harvard University Press, 1986.

Gikandi, Simon. *Writing in Limbo: Modernism and Caribbean Literature*. Ithaca: Cornell University Press, 1992.

Graff, Gerald. *Professing Literature: An Institutional History*. Chicago: University of Chicago Press, 1987.

Beyond the Culture Wars: How Teaching the Conflicts Can Revitalize American Education. New York: Norton, 1992.

Gramsci, Antonio. *An Antonio Gramsci Reader: Selected Writings, 1916–1935*. Ed. David Forgacs. New York: Schocken, 1988.

Guillory, John. *Cultural Capital: The Problem of Literary Canon Formation*. Chicago: University of Chicago Press, 1993.

Habermas, Jürgen. "Walter Benjamin: Consciousness-Raising or Rescuing Critique." *Philosophical-Political Profiles*. Trans. Frederick G. Lawrence. Cambridge, Massachusetts: MIT, 1983, pp. 129–63.

The Theory of Communicative Action. Vol. I: *Reason and the Rationalization of Society*. Trans. Thomas McCarthy. Boston: Beacon, 1984.

The Theory of Communicative Action. Vol. II: *Lifeworld and System: A Critique of Functionalist Reason*. Trans. Thomas McCarthy. Boston: Beacon, 1987.

The Philosophical Discourse of Modernity: Twelve Lectures. Trans. Frederick Lawrence. Cambridge, Massachusetts: MIT, 1987.

Hall, Stuart. "On Postmodernism and Articulation: An Interview with Stuart Hall." Ed. Lawrence Grossberg. *Journal of Communication Inquiry* 10.2 (1986): 45–60.

"Cultural Studies and its Theoretical Legacies." *Cultural Studies*. Ed. Lawrence Grossberg, Cary Nelson, and Paula A. Treichler. New York: Routledge, 1992, pp. 277–94.

Bibliography

Hansen, Miriam B. "Introduction to Adorno, 'Transparencies on Film' (1966)." *New German Critique* 24–25 (Fall–Winter 1981–82): 186–98.
"Mass Culture as Hieroglyphic Writing: Adorno, Derrida, Kracauer." *New German Critique* 56 (Spring–Summer 1992): 43–73.

Heath, Stephen. *Questions of Cinema.* Bloomington: Indiana University Press, 1981.

Hirsch, E. D., Jr. *Cultural Literacy: What Every American Needs to Know.* Boston: Houghton Mifflin, 1987.

Hogan, Patrick Colm. *The Politics of Interpretation: Ideology, Professionalism, and the Study of Literature.* New York: Oxford University Press, 1990.

Hohendahl, Peter Uwe. *Reappraisals: Shifting Alignments in Postwar Critical Theory.* Ithaca: Cornell University Press, 1991.
Prismatic Thought: Theodor W. Adorno. Lincoln: University of Nebraska Press, 1995.

hooks, bell. "Seduction and Betrayal." *Visions* (Fall 1993): 24–25, 51.
Teaching to Transgress: Education as the Practice of Freedom. New York: Routledge, 1994.

Horkheimer, Max, and Theodor W. Adorno. *Dialectic of Enlightenment.* Trans. John Cumming. London: Allen Lane, 1973.

Huyssen, Andreas. "Introduction to Adorno." *New German Critique* 6 (Fall 1975):

Irigaray, Luce. *This Sex Which Is Not One.* Trans. Catherine Porter with Carolyn Burke. Ithaca: Cornell University Press, 1985.

James, C. L. R. *Beyond a Boundary.* New York: Pantheon, 1983.

Jameson, Fredric. *The Political Unconscious: Narrative as a Socially Symbolic Act.* Ithaca: Cornell University Press, 1981.
"Third-World Literature in the Era of Multinational Capitalism." *Social Text* 15 (1986): 65–88.
Late Marxism: Adorno, or, The Persistence of the Dialectic. London: Verso, 1990.
Postmodernism, or, The Cultural Logic of Late Capitalism. Durham: Duke University Press, 1991.
The Geopolitical Aesthetic: Cinema and Space in the World System. Bloomington: Indiana University Press, 1992.

Jay, Martin. *The Dialectical Imagination: A History of the Frankfurt School and the Institute of Social Research 1923–1950.* Boston: Little Brown, 1973.

Jordan, Neil. *A Neil Jordan Reader.* New York: Vintage, 1993.

Kaplan, E. Ann. *Women and Film: Both Sides of the Camera.* New York: Methuen, 1983.

Kaufmann, Stanley. "The Haunted and the Hunted." *The New Republic,* December 14, 1992: 28–29.

Kearney, Richard. *Transitions: Narratives in Modern Irish Culture.* Manchester: Manchester University Press, 1988.

Kincaid, Jamaica. *A Small Place.* New York: Plume, 1989.

Bibliography

King, Thomas R., and Richard Turner. "Disney Agrees to Buy the Distributor of 'Crying Game' at Possibly $60 Million." *The Wall Street Journal*, Southwest Edition, May 3, 1993: B7.

Lacan, Jacques. *Ecrits*. Paris: Seuil, 1966.

"Of Structure as an Inmixing of an Otherness Prerequisite to Any Subject Whatever." *The Structuralist Controversy: The Languages of Criticism and the Sciences of Man*. Ed. Richard Macksey and Eugenio Donato. Baltimore: The Johns Hopkins University Press, 1972, pp. 186–95.

Encore. Book 20 of *Le séminaire*. Ed. Jacques-Alain Miller. Paris: Seuil, 1975.

"Ecrits": A Selection. Trans. Alan Sheridan. New York: Norton, 1977.

The Four Fundamental Concepts of Psycho-Analysis. Ed. Jacques-Alain Miller. Trans. Alan Sheridan. New York: Norton, 1981.

Feminine Sexuality: Jacques Lacan and the "école freudienne." Ed. Juliet Mitchell and Jacqueline Rose. Trans. Jacqueline Rose. New York: Norton, 1985.

L'éthique de la psychanalyse 1959–1960. Book 7 of *Le séminaire*. Ed. Jacques-Alain Miller. Paris: Seuil, 1986.

The Ego in Freud's Theory and in the Technique of Psychoanalysis. Book 2 of *The Seminar*. Ed. Jacques-Alain Miller. Trans. Sylvana Tomaselli. New York: Norton, 1988.

The Ethics of Psychoanalysis 1959–1960. Book 7 of *The Seminar*. Ed. Jacques-Alain Miller. Trans. Dennis Porter. New York: Norton, 1992.

Laclau, Ernesto, and Chantal Mouffe. *Hegemony and Socialist Strategy: Toward a Radical Democratic Politics*. Trans. Winston Moore and Paul Cammack. London: Verso, 1985.

Lazarus, Neil. *Resistance in Postcolonial African Fiction*. New Haven: Yale University Press, 1990.

Lee, J. J. *Ireland, 1912–1985: Politics and Society*. Cambridge: Cambridge University Press, 1989.

Levy, Emanuel. *Small-Town America in Film: The Decline and Fall of Community*. New York: Continuum, 1991.

Lipstadt, Deborah. *Denying the Holocaust: The Growing Assault on Truth and Memory*. New York: Plume, 1994.

Lloyd, David. *Nationalism and Minor Literature: James Clarence Mangan and the Emergence of Irish Cultural Nationalism*. Berkeley: University of California Press, 1987.

Anomalous States: Irish Writing and the Post-Colonial Moment. Durham: Duke University Press, 1993.

Lustick, Ian S. *Unsettled States, Disputed Lands: Britain and Ireland, France and Algeria, Israel and the West Bank–Gaza*. Ithaca: Cornell University Press, 1993.

Lyons, F. S. L. *Ireland Since the Famine*. Revised edition. London: Collins/Fontana, 1973.

Bibliography

Marcuse, Herbert. *Negations: Essays in Critical Theory*. Trans. Jeremy J. Shapiro. Boston: Beacon, 1968.

McBride, Joseph. *Frank Capra: The Catastrophe of Success*. New York: Simon and Schuster, 1992.

McCarthy, Thomas. *Ideals and Illusions: On Reconstruction and Deconstruction in Contemporary Critical Theory*. Cambridge, Massachusetts: MIT, 1991.

McGee, Patrick. *Telling the Other: The Question of Value in Modern and Postcolonial Writing*. Ithaca: Cornell University Press, 1992.

"History's Echo: Joyce, Nationalism, and Decolonization." *Voices from Elsewhere: Essays on Cross-Cultural Studies*. Ed. David Wills and Patrick Mensah (forthcoming).

McGowan, John. *Postmodernism and Its Critics*. Ithaca: Cornell University Press, 1991.

Merod, Jim. *The Political Responsibility of the Critic*. Ithaca: Cornell University Press, 1987.

Metz, Christian. *Psychoanalysis and Cinema: The Imaginary Signifier*. Trans. Celia Britton, Annwyl Williams, Ben Brewster, and Alfred Guzzetti. London: Macmillan, 1982.

Miller, Susan. *Textual Carnivals: The Politics of Composition*. Carbondale and Edwardsville: Southern Illinois University Press, 1991.

Mulvey, Laura. *Visual and Other Pleasures*. Bloomington: Indiana University Press, 1989.

Nairn, Tom. *The Break-Up of Britain: Crisis and Neo-Nationalism*. Second edition. London: NLB, 1981.

Nealon, Jeffrey T. *Double Reading: Postmodernism after Deconstruction*. Ithaca: Cornell University Press, 1993.

O'Brien, Conor Cruise. *Passion and Cunning: Essays on Nationalism, Terrorism and Revolution*. New York: Simon and Schuster, 1988.

Radway, Janice. *Reading the Romance: Women, Patriarchy, and Popular Culture*. Chapel Hill: University of North Carolina Press, 1984.

Rajchman, John. *Truth and Eros: Foucault, Lacan, and the Question of Ethics*. New York: Routledge, 1991.

Roof, Judith. *A Lure of Knowledge: Lesbian Sexuality and Theory*. New York: Columbia University Press, 1991.

Said, Edward. *Culture and Imperialism*. New York: Alfred A. Knopf, 1993.

Sedgwick, Eve Kosofsky. *Between Men: English Literature and Male Homosocial Desire*. New York: Columbia University Press, 1985.

Epistemology of the Closet. Berkeley: University of California Press, 1990.

Silverman, Kaja. *Male Subjectivity at the Margins*. New York: Routledge, 1992.

Taylor, Patrick. *The Narrative of Liberation: Perspectives on Afro-Caribbean Literature, Popular Culture, and Politics*. Ithaca: Cornell University Press, 1989.

Bibliography

Viswanathan, Gauri. *Masks of Conquest: Literary Study and British Rule in India*. New York: Columbia University Press, 1989.

Waldman, Diane. "Critical Theory and Film: Adorno and 'The Culture Industry' Revisited." *New German Critique* 12 (Fall 1977): 39–60.

Watkins, Evan. *Work Time: English Departments and the Circulation of Cultural Value*. Stanford: Stanford University Press, 1989.

Wellmer, Albrecht. *The Persistence of Modernity: Essays on Aesthetics, Ethics, and Postmodernism*. Trans. David Midgley. Cambridge, Massachusetts: MIT, 1991.

Wharton, Edith. *The Age of Innocence*. New York: Macmillan, 1992.

White, Hayden. *The Content of the Form: Narrative Discourse and Historical Representation*. Baltimore: The Johns Hopkins University Press, 1987.

Williams, Raymond. *Marxism and Literature*. Oxford: Oxford University Press, 1977.

Wittig, Monique. *The Straight Mind and Other Essays*. Boston: Beacon Press, 1992.

Yeats, W. B. *The Poems*. Ed. Richard Finneran. New York: Macmillan, 1983.

Zavarzadeh, Mas'ud, and Donald Morton. *Theory, (Post)Modernity, Opposition: An "Other" Introduction to Literary and Cultural Theory*. Washington, DC: Maissoneuve Press, 1991.

Žižek, Slavoj. *The Sublime Object of Ideology*. London: Verso, 1989.

Looking Awry: An Introduction to Jacques Lacan through Popular Culture. Cambridge, Massachusetts: MIT, 1991.

The Metastases of Enjoyment: Six Essays on Woman and Causality. London: Verso, 1994.

Zuidervaart, Lambert. *Adorno's Aesthetic Theory: The Redemption of Illusion*. Cambridge, Massachusetts: MIT, 1987.

Index

Index

commodity, 43, 208
contemporary, 159, 162
dominant and subordinate, 210,
    214–15
expert/technical, 50, 74, 216
hegemonic, 151
high, 1–4, 6, 59
modern, 44
national, 102, 151–52, 208, 210
nativist, 221
patriarchal, 36
political, 171
popular/mass/low, 1–6, 20, 56, 58,
    92, 136, 213
school, 208
versus nature, 132–33, 138, 143–44
Western (European), 203–06, 208,
    210, 215
culture industry, 2–7, 9, 12, 15–16,
    58–59, 66–67, 79–84, 86, 88, 94,
    102–04
curriculum, 59, 202, 207–10, 213,
    217–19
Curtis, Lewis P., 120, 122

decolonization, 123–24
deconstruction, 36, 139, 148, 163–66,
    169–72, 175–76, 179, 181–82,
    186–87, 189–90, 193–96, 199–202,
    204–08, 210–11, 221
de Lauretis, Theresa, 142
de Man, Paul, 205–06
democracy, 42–43, 54, 76, 94–95, 111,
    171–72, 176–80, 189–90, 200–01,
    214–16, 218
Democratic Programme of the First
    Dáil (Ireland, 1919), 96, 111
Derrida, Jacques, 33–35, 52, 62, 91,
    150, 162–69, 171–88, 190–98, 200,
    206–07, 220
desire, 8–10, 27, 30–33, 35–36, 91–94,
    113–16, 119–20, 125–27, 130–31,
    137–38, 140–49, 151–60, 162,
    180–81, 185, 207, 215, 221
determinate negation, 42, 54, 56, 60,
    63, 65, 73–74, 76–77, 94, 106, 151
Devil on the Cross (Ngũgĩ), 18
Dews, Peter, 61–62, 194–97
Dialectic of Enlightenment (Horkheimer
    and Adorno), 43–45, 50, 51, 58,
    75, 80–82
DiFazio, William, 212, 214
différance, 52, 181, 194, 196–98
Disneyland, 56, 59, 66–67
Doane, Mary Ann, 142

D'Souza, Dinesh, 201
Dworkin, Dennis, 23

Eagleton, Terry, 12, 25
Easter Rising, 106, 111
Eliot, T. S., 65, 85

Fanon, Frantz, 151–52
femme fatale, 105, 135
Finnegans Wake (Joyce), 27, 54
freedom, 1–3, 37, 42–43, 54, 124, 133,
    159, 163, 166–68, 170–72, 176,
    178–80, 182–87, 189, 199, 202,
    214–16, 219–20, 222
Freire, Paolo, 214
Freud, Sigmund, 28, 144, 146–47, 153

Gadamer, Hans-Georg, 49, 84
Gaelic Athletic Association, 120
Gallop, Jane, 11
Gasché, Rodolphe, 192
gender, 21, 54, 89, 92, 107, 114,
    136–39, 141, 143–45, 149, 155, 156,
    159, 161, 202, 208, 218
general writing, 165, 174
Genet, Jean, 192
Gikandi, Simon, 122–23, 133
Giroux, Henry A. , 214, 217
*Goals and Objectives for the English
    Curriculum* (LSU), 217
Gödel, Kurt, 164
Goodrich, Frances, 15
Graff, Gerald, 169, 182, 200–01, 218
Gramsci, Antonio, 39, 102, 214–15,
    219
Griffiths, Gareth, 121
Guillory, John, 202, 207–11

Habermas, Jürgen, 47–54, 56–59,
    61–62, 70, 84, 163, 166–67, 169,
    189–93, 200
Hackett, Albert, 15
Hall, Stuart, 17, 21–24, 150
Hansen, Miriam B., 13–14
Heaney, Seamus, 118
Heath, Stephen, 91, 129, 131
Hegel, G. W. F., 48, 59, 73–75, 93,
    123–24, 167, 174, 194
hegemony, 60, 102, 115, 151, 202,
    207–08, 210, 215
Hirsch, E. D., 201, 213
Hitchcock, Alfred, see *Vertigo*
Hogan, Patrick Colm, 163–64, 166,
    170–71, 181–83
Hohendahl, Peter Uwe, 16–17, 84–85

Index

Index

Odets, Clifford, 15
O'Faolain, Sean, 108
Ouloguem, Yambo, 166

Parker, Dorothy, 15
Patriot Games (film), 103–04
Pearse, Patrick, 109–10
pedagogy, 202, 205–12, 217–18, 220–21
political correctness, 38–40, 87, 161
political unconscious, 75, 86, 103
postcoloniality, 18, 106, 108, 110–11,
    115–20, 123, 128, 131–32, 146, 151,
    153–55, 159, 165, 210, 218, 221
postmodernism, 3, 23, 41, 56, 167–68,
    170–71, 218
Proclamation of the Republic (Ireland,
    1916), 96, 111
Proclamation of the Ulster Provisional
    Government (1913), 97
Pynchon, Thomas, 218

race (racism), 21, 54, 89, 93, 97–98,
    106, 109, 113–15, 121–23, 126–27,
    135–36, 145–46, 148–49, 155, 157,
    161, 177, 201, 218
Radway, Janice, 83
Rajchman, John, 147–48, 153–54
Rea, Stephen, 88
reason, 44, 48, 50–51, 55–57, 58–61,
    63–65, 66–67, 78, 163–64, 166–69,
    177, 180–81, 185–86, 188, 196, 220
    communicative, 45, 47, 50, 52–53,
        58–59, 189
    dialectical, 59–60, 63–64, 76, 78
    instrumental, 43–46, 50, 55–60,
        63–64, 66, 71, 74–76, 78
    principle of, 164, 166–68
redeeming contradiction, 7, 36
Reed, Ishmael, 165, 218
republicanism (Irish), 95–96, 98, 100,
    109, 111, 115, 127
Republic of Ireland, 96–97, 99–100,
    102, 109
responsibility, 33, 36, 43, 45, 117, 129,
    157, 162, 171, 177–79, 182–88, 201,
    205–06, 214, 219, 222–23
    social/political, 8–9, 12, 16, 18,
        36–37, 162–63, 172, 216, 218
Riskin, Robert, 14–15
Roof, Judith, 130, 141–42

Said, Edward, 17–19
Schulte-Sasse, Jochen, 16
Scorsese, Martin, see *Age of Innocence*

Sedgwick, Eve Kosofsky, 137–40, 148
sexuality, 9, 30, 89, 92–93, 112–15, 118,
    126–27, 132, 135–52, 154–59, 161
sexual nation, 149–52, 154–55
Silverman, Kaja, 14
Sinn Fein (Provisional), 95–96, 99
sinthome, 27–28, 31–32, 87
slavery, 179, 203–04, 206
Sledge, Percy, 92
Sophocles, see *Antigone*
Spivak, Gayatri Chakravorty, 150
sublimation, 26, 28, 32–33, 35, 153–55
Swerling, Jo, 15

Taylor, Patrick, 124
Terminator, The (film), 83
terrorism, 87–88, 103–04
Through the Looking-Glass, 69
Tiffin, Helen, 121
Tootsie (film), 142
Trauerspiel, 117–18
Tristram Shandy, 13
Trumbo, Dalton, 15

Ulysses (Joyce), 165–66
undecidability, 35, 37, 163–64, 166,
    168–69, 173–75, 179, 182, 185–86,
    188–89, 195, 199, 201, 204–06, 209,
    215, 219–20, 222
university, 19–20, 162–63, 170, 182,
    201–03, 211–12, 214–18, 220, 222

Vertigo (film, Hitchcock), 90
Viswanathan, Gauri, 207

Waldman, Diane, 3
Watkins, Evan, 211–14, 216
Weber, Max, 45, 56, 169
Wellmer, Albrecht, 65
Wharton, Edith, see *Age of Innocence*
White, Hayden, 204
Will, George F., 214
Williams, Raymond, 16–17, 215
Wilson, Michael, 15
Wittig, Monique, 221

Yeats, William Butler, 107, 112, 117,
    131
Yellow Wallpaper, The, 69
Young Ireland, 106

Zavarzadeh, Mas'ud, 202
Žižek, Slavoj, 27, 31, 33–34, 158
Zuidervaart, Lambert, 65, 67, 71